Before this book came out, good information on 529 plans was hard to find. Joseph Hurley has done a terrific job of making it easy to get all the details on these plans. It's well researched and authoritative, yet easy to read. Best of all, there's a thorough analysis of features in every existing plan. You'll learn what these features are, and find the plan that's right for you. This is a must read for anyone who is thinking of using one these plans—or considering an alternative, such as a custodial account or Coverdell education savings account. It has my highest recommendation.

Kaye A. Thomas, Esq.
Fairmark Press Tax Guide for Investors
Fairmark.com

Fortunately, this book is exactly what the title states: a comprehensive and clearly written guide to saving for college.

The CPA Journal

The leading book on 529s.

Jeff Brown
The Philadelphia Inquirer

The definitive guide.

Warren Boroson
Daily Record

Finally, a book explaining college savings programs in a way we can all understand.

Deena B. Katz
President, Evensky, Brown & Katz, named one of the Best
Financial Planners by *Worth* magazine and
author of *Deena Katz on Practice Management*
(Bloomberg Press, 1999)

There is just no option when it comes to figuring out college savings plans: Get your hands on this book.

David Kinchen
Huntington News

Your book is great—I bought two copies, one for my attorney.

Lynn Davis, California

I recently acquired your book, and I think you have done a fantastic job in dealing with the subject in depth and clarity. It is one of the finest handbooks of its type I have ever seen.

Bruce Berger, Writer

Unsolicited Comments Found on the Web:

The best book ever written about saving for college! This book unlocks the secrets of saving for college like the 401k plan did for saving for retirement. A real must for all families to understand.

A fantastic summary of 529 plans. This book should be read by anyone planning to send a child to college.

Terrific guide to a new way to save for college. Highly recommended. This is the first comprehensive analysis that I've seen of an extremely important and relatively new way to save on a tax-deferred basis for your children's or grandchildren's college expenses. It's well-written, comprehensive, and objective, and it gave me enough information to make an informed decision.

THE
BEST WAY
TO SAVE FOR
COLLEGE
A COMPLETE GUIDE TO 529 PLANS

THE
BEST WAY
TO SAVE FOR
COLLEGE

A COMPLETE GUIDE TO 529 PLANS

2005 EDITION

Joseph F. Hurley, CPA

Savingforcollege.com, LLC
Pittsford, New York

Published in the United States by:
Savingforcollege.com, LLC
Corporate Crossings Office Park
1151 Pittsford-Victor Rd, Ste 103
Pittsford, NY 14534
TELEPHONE: (800) 400–9113
INTERNET: www.savingforcollege.com
E-MAIL: Support@savingforcollege.com

Additional copies of this book may be ordered directly from the publisher.

Interior design and typesetting by Desktop Miracles, Inc.

Publisher's Cataloging-in-Publication
(Provided by Quality Books, Inc.)
Hurley, Joseph F.
   The best way to save for college: a complete guide
to 529 plans / Joseph F. Hurley. — 2005 ed.
   p.   cm.
   Includes index.
   LCCN 2004094510
   ISBN 0–9742977–5–5

   1. Prepaid tuition plans—United States.
   2. Education, Higher—United States—Finance.   I. Title.

LB2340.94.H87   2004   378.3'8'0973
                              QBI04–200257

Disclaimer

The author has endeavored to research and write this book with the greatest accuracy possible and with the necessary factual depth to serve as a general guide. However, the reader should understand that there may be both typographical and substantive mistakes within the text of this book. Consequently, this book must be employed as a general guide and not as the rendering of legal, accounting, tax, investment, or other professional services. The reader should, when required, seek the proper professional services in these areas.

The views and opinions expressed herein are those of the author and do not necessarily represent the views and opinions of any professional organization of which the author is a member.

The intent of this book is the education and entertainment of the reader. The author and publisher will not be liable or responsible, if the content of this book causes, or allegedly causes, directly or indirectly, any losses or damages to any person, organization, or entity.

If any purchaser of this book does not want to be obligated by the disclaimer above, you may request your money back in full except for international shipping and handling costs.

All comments received will be considered in future revisions of this book.

Table of Contents

Section One

529 Plans Explained

Section Two

State by State Comparisons

About the Author

Joseph F. Hurley, CPA

Joe Hurley is generally regarded as one of the top Section 529 experts in the country. After the first edition of this book was published in 1999, he founded and is currently CEO of Savingforcollege.com, LLC, an Internet-based publishing and consulting company that focuses on 529 plans. He is a frequent speaker at conferences around the country and is author of many articles for professional journals.

Joe has practiced as a certified public accountant for over 20 years providing tax planning services to individuals, businesses, and tax-exempt organizations, most recently as a partner at The Bonadio Group, a CPA firm headquartered in Pittsford, New York. Joe is a member of the American Institute of Certified Public Accountants, the New York State Society of Certified Public Accountants, and the Financial Planning Association.

Joe became interested in the unique benefits of 529 plans in the wake of the Taxpayer Relief Act of 1997. He wrote several articles and appeared in hearings before the IRS and Treasury in Washington D.C. to provide comments on the proposed regulations issued in 1998 under Internal Revenue Code Section 529. In addition to a professional interest, Joe and his wife Virginia have a personal interest in planning for college costs, with two children ages 18 and 14. To date they have established accounts in over 30 different 529 plans (the large number justified only by the purpose of research).

Aside from offering books, newsletters, and other information services, the author, his company Savingforcollege.com LLC, and his accounting firm are independent with respect to the states and program managers that operate 529 plans. The views and opinions expressed in this book are not conditioned on, or influenced by, the approval of any state official or other employee associated with these programs.

The author does not render personal investment advice. Requests for other consulting and speaking services, and comments about this book, can be directed to Joseph F. Hurley at Savingforcollege.com, LLC, 1151 Pittsford-Victor Rd, Suite 103, Pittsford, New York 14534. You may also contact him via e-mail at jhurley@savingforcollege.com.

Visit www.savingforcollege.com

Here's Why

Our Web site at www.savingforcollege.com is the perfect companion to this book. Here is what you will find when you visit:

- ✦ News about developments in Washington and the states affecting 529 plans.
- ✦ Exclusive "5-Cap Ratings" judging the overall usefulness of each state's 529 plan.
- ✦ An active message board for those with questions, and for those with answers.
- ✦ Joe Hurley's "529 E-ditorials" expressing opinions on a range of topics.
- ✦ Up-to-date descriptions of the programs with links to their official Web sites.
- ✦ Huge listing of useful articles and links.

Hurley updates his site before the states update their own.

ANDREW TOBIAS
Demystifying Finance,
AndrewTobias.com

There is quite a bit of insightful data here. Hurley clearly knows his stuff.

FORBES "BEST OF THE WEB"
Forbes.com

Savingforcollege.com provides the most comprehensive look at the relatively new state-sponsored 529 Plans for college savings.

SENSIBLE INVESTOR'S HONOR ROLL
Sensible-Investor.com

Preface

When I wrote the first edition of this book in 1999, our daughter Megan was in the eighth grade, and our son Chris was still in elementary school. College seemed a long way down the road, but we knew it really wasn't, and my wife Ginny and I had already been taking advantage of the opportunity to save with 529 plans. (In fact, Ginny was in school herself, working towards her master's degree in nursing.)

A lot has happened with our college savings accounts since then. We watched our stock-weighted 529 accounts increase rapidly in value during the boom years of the late 1990s, while our fixed-income accounts lagged behind. Then, as the stock market retreated, so did several of our 529 accounts, and we became thankful for the fixed-income portion of our 529 portfolio that held up so nicely in the face of the bear market. The value of "asset allocation," a term practically hard-wired into the psyche of financial planners, became readily apparent, as did the value of the "age-based" investment approach adopted by so many 529 plans.

We also watched as Congress and our president agreed to legislation in 2001 that made withdrawals from a 529 plan free from federal tax when used for qualifying college costs. I considered the 529 plan to be a good deal before tax exclusion came along; now it became even better. Unfortunately, the new tax benefit came with a catch: the exclusion expires at the end of 2010. By the time the next edition of this book comes out, I hope to be able to report that our elected officials in Washington have taken the appropriate steps to make the exclusion permanent.

Did I mention that our family of four has over fifty 529 accounts spread among 32 different states? As the number of 529 plans proliferated over the past four years, so did our own college investment portfolio. I do not recommend that you do the same, however, or else you will become as overwhelmed with statements, notices, and emails from the programs as we are. The reason we've done this, of course, is for purposes of research: I learn a lot about 529 plans simply by participating in many of them. And don't think that having a huge number of 529 plans means that we have more money squirreled away than we could possibly need for college. The minimum contribution limit in many 529 plans makes this strategy possible.

So where are we now? Megan has just started her first year of college, having enrolled at Cazenovia College in the beautiful village of Cazenovia, New York. We have the "pleasure" of withdrawing money tax-free from her 529 accounts to pay college bills. I can tell you from full-cycle experience, our decision to save using 529 plans is working out nicely. Chris has just entered high school. He'll stay serious about his studies (we hope) and have a great experience over the next four years. Then he goes on to college (we expect) with a financial assist from the 529 accounts we have established for him.

I am thankful for all of the friends and associates who have provided invaluable assistance and support along the way. They include the fine people who work alongside me—Jared Fine, Marie Osypian, Chris Stack, Cheryle Kulikowski, Bob DeRosa, Kelly Ofinowicz; my fellow enthusiasts Kaye Thomas, Esq. and Jeffrey Van Orden; all the dedicated and enthusiastic individuals working for the states and their vendors who have been so cooperative with our many requests and intrusions; and the many investors and advisers around the country who express their support for our mission.

Most importantly, I thank my best friend and wife, Ginny, who has been a source of unwavering support, a valued adviser, and a wonderful mother to our two children.

To Megan and Christopher.
Keep up the great work in school and in life.

Special thanks and love to
Ginny, my wife,
without whom none of
this would be possible.

Introduction

Religion, morality, and knowledge, being necessary to good government and the happiness of mankind, schools and the means of education shall forever be encouraged.
NORTHWEST ORDINANCE, enacted by Congress July 13, 1787

For many young people in our society, a college degree is the key that unlocks the door to opportunity. The evidence comes from studies showing a wide (and increasing) disparity between the incomes of those who graduate from college and those who do not,[1] from the actions of our elected officials as they place college accessibility high on the nation's political agenda, and even from our own college experiences; many of us have seen our lives enriched and improved by the formal recognition of our academic achievements.

But college is expensive, and will become even more so in the future. This means that parents face a formidable challenge in paying for the higher education expenses of their children. Although a considerable amount of assistance is available to ease this burden, in the form of government support, student aid programs, private scholarships, and perhaps some help from grandparents or other relatives, most parents cannot eliminate the need to prepare for the cost of sending their children to college. It becomes a matter of saving.

---

1. Between 1979 and 1999 the earnings of the average full-time college-educated worker rose 16 percent (after inflation), while the earnings of full-time workers with only a high school diploma dropped by eight percent. U.S. Department of Education, *The Condition of Education*, 2000.

This book is all about a remarkable and relatively new savings program available to American families facing future college costs. Its formal name is the qualified tuition program, sometimes abbreviated as QTP, but more often referred to as a "Section 529 plan" or just plain "529 plan." Originally developed by the states, and given special status under federal tax law, it is a savings program you should know about. If you are looking for an effective way to save for your children, your grandchildren, or even yourself, a 529 plan may be a large part of the solution.

Section 529 refers to the specific provision in the Internal Revenue Code, our federal tax law, which describes this particular type of college savings vehicle and lays down some rules that the programs must abide by in order to assure their participants of its tax-beneficial treatment. Until recently, Code Section 529 required that a qualified tuition program be established and maintained by a state. Now, "prepaid" tuition plans offered by post-secondary educational institutions are also eligible, albeit with additional restrictions. The word "tuition" in any of these titles can be a little misleading, because many 529 plans can be used to save for several categories of higher education expenses beyond tuition.

All 50 states, and the District of Columbia, now operate a 529 plan. Some states have more than one. Many of these programs extend an open invitation to you no matter which state your family lives in. In addition, the first-ever institutional prepaid tuition plan, a well-coordinated effort among 200-plus private colleges from across the nation, launched in 2003. The plethora of programs creates a great deal of choice in your selection of a college savings program, and more than a little confusion. By reading this book, you will be better prepared to make the right decisions for yourself and for your family.

How much does college cost?

According to the College Board, the price of one year at the average four-year private college including room and board and other expenses is nearly $30,000, and for the resident student at the average public college or university the price is approximately $12,000. During the past ten years, the annual rate of increase has averaged over five percent.[2]

Since 1980, college prices have been rising at a rate of two to three times the increase in the Consumer Price Index. If this trend continues, the price of a four-year private-college degree for the student enrolling ten years from now will exceed $200,000, and the student at a four-year public institution will pay more than $80,000. More troubling is the fact that median family income has not been keeping pace with rising college costs.

The future is difficult to predict. Recent economic conditions are leading to dramatic increases in tuition and fees at many colleges and universities. Stock market performance has hurt private-college endowments, and state budget woes are being blamed for double-digit hikes at many public institutions. A recovering economy may act to reverse these pressures, although certain other factors—including high demand as more high school graduates choose to enter college immediately, the second baby boom, and increasing costs relating to technology and faculty salaries—suggest that college cost increases will continue to outpace the general inflation indices. If anything can keep a lid on prices, it may be the "long-distance education" movement. Hoped-for efficiencies may eventually materialize and impart downward pressure.

For those who lack sufficient financial resources to simply pay the college bills when they arrive, the traditional means of outside assistance—federal, state, and institution-based financial aid programs—will still be available. Indeed, the money available for student aid has picked up considerably in recent years after a long decline through the 1980s and early 1990s. Since 1992, the federal government's investment in student aid through college scholarships and student loans has more than doubled.[3] But much of this increase is needed just to keep up with higher costs. Moreover, the use of averages fails to reflect the widening income disparity

---

2. Based on data from *Trends in College Pricing 2003* published by the College Board (a nonprofit association serving students, schools and colleges). These figures are for students who are living away from home while attending college.

3. U.S. Department of Education, *Expanding College Opportunity: More Access, Greater Achievement, Higher Expectations*, 2000.

between high and low earners, so the problem of "unmet need" among lower-income students has been growing, not slackening.

How are other families coping with this?

There is no shortage of surveys showing how families view and respond to the challenge of saving for college. The bottom line is that many Americans do not feel adequately prepared.

+ Most Americans believe that a college degree is absolutely essential or very important for young people today (Peter Hart and Associates, 2000), and consider saving for a child's college education to be a top savings priority (Richard Day Research, 1999).
+ Fifty percent of parents, however, do not have a good grasp of the expected cost of college (Yankelovich Partners, 2000), and 48 percent wished they had more information about how to pay for college (Harris Poll, 2002).
+ Two-thirds of parents do not anticipate being able to contribute as much toward the costs of their teen's college education as they would like (Fidelity Investments, 2004).
+ Families with household income below $50,000 are much less likely to be saving for college than families with income above $50,000 (Investment Company Institute, 2004).

Where is higher education on the nation's list of priorities?

Clearly, higher education is regarded in the halls of Congress and state capitols as a national priority worthy of public subsidy. The nature of the subsidy has shifted, however, away from direct support of institutions in favor of tax incentives for individuals. Tax breaks now help the individual who is paying for college, and the one who is saving for college. More money is being invested in dedicated college savings plans than ever before. Soon, many families with children in junior and senior high school will have significant sums set aside for college, and they will be looking for the best college education that money can buy.

The turnaround in education-friendly tax legislation has been remarkable. Before 1996, only a few tax breaks were aimed at helping individuals pay for their own or their children's college expenses. One of these was the exclusion of interest on the redemption of certain U.S savings bonds used to pay for college costs. Another was an employer-provided educational assistance plan, whereby an employee can receive up to $5,250 to pay for undergraduate (and beginning in 2002, graduate) school costs as a tax-free benefit. Income exclusions were also allowed for certain qualified scholarships received by an individual and, in narrow circumstances, for student loan forgiveness.

Other parts of the tax law became downright anti-education in the late 1980s, including the treatment of interest on student loans as nondeductible personal interest, the penalization of taxpayers under 59½ years old for taking distributions out of a qualified retirement plan or an individual retirement account (IRA) to pay for college costs, and the imposition of a "kiddie tax" on investment income of children under the age of 14. For most people, these rules left only one real way to save for future college costs: putting money aside after-tax in a savings or investment account.

Traditional means of saving for college

Many families who could afford to set aside savings for education purposes have done just that. Investment accounts have been established for children and grandchildren, either in the parents' or grandparents' names; in the child's name under the Uniform Gifts or Transfers to Minors Acts; or in special education trusts drafted by attorneys and trust companies. However, these are not tax-advantaged vehicles; zero coupon municipal bonds, stock mutual funds, and even life insurance were often the investments of choice.

The traditional approaches to college saving will continue to be popular with many people, particularly with favorable tax rates on capital gains and dividends. Long-term stock gains successfully shifted to a child's tax bracket may escape federal tax altogether. In addition, the education savings bond program and employer-provided educational assistance plans remain viable for taxpayers who can take advantage of them.

More options now available

Since 1996, Congress has created three new and very significant tax-advantaged ways to invest for college:

+ using a traditional or Roth IRA,
+ saving with a Coverdell education savings account (formerly the Education IRA), and
+ saving with a 529 plan.

And there's even more. The tax law also offers government tax subsidies for the *payment* of college expenses. These include the Hope Scholarship credit, the Lifetime Learning credit, and the renewed deductibility of interest on college loans.

How confusing are all these programs?

Very confusing. The good news in all of this is that tax breaks will help pay for the increasing price of a college education. There is a negative aspect, however, and that is the unprecedented level of complexity faced by families who may wish to take advantage of the new incentives. There are now so many alternatives available that you are likely to have a difficult time selecting the ones that are most appropriate in your circumstances. And some of these options are mutually exclusive; your use of one program may restrict or eliminate the use of another.

Why focus on 529 plans?

Section 529 plans provide some powerful and unique tax advantages not available with other college-savings options. What other tax-advantaged program allows everyone to participate, without regard to age or income level? What other program allows the accumulation of over $250,000 in a tax-sheltered account for one child's future college costs? What other mechanism allows someone with a large estate to immediately reduce that estate by $55,000 per child (or grandchild) without triggering gift tax, and without giving up control of the assets?

The answer is that no other tax-advantaged program provides the combination of benefits 529 plans offer. They are unique and wonderful creations that come in as many different forms as there are states and institutions to sponsor them. They are intended to serve one purpose— providing a way for families of any income level to save for future college costs in the most effective way possible. But they also have investment, tax, retirement, and estate planning implications that reach far beyond this one purpose.

This book will help you make the most effective use of the savings opportunities presented by the 529 plan. It explains the many strategies to consider and choices to make before deciding to enroll in a 529 plan. Once enrolled, 529 accounts continue to need attention, even though they are investments managed by professionals. This book also compares 529 plans to the other alternatives available to a family in saving for college, so that the best options can be selected from the bewildering array of choices.

Glossary

A number of terms used in this book deserve some explanation. An effort has been made to use the most common terminology, although not necessarily the language found in tax law, and to be as consistent as possible in the use of the terms. You will find, however, that the various state programs and other descriptive resources are not consistent in this regard.

529 plan—a qualified tuition program described in Section 529 of the Internal Revenue Code. Referred to in some sources as a **Section 529 Plan** or **QTP**.

Account owner—the person with ownership and control of the 529 account, usually the donor or contract purchaser. Many 529 plans refer to the account owner as the **participant**.

Basis—the sum of all cash contributions, plus the contribution portions of qualifying rollovers to the account, less the contribution portions of distributions previously made. Also known as the **principal of the account**. Tax law refers to basis as the **investment in the account**.

Designated beneficiary—the individual for whom the account or contract is established. All 529 plans require a designated beneficiary be named for each contract or account, except for accounts established by state or local governments or 501(c)(3) organizations for scholarship purposes.

Distribution—an amount of cash withdrawn from a 529 account, or the value of educational benefits provided by a 529 plan. Most 529 savings programs use the term **withdrawal**. If a distribution is used to pay for qualified higher education expenses it is called a **qualified distribution** or **qualified withdrawal**. If a distribution is made for any other reason it is called a **non-qualified withdrawal** or **refund**.

Earnings—the total account value less the basis. A distribution is comprised of an **earnings portion** and a **return of principal**.

Prepaid program—One type of 529 plan (a "savings program" is described below); a program that will pay for one or more years of future college tuition and other specified costs in return for your purchase of a prepayment contract. The person who purchases the contract is known as the **contract purchaser** or **contract owner**. Some prepaid programs offer units, with each unit representing a fixed percentage (often 1%) of one year's tuition. These programs are referred to as **unit-type prepaid programs**, and the purchaser is called the **unit purchaser, unit owner**, or **unit holder**. Tax law refers to an interest in a prepaid program as a prepaid educational arrangement or contract, to the purchaser as the **contributor**, and to the contract owner as the **account owner**.

Private prepaid program—A 529 plan operated by an eligible educational institution (not by a state), as authorized by the Economic Growth and Tax Relief Reconciliation Act of 2001.

Qualified higher education expenses (QHEE) —the post-secondary education expenses incurred by a designated beneficiary that are counted in determining the tax treatment of distributions from a 529 plan. Tax law describes the types of higher education expenses that qualify, generally tuition, fees, books, supplies, equipment, and a limited amount of room and board.

Rollover—a transfer of funds between 529 accounts that is not treated as a distribution because it satisfies certain conditions under Section 529.

Savings program—Another type of 529 plan (a "prepaid program" is described above); a program in which a **donor** makes a contribution to an account that grows in value over time from the investment of the contribution, or by pegging the value of the account to a tuition index. The person who owns the account in a savings program is known as the **account owner.** Tax law refers to the donor as the **contributor,** and to an interest in a savings program as an **educational savings account.** Some states will refer to their 529 savings program as an **investment program** to underscore the fact that accounts can lose value.

CHAPTER

ONE

History of 529 Plans

The states—not the federal government—deserve the credit for inventing 529 plans. Section 529 of the Internal Revenue Code was not even in existence at the time Michigan Governor James J. Blanchard, in his January 1986 State-of-the-State Address, proposed the creation of a new state-run prepaid tuition program "designed to help parents guarantee to their children the opportunity of a Michigan college education." With tuition costs spiraling, such a program would address the increasing anxiety in many thousands of Michigan households. The result of this proposal was the Michigan Education Trust (MET), a newly-created fund to which the state's residents could pay a stipulated amount in exchange for the trust's promise to pay future tuition for a named beneficiary at any Michigan public college or university. The essential benefit was the opportunity to prepay future tuition so as not to be affected by future tuition increases.

The Michigan proposal generated interest in other states, with Wyoming and Florida the first to launch prepaid tuition programs of similar design. Michigan delayed its own launch so that a ruling could be requested from the Internal Revenue Service regarding the tax aspects of the arrangement. The IRS responded to Michigan with both good news and bad news.[1] The good news was that the purchaser of the "prepaid tuition contract" would not be taxed on the accruing value of the contract until the year in which funds were distributed or refunded. The bad news was that the trust itself would be subject to income tax on earnings from invested funds. According to the IRS, it did not qualify as a tax-exempt state instrumentality.

Lacking such exemption, MET went ahead anyway and in 1988 began entering into prepaid tuition contracts with Michigan's residents. Fifty-five thousand individuals signed up for the program. MET paid federal income tax on its investment earnings, and in 1990 filed suit for refund from the IRS. The case was first decided in favor of the IRS, but on appeal in 1994, the Sixth Circuit Court of Appeals reversed the district court judge's decision and found in Michigan's favor.[2]

The irony of the Michigan experience is that MET was forced in 1990 to stop issuing new contracts, due not so much to the burden of paying income taxes, but because it had been selling the prepaid tuition contracts at prices later determined to be too low. When originally establishing contract pricing, program administrators had relied on overly optimistic projections of the rate of return on invested funds in relation to the trust's obligation to pay for rising tuition prices. Simply put, the trust was headed towards insolvency. (The program later resumed with more appropriate pricing and remains today as one of the largest prepaid programs.)

Not long after its 1994 defeat in the Sixth Circuit, the IRS began considering other ways to keep participants in prepaid tuition programs from gaining a tax advantage, one of which was to tax beneficiaries each year on the increasing value of their prepayment contracts. Concerned that such treatment would be a disincentive for savings, Congress passed new legislation authorizing qualified State tuition programs ("QSTPs") as part of the Small Business Job Protection Act of 1996. Section 529 was added to the

---

1. IRS Letter Ruling 8825027
2. Michigan v. United States, 40 F.3rd 817 (6th Cir. 1994), rev'g 802 F. Supp. 120 (W.D. Mich 1992)

Internal Revenue Code by the Act, conferring tax exemption to qualifying state programs, and deferring tax on participants' undistributed earnings.

Although the enactment of Section 529 attracted little notice at the time, it no doubt helped to advance the Clinton administration's highly-publicized agenda to create significant new tax incentives for higher education, an effort that culminated a year later with the Taxpayer Relief Act of 1997 (TRA). The TRA introduced the Hope and Lifetime Learning credits, a tax deduction for interest on student loans, and penalty-free IRA withdrawals for higher education. Substantial changes were also made to Code Section 529 by the TRA, adding room and board to the list of qualifying expenses and providing special estate and gift tax treatment for participants in a 529 plan.

The TRA also gave rise to a new tax-advantaged savings vehicle for college named the Education IRA. Unlike Section 529, which provided that earnings were taxable even when withdrawn for qualified higher education expenses (albeit at the student's tax rate), the Education IRA offered federal tax exemption for the earnings when withdrawn for the same purpose. While this was seen as a significant advantage, the Education IRA was hobbled by age and income restrictions, and by a $500 annual per-beneficiary contribution limit.

With the ink barely dry on the 1997 TRA, the Republican-controlled Congress began pressing to make tax-free Education IRA distributions available to families sending their children to private and parochial grade schools. A bill was drafted to add elementary and secondary school expenses as approved expenses. With much less fanfare, another provision was added to the bill to make Section 529 distributions tax-free, not just tax-deferred, when used for college. Although the bill passed Congress, President Bill Clinton vetoed it, likening the expanded Education IRA to private school vouchers. A similar effort in 1999 failed for the same reason.

The stage was set for President George W. Bush when he took office in January 2001. New tax bills were crafted in both the Senate and the House of Representatives containing the previously-vetoed changes. With strong bipartisan support, the Economic Growth and Tax Relief Reconciliation Act (EGTRRA) of 2001 was signed into law on June 7, 2001. The extension of the Education IRA exemption to include qualifying expenses for kindergarten through 12th grade, along with an increase in the annual contribution limit from $500 to $2,000, were hailed as major accomplishments. (Soon after EGTRRA's enactment, the Education IRA was renamed the Coverdell education savings account, giving recognition to Senator Paul Coverdell as champion of the K-12 provision.) The Section 529 exclusion, although receiving little notice at the time, arguably has had more impact.

EGTRRA made several other significant improvements to the sections controlling 529 plans and the Education IRA/Coverdell ESA. On the 529 front, states would no longer be required to collect a penalty on "non-qualified" distributions made by their programs, as a 10-percent federal tax penalty was now assessed on the federal income tax return. And educational institutions could now establish their own 529 prepaid tuition programs, without any state involvement. Accordingly, qualified State tuition programs were renamed qualified tuition programs, or "QTPs". Most people continue to refer to these programs as 529 plans.

Why do states start 529 plans?

All 50 states, and the District of Columbia, now have 529 plans in operation. Even before Congress fully sanctioned these programs in 1996, nine states operated prepaid tuition programs for their residents. But why? The commitment of staff and other state resources in establishing and maintaining a 529 plan is significant. And until recently, there seemed to be little if any net revenue accruing to the sponsoring state.

As it turns out, states are interested in 529 plans for several reasons. One is the conviction that education is an essential function of state government, and establishing tax-advantaged savings programs targeted for education allows more individuals to obtain a college degree without taking on a crushing debt load. This argument is met with some degree of skepticism, however, since the amount of direct support provided by many states to their public systems of higher education has not kept pace with costs, forcing state schools to increase their tuition levels.

Another incentive for a state to set up a 529 plan is to encourage its residents to attend in-state public colleges and universities. Obviously, this would help keep the state's own institutions financially strong. Although nearly every 529 plan has "portable" benefits, which means that beneficiaries are allowed to use their account to pay for qualified expenses at eligible private and out-of-state institutions, a number of the older programs provide a better investment return to families who choose in-state public institutions. In most 529 plans now, it makes absolutely no difference whether the student attends college within or outside the state operating the 529 plan.

Some cynics believe that the primary motivation for states to commit money in establishing and maintaining 529 plans is political. The programs allow elected officials to look good to the voters. Education is a powerful campaign issue. The governor and state treasurer who champion legislation making it easier for people to afford a college education can easily claim a very "pro-family" stance.

Some of the impetus and support for the expanding 529 market comes from the National Association of State Treasurers, which has formed an affiliate, the College Savings Plans Network (CSPN), as a means to coordinate resources among its members and share ideas concerning state-sponsored programs. Composed of state officials and program administrators, CSPN meets at least annually to discuss issues and communicate ideas and new developments.

What's in store for the future?

Until fairly recently, the future for 529 plans seemed exceptionally bright. New programs had been springing up across the country, creating a wave of enthusiasm among the professional financial community and capturing the interest of the press. Articles and feature stories extolling the benefits of 529 plans were appearing at an increasing pace in the national and regional media. And substantial dollars were finding their way into 529 plans; the $9 billion invested at the beginning of 2001 jumped to nearly $27 billion by the end of 2002.

In January 2003, the 529 momentum was disrupted by the Bush administration's proposal to establish new Lifetime Savings Accounts (LSAs), where individuals of any age and income level could contribute up to $7,500 annually to an investment account, and take withdrawals at any time and for any purpose free from federal income tax. The flexibility and simplicity of the LSA promised to attract a substantial number of college savers, along with their investment dollars. Failing to gain any traction in Congress, the LSA proposal withered, and assets in all 529 plans grew by another $18 billion in 2003, to over $45 billion.

President Bush and the U.S. Treasury Department have not given up on the LSA, and included it again in the administration's fiscal 2005 budget proposal, albeit with a lowered annual contribution maximum of $5,000. As this book goes to press, it is impossible to predict the ultimate fate of the LSA. Even if it were to make it through Congress, the chances of its being further watered down in the process are high. And while any new federal tax-advantaged savings vehicle could significantly impair the growth of 529 plans, the impact would not be fatal. Section 529 plans will continue under any circumstances to offer some key benefits—e.g. state tax breaks, tuition prepayment options, and very high contribution limits—that LSAs could not match.

Assuming the LSA does not see the light of day in its originally-proposed form, it seems certain that, under the 2001 tax law changes and a recovering economy, we will witness an accelerating pace of investment in 529 plans over the next few years. Polls indicate that public awareness of 529 plans still has a ways to go. Many families with children likely to attend college are not yet fully aware of this investment option. This situation is improving, however, due not only to the substantial amount of media coverage, but also because an increasing number of large mutual fund companies and investment brokers are taking on a direct role in the 529 industry.

As recently as June 2000, only four large nationally-recognized investment companies had been selected by the states to manage their 529 college savings programs: TIAA-CREF, Merrill Lynch, Fidelity Investments, and Salomon Smith Barney. Since then, the list has expanded to include most of the country's largest mutual fund companies and financial services firms. These companies are willing to invest substantial sums in advertising and promoting the programs they represent. They see a direct revenue opportunity with 529 plans, and they also see a new tax-advantaged product that will help to round out a menu of products and services to investors.

A significant number of the newer 529 savings programs are now being marketed as "national" college savings plans, despite their state sponsorship. Many of these widely-available programs are being distributed under commission agreements with brokers, financial planners, and other financial advisers. By partnering with the professional investment community, the states are able to offer 529 plans with the look and feel of mutual funds without incurring the associated costs. Registered brokers and investment advisers can directly assist families in understanding 529 plans and selecting appropriate investments, whereas state program administrators are generally prohibited from providing investment advice.

As consumers come to realize that they have a choice among 529 plans, "program shopping" will become more prevalent and some states will find their citizens jumping the border to obtain better-perceived benefits with another state's program. Some individuals will later seek to modify their initial decisions by transferring their accounts from one state's 529 plan to another's.

To protect the viability of their programs, most states appear very willing and even eager to adopt frequent modifications to their 529 plans and provide additional investment alternatives. Several states have added incentives for residents to stay close to home with their college savings, including state income-tax deductions for participant contributions, and even a partial match of contributions. Some residents now enjoy a break on fees and expenses in their home-state programs.

Most of the older 529 plans were developed by the states as prepaid programs, while the majority of newer 529 plans are savings programs (see chapter 5 for a discussion of program types). Many prepaid programs are restricted to state residents and cover only undergraduate tuition and fees. Savings programs are generally more flexible in their application to all the qualifying costs of higher education, and are more familiar to American families accustomed to IRAs, 401(k) plans, and other similar investments.

Savings programs are also easier to administer and less costly to the state, particularly when an outside financial-services company is willing to offer turnkey management under attractive financial arrangements with the state.

In states offering both prepaid and savings programs, separate trusts are maintained and each program operates under its own set of rules. However, they are often packaged under one marketing umbrella and administered by the same agency. Some states are even turning over marketing and operational responsibilities for their prepaid programs to the investment firms managing their savings programs.

Despite the more restrictive nature of prepaid programs, many families continue to be attracted to the "tuition guarantee" they offer and the fact that stock market volatility does not have a direct impact on the value of benefits available through those programs. This does not mean that prepaid tuition programs and their participants are immune to stock market risks, however. A combination of spiraling tuition and low or negative investment performance in the program trust fund can threaten the financial solvency of a prepaid tuition program. Several programs have increased the price of tuition contracts well beyond current public tuition rates, and some have suspended the enrollment into their programs while waiting for financial conditions to improve. At least one program, Colorado's Prepaid Tuition Fund, has no intention of opening back up (although current participants will continue to receive tuition benefits).

The first-ever Section 529 private-college prepaid tuition plan was launched in September 2003. Independent 529 Plan offers tuition certificates redeemable towards tuition at any of 200-plus member colleges and universities. The states will not be involved in this program, which is intended to attract interest from families planning on sending their children to private colleges.

Investment offerings available through 529 savings programs have evolved rapidly. The earliest programs offered a single fixed-income investment. In the late 1990s, several states introduced equity investments as part of an "age-based" investment strategy. This approach, involving a shift in the underlying asset allocation from an equity-weighted portfolio to a fixed-income-weighted portfolio as the beneficiary approached college, was viewed as an appropriate "auto-pilot" investment program under a provision in Code Section 529 that prohibited investment direction by the participant.

The next move was to add "static" or "fixed-allocation" investment options as alternatives to the age-based approach, creating a menu of investment offerings for the program participant. These options appealed to investors who desired more control over their asset allocation, despite the continuing prohibition on investment direction. Fair warning was provided to participants, however, that restrictions contained in Section 529 meant that contributions to a particular investment option could not be redirected later on.

Investors were not truly locked in. A "rollover" made it possible to move funds to another 529 account in the plan with a different investment election, or even to a different state's 529 plan. Originally, however, a rollover was tax-free only if the beneficiary designation was changed to a member of the original beneficiary's family. The 2001 tax law changes made it even easier by permitting a same-beneficiary rollover between programs once in any 12-month period. The IRS, sensing the prohibition against participant investment direction contained in Section 529 had become a paper tiger in the wake of these changes, subsequently announced in September 2001 (Notice 2001–55) that a program could permit investors to change their investment selection once every calendar year, or whenever a beneficiary change took place. No longer was it necessary to transfer 529 funds in order to adjust an account's asset allocation.

Whereas in the past 529 plans were largely viewed as somewhat quirky and of limited usefulness, they have now broken out into the mainstream. Their tax advantages, investment offerings and near-universal accessibility make them attractive to the majority of families in a position to save for college. The states have ceded much of their direct involvement in running the programs to the large financial institutions that can succeed in marketing and managing an investment product. The collegial atmosphere in which state politicians and agency heads have worked together in developing and promoting the concept of a college savings program is being tested by the inevitable forces of free-market competition.

I've seen some articles in the newspapers concerning investigations into 529 plans. What's this all about?

Several recent developments have cast a cloud over some 529 plans. The mutual fund "scandal" that began unfolding during 2003 has directly touched a number of programs using scandal-tainted mutual fund companies as program managers. The reaction by the states to control damage in the wake of investigations by state attorneys general and the Securities and Exchange Commission has been swift if not consistent. At least one state (Oregon) fired its program manager. Other states that may have felt pressure to do the same found themselves constrained by contractual restrictions along with a general desire to avoid major changes in programs that seemed to be working well. In some cases, the states have attempted to blunt the effect of the scandal by expanding their investment menus to include different mutual funds, reducing fees and expenses, and rewriting contracts with their program managers.

Investment regulatory agencies are now scrutinizing the sale of 529 plans, but face an issue as to the scope of their authority. As a state-issued security, an interest in a 529 plan is not subject to the same level of federal oversight as other types of securities and is exempt from registration with the Securities and Exchange Commission (SEC). The Municipal Securities Rulemaking Board (MSRB), a self-regulatory agency created by Congress and subject to SEC administrative oversight, has been busy issuing new investor-protection rules, but its authority extends only to 529 plans sold by brokers. Absent fraud, the direct-sold 529 plans have only their own states to answer to. Whether or not the states will retain the right to self-regulate 529 plans may rest on their success in establishing and maintaining adequate disclosure and reporting standards across all 529 plans. In mid-2004, the College Savings Plans Network approved a set of voluntary disclosure guidelines for 529 savings plans. If these guidelines fail to receive widespread acceptance, Congress may seek legislative changes authorizing the SEC to regulate all 529 plans.

Other public-policy watchdogs are also keeping a close eye on developments in the 529 industry. They are raising such questions as: Are state-sponsored college savings programs a good use of public funds? Do they disproportionately benefit socio-economic groups that do not really need these incentives? Will a program's obligation to pay for tuition influence the pricing decisions of the state's public institutions? Are these institutions becoming too dependent on these programs, and therefore at risk? Will colleges raise their prices, affecting everyone, as more students begin appearing with significant balances in their 529 accounts? Michael A. Olivas and his colleagues at the Institute for Higher Education Law and Governance at the University of Houston Law Center are leading the discussion on several of these issues.[3]

This scrutiny will intensify as attention is focused on the scheduled 2010 expiration of the 2001 EGTRRA tax incentives. Millions of families, with tens of billions of dollars invested in 529 plans, will be anxious to see the exclusion for qualified distributions extended beyond 2010. Our institutions of higher education should be interested as well; many of these families will have sizable savings accounts matched by a desire for the best education this money can buy. Even those families without the financial resources to save for college may have reason to support Section 529 tax incentives. To the extent that higher-income families are willing and able to increase their own savings, we may find that aid dollars can be more effectively directed to those families that truly need the assistance.

---

3. See Michael A. Olivas (ed.), *Prepaid College Tuition Plans—Promise and Problems*, (NY: College Board, 1993), and Barbara Jennings and Michael A. Olivas, *Prepaying and Saving for College, Opportunities and Issues*, Policy Perspectives No. 3 (D.C.: College Board, 2000).

TWO

Why You Should be Interested in a 529 Plan

imply stated, the 529 plan is likely to be your best option for college savings if you have school-age children or grandchildren and are looking to invest significant amounts of money (tens or even hundreds of thousands of dollars). If your savings goals are more modest, the 529 plan can still be competitive with Coverdell education savings accounts (chapter 9) and other college savings options.

As everyone knows, children "grow up too fast." Yet, at the same time, too few parents make a serious attempt to figure out how much it will cost to send their children to college, or consider available options in planning for those costs. Perhaps you expect your child to receive a full athletic or other merit scholarship to a major university. Is your seventh-grader already up to six-foot-four and able to hit four out of five from beyond the three-point line? Was she the national champ in her age group for the 200-meter butterfly? Has he been the headline performer at Carnegie Hall? If so, congratulations! College costs should not be a problem for you, assuming your child's injury-free dedication to the sport or other activity continues through high school. If not, welcome to the group of us who cannot count on a full scholarship and need to face the prospect of coming up with the resources to fund our child's education.

Let's face it, just meeting everyday expenses is challenging enough, never mind trying to save significant dollars on top of that. The task of putting aside enough money to pay for college often seems overwhelming. It is difficult to conceptualize the amount that the experts are telling us a private college will cost in 2022 when today's newborn will be enrolling. A quarter-million dollars? Why even bother to try?

Some of us think a safety net will always exist. "If it turns out that I can't afford to pay my kid's college expenses, I know there will be other ways to handle it." Thanks to our educational institutions and government, a safety net currently does exist, in the form of federal, state, and institution-based financial-aid programs. But even with the programs now available—including loans, grants, and work-study—many qualified students and their families face financial pressures that impact their desire and ability to attend college. Furthermore, we see that loans, not grants, are the fastest growing component of financial aid.

Finally, some parents are unwilling to establish dedicated college savings accounts even when they have the resources to do so, because they do not like to give up control of assets. Putting assets in Uniform Transfers to Minors Act accounts is always an option, but how do you eliminate the risk that the child will decide to fund an "alternative" lifestyle that does not include college? You can place the assets in trust with provisions that prevent unauthorized use of the funds, but the establishment of the trust may involve significant time and money, and then it requires annual maintenance. Many parents simply contribute the maximum allowable amount to qualified retirement plans, buy a nice house with some appreciation potential, and put whatever's left over into mutual funds.

Section 529 plans offer many features and tax incentives to overcome families' reluctance to save for college. No matter what circumstances a family may be in—large or small, low-income or high-income, decided on a particular college or undecided, transient or settled—there are programs available to accommodate college saving desires in simple, flexible, and tax-efficient ways. In fact, 529 plans offer advantages even to those without school-age children or grandchildren. Who's to say that the older individual will not want to return to school at some point in the future? We see more "nontraditional" students enrolling in post-secondary schools every year, for graduate work, for a change of career, or just for enjoyment and self-improvement. A 529 plan can be a great way to save for this possibility, even if the idea is eventually abandoned.

What's so great about 529 plans?

Here are the advantages, in a nutshell:

Federal income tax advantages

+ Earnings build up in your account on a tax-deferred basis.
+ Distributions from your account that are used for certain qualifying college costs are tax-free. (As explained in chapter 3, this benefit is currently scheduled to expire at the end of 2010.)

Estate and gift tax benefits

+ Your contributions to a 529 account are treated as completed, present-interest gifts to the beneficiary for purposes of the federal gift tax and generation-skipping transfer tax. This means that the money comes out of your taxable estate, and the gifts qualify for the $11,000 annual gift-tax exclusion.
+ A special election allows your contributions to be treated as if they were made over a five-year period for gift and generation-skipping transfer tax purposes. This means that $55,000 can be contributed to a 529 plan account gift-tax free (assuming you make no other gifts during that five-year period).

Availability and flexibility

+ Unlike so many other tax breaks, a 529 plan imposes no income limitations. A high-income individual can take advantage of a 529 plan when other alternatives (such as a Coverdell education savings account) are not available.

✦ In most 529 plans, over $200,000 can be contributed to an account for a single beneficiary. At $2,000 per year, a Coverdell education savings account just doesn't measure up.

✦ Despite the treatment of your contributions as completed gifts, you still retain ownership and control of the account. This creates powerful and unique advantages. You, and not the beneficiary, decide when to take distributions and for what purpose. You can substitute the beneficiary of the account; you can even revoke it. Any concern that you may have about losing control of significant assets is greatly diminished.

Investment benefits

✦ Section 529 plans offer different investment approaches, providing the opportunity to select an approach that parallels your own investment objectives. Some programs offer a way for your savings to keep up with increases in tuition costs; others offer a menu of investment options ranging from low-risk, fixed-income funds to higher-risk stock funds; while still others use portfolios allocated among stocks, bonds and money market investments tailored to the age of your beneficiary. Many programs have no residency requirements, making the range of savings options available to all.

✦ You can obtain professional investment management at a reasonable cost. Fees and expenses will vary considerably among 529 plans, and they should always be a factor in your decision to invest. But for most families the tax benefits of a 529 plan outweigh the extra expense, and the sponsoring states are intent on keeping the costs as low as possible, particularly for their own residents. Some programs utilizing mutual funds are able to acquire the lowest-cost "institutional" shares, thereby reducing the overall expense to you.

✦ Many programs accommodate automatic payment plans through payroll deduction or electronic funds transfer from your bank account, making education budgeting simple and providing the discipline that some parents need.

State tax benefits

+ Most states follow federal income tax treatment in excluding the earnings in your 529 account from state and local income taxes, and many offer a deduction or tax credit for all or part of your contributions into their programs.
+ A few states also provide other financial benefits to program participants, such as scholarships, matching contributions, or favorable state-aid treatment.

Asset protection

+ In some states, the law provides specific protections from creditors' claims.

If these programs are so great, why doesn't everyone know about them and use them?

The answer is that everyone *should* be aware of 529 plans, and in fact the word has been spreading. Surveys show that with each passing year more Americans gain familiarity with 529 plans.

Growth in 529 assets has been impressive. At the beginning of 2002 there was approximately $14 billion in all 529 plans. This figure had increased to over $45 billion by the start of 2004. It is reasonable to expect continued rapid growth over the next few years.

What accounts for the popularity of 529 plans? We can point to several factors:

+ **Wide availability and full public acceptance of 529 plans.** Although several states have a tuition savings program dating back to the late 1980s, it was not until 1996 that Section 529 was added to the Internal Revenue Code, and the majority of programs now in operation are new since 1997. Every state has at least one 529 plan, many states have two, and a few have three or more. Educational institutions now have the authority to develop and offer their own 529 prepaid programs.

✦ **An outpouring of media interest** in 529 plans, particularly in the wake of the tax law changes in 2001 that granted a federal income-tax exemption for qualified distributions. Many personal finance periodicals, including Money, SmartMoney, and Kiplinger's Personal Finance Magazine, regularly mention 529 plans. Many of the country's top financial writers now recognize the advantages of 529 plans and recommend them through their books, Web sites, public appearances, and newspaper columns.

✦ **Increased awareness of 529 plans among the professional investment and insurance community.** Before 2001, most brokers, investment advisers, and financial planners had little reason to promote 529 plans over other more traditional investment products because none of the state programs paid a commission. That has all changed now. Every segment of the professional planning community—hourly fee-based, asset fee-based, commission-based, or some combination—has a way to introduce 529 plans into its clients' portfolios and be compensated for their advice and guidance. In fact, we now see that broker-sold 529 plans are the fastest-growing component of new account growth, reflecting the large number of investors who rely on financial professionals in making investment decisions. For those individuals who wish to conduct their own research and make their own investment decisions while incurring lower fees and expenses, "direct-sold" 529 plans will always be an option.

✦ **Workplace enrollment.** Many employers are receptive to the idea of facilitating employee use of 529 plans by offering group enrollment and payroll deduction. As an after-tax voluntary deduction program, a workplace 529 program has no payroll tax implications, no discrimination testing, and few, if any, eligibility requirements. Hence, this additional "benefit" can be made available to employees at low or no cost to the company. Special considerations come into play, however, in deciding which particular 529 plan or group of plans to offer under a group-enrollment format. Since the dollars being contributed are coming from the employee, it is incumbent upon the employer to consider whether the 529 plans selected are the ones that offer the best benefits to their particular employees.

✦ **Private company affiliations.** An increasing number of private companies view higher education as a national priority and have recognized 529 plans as a way to help families that are facing the challenge of paying for college costs. Customer loyalty programs are one type of enterprise that see a nice fit with 529 plans. By using particular credit cards or buying particular products, you earn "rewards" that can be automatically deposited into your 529 accounts. While Upromise (www.upromise.com) appears to be the largest such rewards program with over 5 million families signed up, others may easily be found on the web by typing "college savings rewards" into Google or other search engines.

But don't 529 plans require that I send my child to an in-state public school?

This is one of the most common misconceptions about 529 plans. In fact, every state's 529 plan permits your account to be used at colleges and universities anywhere in the United States (and in many foreign countries as well). Some 529 plans provide better benefits for in-state schools, but none lock you into a specific institution or state public education system.

I've heard about the program in my state and it doesn't really excite me. That leaves me out, right?

Not at all. You should consider other states' programs. Many of the best 529 plans are operated by states that impose no residency restrictions. They are open to all.

I have already set up an account in my state. So I guess I'm all set.

Guess again. Have you selected the program with the best benefits? If not, you may be better off transferring your account to a different state's 529 plan. If transfer is not a viable option (because of certain restrictions under federal law or penalties and fees imposed by some 529 plans), you can leave your current account where it is and open a second account (or third account, etc.) with another state that offers a more attractive program.

My broker tells me I am better off using his recommended mutual funds to save for college costs. Is he right?

Your broker may be right, but it really depends on your particular circumstances and investment objectives. The better question is: How much does your broker or financial planner know about 529 plans? Until recently few did, and many felt threatened by the concept of a 529 plan, viewing it as a competitive product that did not pay commissions. That situation has largely changed now that many states have approved commissions for 529 plans distributed through investment advisers. Financial professionals across the country, including commission-based advisers as well as fee-only planners, have begun embracing 529 plans as a potential solution for clients, and are finding ways to effectively incorporate them into long-term financial plans. Knowledge level remains the key, however. If you rely on a broker or financial planner in making investment decisions, be sure the adviser is up to speed on the technical and comparative aspects of 529 plans. To locate such a professional in your area, try using the "Find a 529 Pro" directory at www.savingforcollege.com.

My child is a senior in high school. Isn't it too late for me to start using a 529 plan?

Not necessarily. Assess your potential for tax savings by looking at your most recently filed income tax return. Did you pay any tax on interest, dividends, or capital gains distributions? If you did, a 529 plan represents an opportunity to convert taxable investment income into tax-free investment income. Even if the account has a life of only a few years—remember that it will usually take two to five years or even longer to earn a degree—you will be saving taxes. In fact, many parents facing college bills in the near future want to have their money in safe, interest-paying investments. This is the where the tax protection of a 529 plan provides the greatest advantage.

It gets even better if you live in a state that offers a tax deduction for contributions to the home-state 529 plan. Instead of paying college bills out-of-pocket, you can reap the benefit of a state income tax deduction by first making a contribution to the 529 plan, and then using your account to pay the bills. Bottom line: college expenses become a write-off for state income tax purposes.

Section 529 plans sound too good to be true. Won't the IRS or Congress shut them down?

Not likely. Millions of American families are now investing in 529 plans and there is every indication that our elected officials in Washington want to see them become more popular, not less. This point was underscored at a June 2004 hearing held by the House Financial Services Subcommittee on Capital Markets. "The success of 529 tuition savings plans is good news," declared Rep. Michael G. Oxley in his opening statement.

There must be some disadvantages to 529 plans. What are they?

No single investment, including a 529 plan, is the perfect option for every investor. The comparative advantages and disadvantages of 529 plans are discussed throughout this book. The fact that most 529 plans charge a fee to participants, as mentioned earlier in this chapter, is certainly one of the most obvious considerations. Here are some other significant disadvantages.

+ Section 529 plans are confusing. It is difficult to understand all the considerations and options relating to 529 plans. There are plenty of places where you can learn about IRAs, savings bonds, and the like, and the rules for these programs are fairly straightforward—one sponsor's IRA is not going to be much different from another. The same is not true for 529 plans. The rules surrounding 529 plans invite many questions and planning considerations. And rather than one basic model, there are several to choose from. Each 529 plan has unique features that make comparisons between different programs tricky. Many financial and legal advisers have not yet learned enough about the programs to effectively counsel their clients in this area. You can find some helpful articles in the financial press, and the materials available from the programs themselves provide a great deal of useful information. In addition, the Securities and Exchange Commission and certain industry groups such as the National Association of Securities Dealers, Inc. (NASD) and the Securities Industry Association (SIA) have recently begun efforts to provide general 529 information to the investing public. But apart from this book and the information on our companion Web site at www.savingforcollege.com, there is currently little comprehensive literature available from independent sources.

✦ The lower tax rates on capital gains and dividends do not apply to gains in your 529 account. Of course, if things work out right your earnings will be entirely tax-free, but if any part of a withdrawal turns out to be taxable as a "non-qualified distribution," it is taxable at ordinary income rates. There will also be a 10 percent penalty on earnings, unless an exception applies.

✦ If your account loses value, you cannot simply sell the investment and claim a capital loss. Under certain circumstances you may be able to claim a miscellaneous itemized deduction in the year you completely liquidate a 529 account, but many taxpayers will find little or no tax benefit in doing this.

✦ Investment selection in a 529 savings program is limited (although less so than in the past), and your ability to change investments is somewhat restricted. The ultimate responsibility for your account rests with the state agency or other person acting as trustee under the program trust. They make the rules, and they can change them. To date, almost all program changes have been beneficial to the participant but that may not always be the case.

✦ You may decide to invest with a particular 529 plan based in part on the program's selection of a particular mutual fund company or financial services firm as program manager, only to find that the program manager is replaced in a later year with a different investment firm. The contracts between the state and the outside program manager have terms lasting anywhere from two to 30 years, and at the end of that term the state can decide to bring in someone new. If that happens, it is likely that your account will have new investments and different expenses.

✦ The fact that you retain ownership and control over the account may work against you in certain situations. For instance, an account owner applying for Medicaid in the future may find that the state Medicaid agency requires that the 529 account first be used to pay for medical and long-term care expenses before Medicaid payments can begin. Another risk is that creditors attempt to reach your account for unpaid debts. These issues are usually controlled by state law, and some states do provide specific protections for participants in their 529 plans (seek advice from an attorney). Federal bankruptcy protection does not extend to 529 accounts although as this book went to press both houses of Congress had passed bills that would provide some level of bankruptcy protection to 529 accounts.[1]

✦ Your 529 account, and any distributions from it, can impact the student's eligibility for need-based financial aid. This particular issue is covered in detail in chapter 4 and throughout the other chapters in this book.

---

1. See Senate Bill S.420. Generally, up to $5,000 in contributions made to a 529 plan between 365 days and 720 days prior to the filing of the bankruptcy petition, and any amount of contributions up to program limits for contributions before that time, would be excluded from the account owner's or contributor's bankruptcy estate and would therefore be protected from creditor claims. There are certain requirements as to the relationship of the debtor and the 529 account beneficiary.

I'm not sure I like the idea of the state holding my money. What's to prevent the state from appropriating the program funds for other purposes?

In most states, your contributions and account earnings are maintained in a separate legal trust that cannot be reached by the state for other purposes. If you have concerns about this, you should not hesitate to contact the program administrator in the state operating the program and obtain specific assurances.

I have heard that I cannot count on my withdrawals being tax-free when my child goes to college because the law will change in 2011. Is that right?

The changes made to Code Section 529 by the Economic Growth and Tax Relief Reconciliation Act of 2001 are scheduled to expire at the end of the year 2010. Unless Congress acts to renew these rules before then, we automatically revert to pre–2002 Section 529 treatment. This means that qualified withdrawals would no longer be tax-free (the earnings portion would be taxed to the beneficiary) and other provisions would change as well. While there are no guarantees, it is difficult to believe that Congress will fail to preserve the 529 exclusion considering that millions of families will have a direct interest in these programs by the time 2011 rolls around.

My employer has recently started promoting a payroll deduction plan for college savings. Is this something I should consider?

Contributing to a 529 plan through payroll deduction can be a simple and relatively "painless" way to budget for college savings. Your employer may be interested in helping you learn more about the benefits of saving with a 529 plan and may even offer assistance in the enrollment process. Often the support and education is provided directly by a 529 program manager, or a financial adviser representing a 529 plan, under special arrangement with the employer. You will usually have the opportunity to attend special educational sessions, study program materials, and get your questions answered.

You should not assume that your employer's 529 plan is the best one for you. You will always have the option to establish an account on your own. Some employers will offer payroll deduction for two or more 529 plans so you have some choice in selecting the best program for you. Employers will generally disclaim any responsibility for determining your suitability for the investment.

Contributions to a 529 plan through payroll deduction are made on an after-tax basis. Unlike a 401(k), your contributions are not subtracted from your taxable earnings, and they generally do not involve any payroll taxes or discrimination testing on the part of the employer.

I see that 501(c)(3) exempt organizations can open accounts in many 529 plans, but why would they want to?

Under the law, a charitable organization opening a 529 account as part of a scholarship program is not required to name a beneficiary to the account. While the ability to defer the designation of beneficiary until awarding the scholarship is crucial, most scholarship-granting organizations will still have little reason to use a 529 plan. They do not reap any benefit from the tax exemption under Section 529 (charitable organizations do not pay tax on investment income anyway), and most have already established internal policies controlling the investment of their scholarship funds. However, other organizations that do not currently have a scholarship program might be interested in starting one, if it was easy to administer. A 529 savings program can fill this role by offering professional investment management and account administration at low cost. Many 529 program managers will be eager to facilitate the objectives of the scholarship program, including the processing of scholarship withdrawals to the institutions attended by scholarship recipients. There might also be valuable cross-promotional opportunities between the charity and the 529 plan.

THREE

Section 529 Overview

This chapter describes the provisions of Code Section 529, including the tax benefits for the participant, the tax rules for withdrawals, and the various qualification requirements. It is a fairly technical chapter that includes information needed by the professional adviser who will be working closely with clients considering these investments.

Unfortunately, the amount of guidance coming from the Treasury Department and IRS discussing Section 529 and other education tax provisions has not been sufficient to address all the questions that can arise. Proposed regulations under Section 529 were issued in August 1998, and were helpful at the time, but they have become obsolete as a result of the Economic Growth and Tax Relief Reconciliation Act (EGTRRA), signed in June 2001. The IRS considers the issuance of final regulations under Section 529 to be a "priority," but that does not necessarily mean we will see them anytime soon.

Regulations are important because they describe the rules that the programs, and individual taxpayers, must follow in order to be in compliance with Section 529. The literal reading of the law must be coordinated with the practical demands placed on the programs and their participants.

The Treasury Department faces some particularly difficult issues in developing regulations under Section 529 due to the unique character of these programs.

Meantime, we can look to other IRS documents for some help. Notices, rulings, publications, and the tax forms themselves (along with their instructions) provide direction but not a lot of detail. The best place for taxpayers to find official IRS guidance is Publication 970, Tax Benefits for Higher Education, available on the Web at www.irs.gov.

Several of the rules described below are scheduled to change in 2011 following the sunset of EGTRRA. Unless new laws extend or modify the provisions of Section 529, the treatment of 529 plans and their program participants will revert to pre–2002 laws. Because it appears somewhat likely that Congress and the President will agree to act on these provisions before that time, pre-EGTRRA Section 529 provisions are not fully detailed in this chapter.

What is a 529 plan and who can participate?

A 529 plan is a program designed to help families prepare for the cost of post-secondary education that meets certain requirements contained in Section 529 of the Internal Revenue Code for a "qualified tuition program" or "QTP." Section 529 serves two basic purposes.

First, it grants tax-exempt status to 529 plans. Without statutory protection, the state-owned trust holding the investment assets could be taxed on its undistributed investment income.[1] Further, trust earnings will not be considered "debt-financed" income, if the only liability of the program is to investors, and so the tax on unrelated business income is not applied.

Second, Section 529 describes the federal tax treatment for program participants, both for income tax purposes and for estate, gift and

---

1. Tax-exempt status is already provided to states and their political subdivisions under Code Section 115. The central issue in Michigan v. United States (6th Cir. 1994) (discussed in chapter 1) was whether the Michigan Education Trust was an instrumentality of the state and thus protected from imposition of tax. The IRS felt the MET was not a state instrumentality. Several other state programs could be challenged on similar grounds if not for Code Section 529.

generation-skipping transfer tax purposes. In some ways, the treatment prescribed by Section 529 as it relates to participants directly contradicts the "normal" rules under other provisions of the tax law.

Only two groups can offer a 529 plan. The first includes any state or state agency or instrumentality ("state"). The second includes any eligible educational institution. An institutional or "private" program could not be qualified under Section 529 prior to the EGTRRA changes, and in order to qualify now it must meet additional requirements and provide certain protections as discussed below.

A state-sponsored 529 plan is one that permits a person to either (1) purchase tuition credits or certificates on behalf of a designated beneficiary which entitle the beneficiary to the waiver or payment of his or her qualified higher education expenses, or (2) make contributions to an account which is established for the purpose of meeting the qualified higher education expenses of the designated beneficiary.

The first type of program described in the preceding paragraph is commonly referred to as a "prepaid" tuition program, while the second type is commonly referred to as a college "savings" program or college investment program. A savings program can be viewed as a kind of state-sponsored mutual fund—a participant's contributions to the program are invested and the value of the participant's account is determined by the investment performance of the underlying securities. It is not uncommon for the media to describe 529 plans as only referring to the savings programs.

In prepaid programs, the participant's "return" is not linked directly to investment securities. Some prepaid programs operate like futures contracts, where the participant purchases a contract that obligates the program to deliver a certain bundle of tuition or other benefits in the future, while others act like index funds, where the participant purchases redeemable "units" or "credits" whose value is pegged to average in-state public tuition or to some other tuition inflation index. In some significant ways, these unit-type prepaid programs have more in common with the savings programs than they have in common with the contract-type prepaid programs, and a couple of states have even relabeled their unit programs, replacing the word "prepaid" with the term "guaranteed savings."

An eligible educational institution that desires its own 529 plan is limited to offering a program that falls only into the first category, i.e. prepaid programs. In addition, it must hold its program assets in a "qualified trust," which is one that meets certain standards normally applicable to individual retirement accounts.

When you establish an account in a 529 plan, you are required to name one living individual as designated beneficiary of the account. Typically, this is your child or grandchild, but it is not necessary that the beneficiary be related to you in any way. Multiple beneficiaries require multiple accounts. It is also acceptable in most, but not all, 529 plans for you to name yourself as beneficiary of the account you establish.

Accounts established by a state or local government (or agency or instrumentality thereof) or by a 501(c)(3) exempt organization as part of a scholarship program are not required to name a designated beneficiary. Beneficiaries can be selected at the time of distribution, and one account can be used to assist multiple students in paying for college costs.

Almost anyone can participate in a 529 plan. There are no income or age limitations on either the account owner, the contributor (if different), or the designated beneficiary. There is no requirement that the participant reside in the sponsoring state or that the beneficiary attend a school located in that state. The 529 plan can establish its own restrictions, however, and so it is important to distinguish the flexibility permitted under federal law from the rules of the program itself.

What other requirements must a 529 plan meet?

All 529 programs must meet the following requirements in order to qualify under Section 529. (Note that a state-sponsored 529 plan is not required to apply for a ruling or determination from the IRS as to its qualified status, although several states have requested, and some have received, such a ruling. An institution-sponsored program, however, is required to apply for and receive a determination from the IRS that it meets the requirements for qualification as a prepaid program under Section 529.

At the time this book was published, only one institution-sponsored program, called Independent 529 Plan, had received such a determination from the IRS.)

1) The program can only accept contributions in cash, including check, money order, and credit card. Many 529 plans also permit electronic funds transfer from a bank or investment account. Contributions may not be made with investment securities or other types of property. To transfer other investments into a 529 plan you will need to liquidate those investments, possibly triggering taxable income or capital gains. Under certain conditions, you may be able to transfer funds from an existing Coverdell education savings account or qualified U.S. savings bonds without triggering tax. These rules are explained more fully in later chapters.

2) The program must provide a separate accounting for each designated beneficiary. Separate accounting does not mean separate investing, and contributions are typically commingled in the program trust for investment purposes.

3) The program may not permit you or your designated beneficiary to direct the investment of your account. The tax law is specific: investment direction must be left to the sponsoring state. Although this somewhat paternalistic provision appears to be very limiting, a savings program can in fact provide substantial investment choice and flexibility to the account owner. Many of the programs now offer a menu of investment options. A contribution can be directed to one of these options, or in some 529 plans can be spread among the options (others might require that separate accounts be established if you want to invest in more than one investment option). Further, as a result of Notice 2001–55 issued by the IRS in September 2001, a 529 plan that "allows participants to select only from among broad-based investment strategies designed exclusively by the program" may now permit an account owner to change investment strategies once per calendar year.[2] Although it is not entirely clear yet what the IRS means by "broad-based investment strategy,"

---

2. Notice 2001-55, 2001-39 IRB (Sept. 24, 2001)

the Notice seems to suggest that you will be allowed to reallocate your account among available investment options, subject to program approval. There are other ways to exercise some degree of investment control. In most 529 plans, you may switch investments any time you change the beneficiary. You can also roll over your account to another state's program that has different investment offerings, subject to the rules for qualifying rollovers (discussed below).

4) The program may not allow accounts to be pledged by the account owner or designated beneficiary as security for a loan.

5) The program must provide adequate safeguards to prevent contributions on behalf of a designated beneficiary in excess of those necessary to provide for the qualified higher education expenses of the beneficiary. Almost all 529 plans currently place a specific dollar limit on contributions, typically expressed as an account balance limit. An account balance limit means that new contributions will not be accepted once the account value reaches a specific level, although it will not prevent the account from growing beyond that limit based on investment performance.

The IRS proposed regulations provide a safe harbor to programs that limit contributions on behalf of a designated beneficiary to an amount determined by actuarial estimates necessary to pay tuition, required fees, and room and board expenses of the designated beneficiary for five years of undergraduate enrollment at the highest-cost institution allowed by the program. Many programs have abandoned the safe harbor and include graduate school costs and other qualified expenses in the computation of their contribution limits, presumably with assurances from the IRS or legal counsel that they will not jeopardize qualification under Section 529. (In a private letter ruling issued to New York's 529 savings program, the IRS approved a limit based on four years of undergraduate expenses and three years of graduate school expenses.) You will find some 529 plans with account balance limits in excess of $300,000.

The limitation on contributions is imposed by the 529 plan on a per-beneficiary basis. If there is more than one donor to the account, or if there is more than one account in the program for a particular beneficiary, the accounts must be combined for purposes of determining total contributions. The proposed regulations do not, however, prohibit a designated beneficiary from maintaining accounts in different states and contributing a combined amount that exceeds the individual program limits. Congress presumably did not intend that the "stacking" of accounts be used as a way to circumvent the safeguards imposed by any one program, so it would be reasonable to anticipate that final regulations will impose additional requirements. Some states have started to require a representation from the donor that accounts in multiple programs are not being used as a way to make contributions beyond the level that can be reasonably supported as appropriate for the beneficiary's future higher education needs.

I see some mutual fund companies advertising their own 529 plans. Can any investment firm offer a 529 plan?

No. The reason you see advertisements for 529 plans from mutual fund companies, broker-dealers, and banks is that many of the state-sponsored 529 plans have outsourced program management and marketing to these firms. Tax law requires that the state or institution "establish and maintain" the program but does not prohibit the sponsor from hiring a vendor to assume the investment and operational duties. These vendors also have a direct interest in the success of the programs, as their fees are typically based on the level of assets under management in the program. Under the proposed regulations, in order to meet its duty, a state must set all the terms and conditions of the program and be actively involved on an ongoing basis in the administration of the program, including supervising all decisions relating to the investment of assets contributed to the program.

What are the federal income tax rules for 529 plan participants?

Your contributions to a 529 plan are not deductible in computing your federal income tax. Your initial tax savings come from the deferral of income; earnings in your account remain tax-free until they are distributed. Distributed earnings may or may not be subject to tax, depending on whether the beneficiary incurs sufficient qualified higher education expenses (QHEE) during the year. QHEE are defined on page 49.

As 529 funds are withdrawn, or payments are made on behalf of the beneficiary, the program administrator is responsible for sending Form 1099-Q to you or to your beneficiary after year-end showing gross distributions, earnings, and basis. You will need the gross distributions and earnings figures when completing your federal income tax return to determine how much of the earnings, if any, is subject to tax. Basis always comes out tax-free.

If the account beneficiary has incurred QHEE that in total are equal to, or greater than, the total distributions from all 529 accounts as reported on Forms 1099-Q, the distributions are excluded from taxable income in their entirety. If, however, total QHEE are less than total distributions, only a portion of the distributed earnings is excluded from income. The remainder is taxable as ordinary income, as expressed by the following formula:

$$\frac{\text{Gross Distributions} - \text{QHEE}}{\text{Gross Distributions}} \times \text{Earnings} = \text{Ordinary Income}$$

If withdrawals are made from a Coverdell education savings account for the same beneficiary during the year, QHEE must be allocated between the 529 distributions and the Coverdell withdrawals. This is because withdrawals from a Coverdell ESA follow the same general taxation rules as distributions from a 529 plan. Publication 970, available from the IRS, suggests a pro rata allocation of expenses, but apparently will permit any other reasonable method. Coverdell ESAs are discussed in chapter 9.

A question that does not appear to be fully resolved is whether your payments for QHEE must match up with the distributions from your 529 account in the same taxable year. While this will not be a concern when the program makes qualifying payments directly to the school or third-party vendor, it can become an issue if you make the payments yourself and request withdrawals from the 529 plan as "reimbursement." For example, let us assume you pay the tuition bill on December 20 and immediately request a withdrawal from your 529 account. If it takes the program administrator two weeks to process your request and issue the distribution check, you risk having insufficient QHEE in the year of the withdrawal. Until further guidance is issued by the IRS, you should assume that QHEE and distributions will be accounted for on a cash basis and that 529 account withdrawals and the payment of qualified expenses must occur within the same calendar year.

Earnings subject to tax because they are part of a non-qualified distribution will also be subject to a 10 percent federal additional tax. This tax, which represents the penalty for using a 529 account for purposes other than higher education expenses, is computed on Form 5329 and paid with the recipient's federal income tax return. Before 2002, the law required that a 529 plan itself impose a "more than de minimis" penalty on non-qualified distributions, and 10 percent-of-earnings was the standard penalty among savings programs. This requirement has now been lifted, and the states have eliminated their own penalties.

Note the following exceptions to the 10 percent federal additional tax:

✦ The distribution is made because the beneficiary is disabled—i.e., unable to engage in any substantial gainful activity because of a physical or mental condition and the condition is of indefinite duration or is expected to result in death.

✦ The distribution is made because the beneficiary received a tax-free scholarship or allowance, to the extent the distribution does not exceed the scholarship or allowance.

✦ The distribution is paid to the beneficiary (or to the beneficiary's estate) on or after the death of the beneficiary.

✦ The distribution is included in income only because total qualified higher education expenses were reduced by tuition and related expenses used in computing the Hope credit or lifetime learning credit.

How does the 529 plan administrator calculate the earnings portion of a distribution?

For each distribution, the administrator subtracts the "principal portion" from the amount of the distribution, leaving the earnings portion.[3] In a 529 savings program, the principal portion is determined by the following equation:

$$\frac{\text{Basis}}{\text{Value of account}} \times \text{Distribution} = \text{Principal portion}$$

Basis generally refers to the total contributions into the account less prior distributions of principal. The value of the account is typically determined on the day of distribution.

The calculation is slightly different in a prepaid program. The total amount of distribution is based on the current value of the tuition and other education benefits your beneficiary receives during the year. The principal portion is calculated based on the number of tuition credits used or redeemed during the year as a percentage of total credits purchased. For example, if you originally purchased eight semesters of tuition and you use the program to pay for two semesters in a year, the principal portion is two-eighths or 25 percent of the amount you paid for the prepayment contract. Some of the "unit-type" prepaid programs deviate from this approach and use a "first-in/first-out" approach in assigning basis to redeemed units.

For purposes of this pro rata calculation, all accounts in the program with the same account owner and designated beneficiary must be treated as one account. Accounts in a prepaid program do not have to be aggregated with accounts in the same state's savings program.

Before 2002, when accounting for distributions, a program administrator was required to aggregate all accounts maintained for the same beneficiary in any of that state's 529 plans, even where there were different account owners. Furthermore, the program administrator was required to treat all distributions as being made on the last day of the year. These rules caused unforeseen difficulties and were loosened with the EGTRRA changes and IRS Notice 2001–81.[4]

---

3. Section 529 applies the provisions of Section 72 to the extent the distribution is not excludable under any other section of the Code (e.g. Section 117 scholarship exclusion).
4. Notice 2001-81, 2001-52 IRB (Dec. 7, 2001)

A 529 program administrator will need to track your account's basis in order to satisfy the distribution reporting requirements. Rollover contributions from another 529 plan, and tax-free transfers from Coverdell education savings accounts and qualifying U.S. savings bonds, pose a special challenge to program administrators because these transfers include untaxed earnings. (These types of transfers are discussed in further detail below and in later chapters.) The basis of contributions associated with these transfers must be adjusted for their untaxed earnings. IRS Notice 2001–81 prescribes the procedures a 529 plan must now employ to ensure that this information is properly recorded.

The government's decision to make program administrators responsible for determining the earnings portion of a distribution lifts some of the paperwork burden from your shoulders. You do not have to maintain your own tax basis records.

Reporting 529 distributions on your tax return will be anything but simple, however, because of the changes made to Section 529 by EGTRRA. Before EGTRRA, you had only to provide evidence to the 529 plan administrator that distributions were being used for qualified higher education expenses. If you couldn't do so, the program would assess a penalty. Because the requirement for a program-imposed penalty is now removed, the 529 program administrator is no longer required to verify the use of distributions unless those procedures remain part of state law or program rules.[5] Now it is up to you, the program participant, to account for qualified higher education expenses with your federal income tax return, and provide proof of these expenses in the event your return is examined by the IRS.

Who receives the Form 1099-Q, the account owner or the beneficiary?

This is an important question in the case where distributions from a 529 plan are not fully excluded from income. If you (the account owner) are treated as the recipient, the earnings portion of the non-qualified distribution will

---

5. Some states, however, may continue to require that the use of distributions for qualified higher education expenses be verified by the program administrator. For example, a program might impose a penalty, additional fee, or recapture tax on non-qualified withdrawals only.

be taxable to you at your marginal tax bracket. If your beneficiary is treated as the recipient, the earnings portion of the distribution will be taxable to him or her at a possibly lower tax bracket. The IRS says that distributions paid directly to the eligible educational institution are to be reported to the beneficiary as recipient. For any cash withdrawals, the Form 1099-Q will be sent to the person who received the funds as determined under the rules of the 529 plan.

> *Example:* Mr. Brown establishes an account with a 529 plan for his daughter Kelly and makes a one-time contribution of $10,000. Five years later, once Kelly has started college and the account has grown to $15,000, Mr. Brown requests a $9,000 withdrawal from the account made payable to Kelly. Kelly will receive a Form 1099-Q after the end of the year showing $9,000 in total distributions and $3,000 as the earnings portion. The earnings portion is one-third of total distributions, based on the ratio of account growth at the time of distribution ($5,000) to total account value ($15,000). If Kelly can show that she incurred at least $9,000 of qualified higher education expenses during the year, the entire distribution is federally tax-free. If Kelly can only show $5,000 of QHEE, then 5/9ths of the $3,000 earnings portion will be tax-free and 4/9ths, or $1,333, will be subject to tax on Kelly's federal income tax return as ordinary income. She will also incur a 10% additional tax ($133).

What about state taxes?

State tax laws are not uniform, but here, generally speaking, is the way it should work for most:

+ Opening a 529 account is a state other than your own does not subject you or your beneficiary to that state's income tax.
+ You or your beneficiary will be required to pay income tax on the distributed earnings in *your* state of residency, assuming it imposes

an income tax, unless your state grants a specific exemption or follows federal law that excludes qualified distributions.

✦ State treatment will follow federal treatment regarding the amount and timing of income, and in determining who reports the income (you or the beneficiary).

How might the states deviate from this approach? One concern is that the state sponsoring the 529 plan may decide that it can collect taxes from non-resident participants in that plan. This is unlikely, however, because income from intangible investment assets is generally sourced in the state where the taxpayer resides and not the state that offers the investment.

Another concern could arise for residents in a state that does not conform its rules to the federal computation of adjusted gross income (AGI). Most states use federal AGI or taxable income as a starting point for state taxable income, but some start with their own definition of "gross income." These states include Alabama, Mississippi, and Pennsylvania. The risk in any non-conforming state is that the state will not recognize the Section 529 income tax rules, i.e., deferral of income and exclusion of income on qualified withdrawals.

Some states will conform to the federal computation of AGI as of a specific date, but any changes to the federal tax laws after that date are not automatically incorporated into the state tax calculation. You should attempt to find out how your state handles 529 accounts, and whether accounts in out-of-state programs are treated differently than accounts in the state's own 529 plan. State tax consequences of a 529 distribution can also be uncertain in a year in which you or your beneficiary moves between states.

What are qualified higher education expenses?

The definition of "qualified higher education expenses" or "QHEE" is critical in determining the tax consequences of a distribution from a 529 plan. As discussed above, distributions are fully exempt from federal income tax only if the beneficiary incurs an equal or greater amount of QHEE.

QHEE means tuition, fees, books, supplies, and equipment required for enrollment or attendance on a full-time or part-time basis at an eligible educational institution, plus, in the case of a "special needs beneficiary," any "special needs services."[6] In addition, QHEE includes room and board expense (both on-campus and off-campus) for students enrolled in certain college programs on at least a half-time basis.[7] The student's qualifying expenses must be reduced by any tax-free scholarships or payments, and by educational assistance allowances provided under certain federal programs.

QHEE under current law does not include the cost of transportation or personal expenses, even though they may be considered part of the "cost of attendance" for federal financial aid purposes. Repayment of student loans also does not qualify.

Eligible educational institutions are defined by reference to Section 481 of the Higher Education Act of 1965 and include any accredited post-secondary educational institutions offering credit toward a bachelor's degree, an associate's degree, a graduate or professional degree, or another recognized post-secondary credential. Certain proprietary institutions and post-secondary vocational institutions also are eligible institutions. The institution must be eligible to participate in Title IV U.S. federal financial aid programs. To determine if a particular institution has been assigned a federal school code by the Department of Education, and presumably eligible under Section 529 as meeting these requirements, you may enter

---

6. A "special needs beneficiary" is to be defined by Treasury Department regulations, which have not yet been issued.

7. The amount paid for room and board as QHEE cannot exceed (i) the allowance applicable to the beneficiary for room and board included in the "cost of attendance", as defined in section 472 of the Higher Education Act as in effect on June 7, 2001, as determined by the eligible educational institution for that period, or (ii) if greater, the actual invoice amount the beneficiary residing in housing owned or operated by the eligible educational institution is charged for room and board costs for that period. The room and board costs must be incurred during an academic period during which the student is enrolled or accepted for enrollment in a degree, certificate or other program (including a program of study abroad approved for credit by the eligible educational institution) that leads to a recognized educational credential awarded by an eligible educational institution. A student will be considered to be enrolled at least half-time if the student is enrolled for at least half the full-time academic workload for the course of study the student is pursuing as determined under the standards of the institution where the student is enrolled. The institution's standard for a full-time workload must equal or exceed a standard established by the Department of Education under the Higher Education Act.

the name of an institution at the Department of Education's Web site at http://www.fafsa.ed.gov/fotw0405/fslookup.htm. Many foreign universities are included on the list. Some states have requested that the IRS provide an official listing of eligible educational institutions, but so far none has been published.

Can I claim the Hope or Lifetime Learning credit in the same year that I withdraw from my 529 account to pay for college?

Yes, the Hope or Lifetime Learning credit (see box below) can be claimed regardless of whether funds used for qualified tuition and related expenses come from a 529 account. However, in order to prevent "double-dipping," Section 529 requires that QHEE be reduced by any expenses used to determine the Hope or Lifetime Learning credit. Unless you incur an amount of QHEE out of pocket (viz. not funded by 529 account distributions) that is at least equal to the amount of tuition and related expenses used in determining the Hope or Lifetime Learning credit, some portion of your 529 distribution will no longer be qualified and will become subject to income tax. The 10 percent penalty tax will not apply in these circumstances.

> *Example:* Eric, a second-year college student, has his own 529 account. He withdraws $20,000 from the account during the year to pay for all of his QHEE, including $8,000 in tuition. The entire $20,000 withdrawal would be tax-free, except that Eric claims the maximum $1,500 Hope credit against $2,000 of his tuition. He must reduce his $20,000 QHEE by $2,000, leaving $18,000. This means that $2,000 (or one-tenth) of his 529 withdrawal is no longer qualified. If we assume the earnings portion of the withdrawal is $5,000, then one-tenth of $5,000, or $500, is taxable to Eric as ordinary income (but is not subject to a 10 percent additional tax). If Eric's marginal federal tax bracket is 15 percent, he incurs $75 in federal tax.

You may elect to waive the Hope and Lifetime Learning credit if you decide that its negative impact on 529 distributions is greater than the amount of credit. This will occur in a relatively small number of cases because the benefit of the credit will nearly always outweigh the tax on that portion of your 529 distributions.

Note that similar coordination rules apply to withdrawals from a Coverdell education savings account. Furthermore, if withdrawals are taken from both a Coverdell ESA and a 529 account in the same year for the same beneficiary, the QHEE must be divided between them to determine the amount of tax exclusion on the withdrawals from each type of account. See chapter 9 for more information.

How about the above-the-line deduction for qualified tuition and related expenses? Can I claim the deduction for expenses I pay using funds from my 529 account?

If you are eligible to claim the above-the-line deduction ("Section 222 deduction") for up to $4,000 of qualified tuition and related expenses in 2004 and 2005 (increased from $3,000 for 2002 and 2003), the use of your 529 account may affect the amount of deduction you can claim. The earnings portion of a 529 distribution used to pay qualified tuition and related expenses will reduce the deductible amount. The IRS has not yet described how to allocate your 529 distributions between qualified tuition and related expenses, which reduce the total Section 222 deductible amount, and other qualified higher education expenses such as books and room and board that are eligible for Section 529 purposes but not for Section 222 purposes.

The Credits and Deduction for Tuition Payments

The 1997 tax-law changes gave birth to two new credits, the Hope Scholarship credit and the Lifetime Learning credit, available to taxpayers with incomes below a certain level who incur qualified tuition and related expenses. The credits are nonrefundable, so the amount you claim cannot be greater than your tax liability excluding the credits. You may elect to claim the credits by attaching Form 8863 to your original or an amended federal income tax return. The 2001 EGTRRA created an above-the-line deduction for the same category of expenses. The deduction is available to eligible taxpayers only for the years 2002 through 2005, but may not be claimed in any year you elect to claim the Hope or Lifetime Learning credit. The rules surrounding the Hope and Lifetime Learning credits were already complex; the introduction of a new and competing deduction will make tax planning and return preparation all the more difficult.

Hope Scholarship credit

The Hope credit is equal to 100 percent of up to $1,000 of qualified tuition and related expenses paid by a taxpayer during the taxable year for the qualified educational expenses of a student during any academic period beginning in each taxable year, plus 50 percent of such expenses over $1,000. The maximum credit is $1,500 per year per student. These limits will be increased in the future based on cost-of-living adjustments. The Hope credit may be claimed only twice. The student cannot have completed two years of post-secondary education before the start of the taxable year, and must be at least a half-time student.

For purposes of this credit, the term "qualified tuition and related expenses" means tuition and fees required for the enrollment or attendance of (1) the taxpayer, (2) the taxpayer's spouse, or (3) any dependent of the taxpayer, at an eligible educational institution. Qualified expenses are reduced by tax-free scholarships and allowances.

Lifetime Learning credit

The Lifetime Learning credit is equal to 20 percent of up to $10,000 ($5,000 for years before 2003) of the qualified tuition and related expenses paid by the taxpayer during the taxable year for education furnished during any academic period beginning in the taxable year. The maximum credit beginning in 2003 is $2,000 per year per taxpayer (not per student). Tuition and related expenses for any course of instruction taken at an eligible educational institution to acquire or improve job skills of the individual are qualified. There is no limit to the number of years in which the Lifetime Learning credit can be claimed.

The same expenses cannot be used for both a Hope credit and a Lifetime Learning credit. Any expenses used in determining a Hope or Lifetime Learning credit will reduce total qualified higher education expenses used in calculating the tax exclusion for distributions from a 529 plan or Coverdell education savings account. Proper coordination and planning will maximize the benefits of these credits and exclusions over the course of a family's college years.

The Hope and Lifetime Learning credits are not available to taxpayers whose modified adjusted gross income (MAGI) exceeds specified levels. For single taxpayers, the credits are lost at $52,000 of MAGI in 2004, and for married taxpayers filing joint returns the credits are lost at $105,000. For single taxpayers with MAGI between $42,000 and $52,000, and for married taxpayers filing a joint return with MAGI between $85,000 and $105,000, a partial credit is available.

If you claim your child as a dependent, only you may claim the Hope credit or the Lifetime Learning credit with respect to your child's qualifying educational expenses. Your child may claim the credit if you do not claim the child as a dependent on your tax return. (An otherwise dependent child cannot claim a personal exemption, however, no matter what the parent decides to do about claiming the dependency exemption.)

Your ability to decide whether to claim your child as a dependent provides significant latitude. If your income falls above the limits, and your child's income falls below the limits, the child may derive a tax benefit from the credits when you cannot. You will lose the benefit of the dependency exemption, but some high-income parents are unable to derive full benefit from the dependency exemption anyway, due to the income phase-out of the exemption. In that case, you would make the easy decision to forego claiming your child as a dependent, and thereby allow the child to apply the education credit against his or her tax liability.

The above-the-line tuition deduction

Beginning in 2002, an eligible taxpayer may claim an above-the-line deduction under Section 222 of the Internal Revenue Code for a limited amount of qualified tuition and related expenses. These are the same expenses that qualify for the Hope and Lifetime Learning credits, and are mutually exclusive. You may not claim the deduction for yourself or your dependent student in any year in which you or that student claim the Hope or Lifetime Learning credit.

To be eligible for the deduction, you must not be a married individual filing separately or the dependent of another individual and your MAGI must be below a certain level. If your MAGI is $65,000 or less ($130,000 or less on a joint return), you may deduct up to $3,000 in qualified tuition and related expenses in 2002 and 2003, and up to $4,000 in 2004 and 2005. If your MAGI exceeds $65,000/$130,000 but does not exceed $80,000 ($160,000 on a joint return), you may deduct up to $2,000 in qualified tuition and related expenses in 2004 and 2005 only.

You must reduce your total qualified tuition and related expenses by the excluded earnings from 529 plan distributions, Coverdell ESA withdrawals, and qualified U.S. savings bond redemptions, which are used to pay for such expenses.

What are the federal gift and estate tax rules under Section 529?

Section 529 prescribes that the contribution to a 529 plan account is a completed gift for estate and gift tax purposes. The gift is from the individual contributor to the designated beneficiary (assuming the contributor and beneficiary are not the same person). This rule applies despite the fact the account owner retains ownership rights that would otherwise cause the assets to remain in his or her estate. A further advantage is that the funding of the account is treated as the gift of a "present interest" qualifying for the annual $11,000 gift tax exclusion. Finally, Section 529 provides that the contributor may under certain circumstances elect to treat the gift as occurring ratably over a five-year period, so that the $11,000 exclusion can be leveraged to as much as $55,000 in a year. Chapter 8 describes these rules in more detail.

Can I change the beneficiary of my 529 account?

Section 529 allows the account owner to replace the current designated beneficiary with a new beneficiary who is a "member of the family" (see box below). All 529 plans accommodate a change in beneficiary without imposing a penalty, although some may have age or residency restrictions, and some may charge a fee. There are no federal income tax consequences of a beneficiary change; however, there can be gift tax consequences when the new beneficiary is at least one generation below the old beneficiary, as discussed in chapter 8.

Can I transfer my account from one state's 529 plan to another state's 529 plan?

Yes, a qualifying rollover will not be treated as a distribution for federal income tax. A transfer of assets from one state's plan to another for the same beneficiary is a qualifying rollover, but this type of rollover can be done only once every 12 months. However, there is no limit on the frequency of rollovers where the beneficiary is replaced with a qualifying member of the family. A rollover can be transacted either through a direct "trustee-to-trustee" transfer (program permitting), or by a withdrawal of funds followed by the contribution of equivalent funds within 60 days to a different 529 plan. Be sure to find out how the 529 plan you are investigating handles rollover requests, as there may be restrictions imposed by the program. Many prepaid programs will treat such a request as a cancellation of the contract.

Member of the Family

Regarding beneficiaries, "member of the family" means an individual who has one of the following relationships to the current beneficiary:

+ A son or daughter (natural or legally adopted), or a descendant of either;
+ A stepson or stepdaughter;
+ A brother or sister (by whole or halfblood), or stepbrother or stepsister;
+ The father or mother, or an ancestor of either;
+ A stepfather or stepmother;
+ A niece or nephew;
+ An aunt or uncle;
+ A son-in-law, daughter-in-law, father-in-law, mother-in-law, brother-in-law, or sister-in-law; or
+ The spouse of the designated beneficiary (who must have the same principal place of abode) or the spouse of any of the relatives listed above (who must have the same principal place of abode).
+ A first cousin (added by EGTRRA)

Can a corporation or trust be the owner of a 529 account?

Yes, Section 529 refers to a "person," defined under Section 7701 of the Code as an individual, a trust, estate, partnership, association, company or corporation. Many 529 plans permit legal entities to establish accounts, although some do not. There will be special tax considerations whenever a non-individual taxpayer is account owner, and some of the issues surrounding entity ownership have not been fully explored or tested. For corporations, the compensation rules (Code Section 83) must be considered, and perhaps also the anti-tax shelter provisions. For certain trusts, the effect of 529 plan distributions on "distributable net income" has to be considered. Your attorney and accountant should be consulted in these matters.

Can I transfer the ownership of my account to someone else?

Nothing contained within Section 529 prohibits or regulates a transfer of account ownership. It is up to the individual 529 plan to provide rules concerning transfer of account ownership. Some programs will accommodate a request to transfer account ownership while others expressly prohibit such transfers prior to the owner's death or legal incapacity. The mere transfer of ownership appears to have no federal income, gift, or estate tax consequences. However, a new account owner will generally have all rights associated with original ownership including the power to revoke the account.

What happens to my account if I die?

The death of the account owner does not cause a 529 account to terminate. Instead, all rights of ownership and control over the account are passed to a successor account owner. The identity of the successor owner depends on the rules of the program and state law. Most 529 plans now permit you to name a successor owner on the account application or upon later submission to the program administrator. The program rules may specify the account owner in other situations, i.e. you fail to name a successor account owner, or the person you name as successor declines the appointment or predeceases you. For example, the 529 plan may specify that, in the absence of a named successor, the beneficiary of the 529 account will become account owner unless the beneficiary is a minor, in which case the beneficiary's living parent or guardian will become account owner. In any situation where there is no clear successor under the terms of your account or the rules of the program, ownership will pass according to your will or your state's laws of intestacy. If you live in a state with a community property law, consult with your attorney regarding the treatment of your 529 account.

FOUR

Financial Aid Considerations

We now turn our attention to one of parents' most significant concerns: the impact of a 529 account on financial aid awards. Although the rules in this area may change in the future, guidance from the U.S. Department of Education helps define how college financial aid administrators should be treating 529 plans in the federal financial aid application process.

Although saving for college with a 529 plan will usually reduce a student's financial aid eligibility, saving for college through other means can have an adverse impact that is, in many cases, worse than a 529 plan. The precise effect will depend on the category of 529 plan or other investment, as well as the particular policies of the institution. This process is explained below.

The authorization for federal financial aid comes from Title IV of the Higher Education Act of 1965, as amended (HEA). Financial aid packages consist of any combination of grants, work-study, and loans. A student's financial need is determined by the institution as the difference between that particular institution's cost of attendance (COA)[1] and the student's expected family contribution (EFC). The EFC represents the amount the family can be expected to contribute towards a student's college costs based on its own financial situation.

The EFC is calculated using data submitted to the Department of Education on a form known as the Free Application for Federal Student Aid (FAFSA). The FAFSA is filed by high school seniors after January 1 in their final year of high school. In subsequent college years, the student files an abbreviated Renewal FAFSA. Under the EFC formula, 50 percent of the student's income (net of an income protection allowance of $2,420 for the 2004-2005 award year and allowances for federal, state, and social security taxes), and 35 percent of the student's assets are assumed to be available to pay for college costs.

For dependent students, the formula also assumes that between 22 percent and 47 percent of the parents' income and at most 5.6 percent of the parents' assets are available to pay for college costs. The parents' income is reduced for this purpose by tax allowances and a maximum $3,000 employment expense allowance. The formula also provides "protection allowances," one for parental income based on the household census (e.g., the income protection allowance for two parents and one student in the household is $17,060) and one for assets based on whether there is one parent or two and on the age of the older parent (e.g., the asset protection allowance for two parents with the oldest being 45 is $42,100).

Parental contribution to EFC is pro-rated to each member of the family attending college in the upcoming year. This pro-ration can have a dramatic effect and many families that would not qualify for financial aid with one student in college may qualify when they have two or more family members in college at the same time.

The FAFSA is based largely on income as reported on the student's and parents' tax returns for the year prior to the year in which the student

---

1. COA includes tuition, fees, room and board, books, supplies, transportation, and personal expenses. Some institutions will choose not to include transportation and personal expenses in the COA figure.

enters college (e.g., 2003 tax return for students enrolling in fall 2004), along with asset values as of the date on which the form is filed. The EFC is automatically zero for a dependent student with parents who earn $15,000 or less and where the student and parents are eligible to file Form 1040A or 1040EZ, or where they are not required to file any income tax return.

A separate formula is used for independent students without dependents, and another for independent students with dependents. A student is automatically considered independent if he or she is at least 23 years old, a veteran of the armed forces, a master's or doctoral candidate, married, or declared independent by a court, or if he or she has legal dependents other than a spouse. Parental assets and income are not considered in the need analysis for these students. The Department of Education maintains an extensive library of publications and other materials relating to federal financial aid on the Web at www.ed.gov.

Does all need-based aid come from the federal government?

No, most states also maintain need-based grant programs. Many of these programs use the federal methodology while others use state-developed criteria. In some states, the determination of student eligibility for state-funded programs does not count balances in the state's own 529 plan. This can be an attractive incentive.

Many institutions, primarily private colleges, provide substantial amounts of gift aid out of their own endowments and other funds. A large number of these colleges utilize an alternative approach in determining need known as the "institutional methodology," developed by The College Board and administered by its affiliate College Scholarship Service (CSS). To apply for grants at colleges that use the institutional methodology, a student must complete an application called the PROFILE. The PROFILE is similar to the FAFSA in that it follows the same general approach and is used to compute the applicant's expected family contribution. But there are also many differences between the forms, some of which are significant. For example, the PROFILE application requires information about equity in the home and family farm, which are exempt assets under the federal methodology. It will also provide information to the financial aid administrator about any retirement accounts owned by the student. The rest of this chapter focuses primarily on the federal methodology, not the institutional methodology; as you read through it, keep in mind that the treatment of 529 plans can differ. For example, the PROFILE makes no distinction between 529 prepaid programs and 529 savings programs, and treats both types as parental assets.

Does the federal methodology distinguish between Section 529 prepaid tuition programs and savings programs?

Yes. Even though both types of 529 plans receive the same federal income tax treatment, they are treated very differently for purposes of federal financial aid.

Families participating in a prepaid tuition program can be severely disadvantaged in the federal financial aid process. The Higher Education Act specifically provides that "prepaid tuition plans shall reduce the cost of attendance by the amount of pre-payment." This means that the value of a prepaid tuition contract is not included as an asset on FAFSA forms, but any payments made from a prepaid program for a student's tuition and other expenses are treated as an additional "resource," or as a reduction in the cost of attendance, in the same manner as a scholarship or a grandparent's direct payment of tuition. They reduce a student's financial need, and thus financial aid, on a dollar-for-dollar basis. Beneficiaries should inform the institution they wish to attend that they have prepaid tuition contracts and indicate the amount of the contract benefits to be paid out. Even if not informed of the existence of a prepaid tuition contract, the institution will discover it when it receives payment from the program, and will make adjustments to the student's aid award.

Many financial planners will fault the prepaid programs for not warning the purchaser more fully about the financial aid implications of such a contract. In many cases where the program enrollment materials fail to provide detailed explanation of this issue, the criticism appears justified. However, keep in mind that some financial aid programs may not be impacted. For instance, a prepaid tuition contract will not affect eligibility for a federal Pell grant or most state grants, and a federally subsidized Stafford loan (subject to certain limits) will still be available to the extent the contract does not cover the "unmet" financial need of the student. But a prepaid tuition contract will reduce the chance of receiving work-study, a federal Perkins loan, or a Federal Supplemental Educational Opportunity Grant (FSEOG).

The federal financial aid treatment of assets in a 529 savings program works out much better for most families. The Department of Education takes the position that the account is an asset of the account owner. If the account owner is the student's parent, the value of the account will be assessed at a maximum 5.6 percent rate, and if the account owner is the grandparent or some other relative it will not be counted at all on the asset side of the EFC equation.

Note that all assets are disregarded if the family qualifies for the "simplified EFC formula." In order to qualify for this beneficial treatment, the dependent student and parents must have adjusted gross income less than $50,000 and meet all of the requirements to be eligible to file Form 1040A or 1040EZ (rather than Form 1040). Qualifying families might actually prefer a 529 because it will never trigger capital gains. If a student or parent were to invest in mutual funds or other securities, and then sell shares during the base year requiring Schedule D reporting on Form 1040, the family would not be able to take advantage of the simplified EFC formula.

Aren't the distributions from a 529 plan included as "income" when calculating a student's financial aid eligibility?

Tax-free withdrawals from a 529 savings account owned by the parent or the student are *not* to be included in financial aid income, according to a letter announcement released by the Department of Education in January 2004. This "clarification" came as welcome news. Prior to 2002, the earnings portion of a qualified withdrawal was reported on the student's federal income tax return, and thus was included in financial aid income. When the tax law was changed to exclude post-2001 qualified 529 withdrawals from federal income, experts were left to wonder if the Department of Education would require an add-back for financial aid purposes.

If the federal income tax exclusion for qualified 529 withdrawals is allowed to expire at the end of 2010, we can assume that the earnings reported on the student's tax return will once again be included as student income in computing the expected family contribution.

Withdrawals from a 529 savings account owned by a grandparent, relative, or other acquaintance and used to pay a student's college expenses will presumably be added to financial aid income as untaxed income, thereby reducing financial aid eligibility. Grandparents especially should be aware of this effect, since many people are under the false impression that a grandparent-owned 529 account is "invisible" for financial aid purposes.

The earnings portion of distributions from a 529 prepaid program should be excluded from student income in computing EFC in any case, since the benefits already reduce aid eligibility on a dollar-for-dollar basis. Whether aid applicants and financial aid administrators know enough about the interaction of tax law and federal financial aid to make the appropriate adjustments for prepaid contract holders is less certain.

Does it make sense that prepaid and savings programs are treated so differently?

Not really. Prepaid programs and savings programs share many of the same basic features, and in some states the 529 plan is actually a prepaid-savings hybrid.

For example, programs in Pennsylvania and Ohio that were previously classified as prepaid are now labeled "guaranteed savings" programs. By changing the name and making other operational adjustments, Pennsylvania program authorities expect that their participants will be entitled to favorable financial aid treatment. They appear to be justified in claiming savings-program status (and so might some other unit plans that have not yet adopted the "guaranteed savings" label). The units are redeemed in a manner similar to any 529 savings program, except that the valuation is based on an index of average tuition prices rather than underlying stock and bond funds.

Many in the 529 community are actively lobbying Congress for an amendment to the financial aid laws that would treat 529 savings plans and 529 prepaid programs equally. This issue will likely be considered as Congress takes up the reauthorization of the Higher Education Act sometime during 2005. Until financial aid parity actually comes about, however, a family with little in the way of financial resources may want to think twice before committing scarce dollars to a prepaid tuition contract. Unless the student is eligible for a Pell grant, a 529 savings program will likely provide a better financial aid result.

How does a 529 savings account compare to other investment alternatives?

A 529 savings program is treated more favorably than several other college investment alternatives. Take custodial accounts, for example. Many families discover too late that the transfer of investment assets to a child's UTMA or UGMA account in an effort to reduce income taxes will have negative financial aid consequences. Student-owned investments, including UTMA/UGMA assets, are assessed much more heavily than parental assets.

Before 2004, families with Coverdell education savings accounts faced the same predicament—a Coverdell ESA was treated as an asset belonging to the student. But that has now changed. The letter announcement released by the U.S. Department of Education in January 2004 (described above) includes the following statement:

> Coverdell Education Savings Accounts and 529 College Savings Plan receive equal treatment in the calculation of federal financial aid eligibility. Specifically, both can be regarded as assets of the parent if the parent is the owner of the account, rather than the student, and thereby displace a smaller amount of financial aid.

The problem with the Department of Education's new position on the Coverdell ESA is that it seems to ignore one of the most important differences between 529 plans and Coverdell ESAs, i.e. a parent retains all ownership rights with the 529 plan but not with the Coverdell ESA. A Coverdell ESA is under a custodian's or trustee's control, similar to the UTMA/UGMA. Regardless, families should accept the recent policy change at the Department of Education as good news and more reason to favorably consider the Coverdell education savings account when formulating a college savings strategy.

A traditional or Roth IRA is generally considered to be a favored type of investment when it comes to financial aid eligibility, but in fact may have negative financial aid consequences to the unsuspecting family. Qualified retirement accounts, including IRAs, are excluded from the asset side of the EFC computation and, as discussed in chapter 11, penalty-free withdrawals from an IRA may now be taken to pay for college. The problem is with the income side of the EFC computation; the entire withdrawal (principal and earnings) is added into income in the EFC calculation. Aid-eligible families with retirement assets should not plan on tapping those accounts to pay for college.

Families using 529 plans should realize that they can reduce or eliminate any negative impact the investment might have on financial aid availability. The choice of designated beneficiary and the decision of when and how to take withdrawals (qualified or non-qualified) could make a significant difference. For further discussion of this, see chapter 12, "Managing Your 529 Account."

Some institutions have indicated that 529 savings programs would be given added weight in the packaging of a student's financial aid award, despite the position of the Department of Education. Institutions have significant latitude in this area because the Higher Education Act specifically prohibits the Department of Education from prescribing regulations to carry out the need analysis provisions in the law.

Of course, many families will never expect to qualify for financial aid regardless of who is credited with the assets and income. For them, the financial aid implications of a 529 plan, or any other investment alternative, will be of little concern. Others who do qualify may discover that financial aid means loans and work-study, not grants or scholarships. Their concerns about the financial aid consequences of investment decisions may also be tempered.

Federally-Funded Student Aid

✦ **Federal Pell Grants**—Non-discretionary grants awarding up to $4,050 per year to applicants with an "expected family contribution" of less than $3,851 (2004–2005 award year).

✦ **Federal Supplemental Educational Opportunity Grants** (FSEOG)—Up to $4,000 per year allocated by the institution to students with financial need.

✦ **Federal Stafford Loans**—Low-interest loans directly from the government (Federal Direct Loan Program), or guaranteed by the government (Federal Family Education Loan Program), available to all students, but subject to annual borrowing caps. Limited interest subsidy is available to students determined to have financial need.

✦ **Federal PLUS Loans**—Similar to Stafford, but made to creditworthy parents of students.

✦ **Federal Perkins Loans**—Up to $4,000 per year ($6,000 for graduate study) of five percent-interest loans allocated by the institution on the basis of financial need.

✦ **Federal Work-Study** (FWS)—Funds provided by government for an institution's part-time employment of students with financial need.

FIVE

Prepaid vs. Savings

Section 529 plans come in only two basic forms: prepaid and savings. But categorizing any given program is not always simple. Some plans contain features that are common to both prepaid and savings programs. They act like a prepaid program under some conditions, and like a savings program under different conditions. Some states even combine their separate prepaid and savings programs in a single package, marketed to the public as one program with different options.

If your state operates a prepaid program that may be of interest, one of your first steps should be to check whether the program is accepting new enrollments. Several states, including Colorado, Ohio, Texas, and West Virginia have temporarily or permanently suspended enrollment into their prepaid programs. Other states may follow suit if program financial solvency is further stressed by increasing tuition levels.

What is a prepaid program?

A prepaid program is one involving the purchase of tuition credits or certificates that entitle the beneficiary to a waiver or payment of future qualifying college costs. In essence, future tuition is being purchased today. The price you pay now is not necessarily equal to current tuition levels, although current tuition is always a factor when a prepaid program establishes its prices.

There are three types of prepaid programs. The most prevalent is the state-sponsored **"contract" program**. In return for your upfront cash payment, or your commitment to a series of cash payments, you receive a promise from the program that it will pay for future tuition and mandatory fees at public colleges, universities, or community colleges located in the state. The contract may cover a period from one semester to five years, depending on the program's options and the amount of tuition you wish to purchase. If your beneficiary attends a private or out-of-state school, the program will determine the value of your contract under a pre-set formula and make payments in an amount not to exceed that value.

The second type of prepaid program, also state-sponsored, is a prepaid/savings hybrid that is sometimes referred to as a **"unit" program**. It typically involves the purchase of tuition units or credits that represent a fraction (e.g. one percent) of the average yearly tuition and fees at public institutions in the state. These units change in value each year as average in-state tuition and fees increase. They are redeemed in the future to pay for tuition and fees, and in most cases, they can be redeemed for other qualified expenses as well (room and board, books, supplies, and equipment).

Categorizing the unit program as either prepaid or savings remains a matter of debate; it makes a difference because prepaid programs and savings programs are treated differently in determining student eligibility for federal financial aid (see chapter 4). In 2000, Pennsylvania reconfigured its 529 plan, TAP, in an effort to secure more favorable financial aid treatment for its participants. Previously recognized as a unit-type prepaid program, TAP is now characterized as a "guaranteed savings" program. Similarly, Ohio has repositioned its unit-type prepaid program (the oldest such program in the country) as the "Guaranteed Savings" option alongside the more conventional investment options in its CollegeAdvantage Savings Plan. Tennessee and Washington have unit programs that have not yet adopted the "guaranteed savings" label, but perhaps should do so.

The third type of prepaid program, referred to here as a **"voucher" program**, depends on the voluntary participation of one or more educational institutions, and may combine both private and public schools. Payments into the program are worth a pre-determined percentage of tuition and fees at each institution. For example, a multi-institution prepaid program may provide that a $5,000 contribution is worth 50 percent of one year's tuition at participating College A, and 30 percent at College B. If your child attends one of those participating institutions, the tuition bill is reduced by the stated percentage. If your child attends a non-participating institution, or decides not to go to college at all, you can request a return of your payments adjusted for interest, investment performance of the program fund, or other factors as described in program materials. The Massachusetts U.Plan, with several dozen Massachusetts private and public institutions, was the first to offer a voucher-type prepaid program. However, it does not qualify as a 529 plan under the federal requirements (it issues Massachusetts general obligation bonds and so the interest is free from federal and Massachusetts state income tax). Independent 529 Plan, a private-college prepaid program, launched its voucher program in fall 2003. It is a 529 plan.

Here is another way to think about the three different types of prepaid programs: A contract program works like a futures contract, a unit program like an index fund (the index being average tuition at selected schools), and a voucher program like a discount coupon. All three rely on the program trust fund (made up of participant payments or contributions) to generate an investment return sufficient to cover the program's liability for future tuition payments and unit redemptions.

What is a savings program?

A 529 savings program is a more familiar type of tax-deferred investment, in many ways similar to a variable annuity or an individual retirement account. Contributions are made to a trust fund that is invested in mutual funds and other financial instruments. The idea is that your account will grow in value over time to keep up with, or preferably surpass, the increasing price of a college education.

Before Congress enacted Internal Revenue Code Section 529 in 1996, several states had prepaid tuition programs but only one state, Kentucky, had a pure savings program. Since 1996, a majority of the new 529 plans are savings programs. There appear to be a couple of reasons for this phenomenon. One is that savings programs offer the potential for higher investment returns than prepaid or guaranteed savings programs. Accounts are usually invested in equity and bond mutual funds that have historically outpaced the increases in college expenses.

The other reason is that savings programs are easier and cheaper for a state to administer, especially when the outside vendor that handles the investments also agrees to handle much of the program administration and marketing. Recently, several states have launched new or redesigned programs in which the program fund is charged a fee that is shared by the program manager and the state treasury, in effect making the program a source of revenue for the state.

What are the major differences between prepaid and savings programs?

Choosing the right type of 529 plan is important, because there are significant differences between them. Most people evaluating alternative 529 plans will, quite naturally, focus attention on the investment aspects of the programs being considered. After all, we all want our investments to do as well as possible. Historically, over long periods of time, stocks have outperformed many other investments, and certain types of common stocks have done better than others. On the other hand, stocks generally carry more investment risk than most other types of investments.

Nearly all 529 plans, of either variety, employ professional investment managers to maximize potential return within a certain level of risk. In a savings program, the investment management is applied directly to the assets in a participant's account. In a prepaid or guaranteed savings program, the investment management is applied to the program fund to ensure that the program will be able to pay for future tuition or unit redemptions. Because a participant will have no choice in the state's selection of investment managers, the participant must rely on the judgment of program officials.

While most savings programs offer the advantage of unlimited upside investment potential, prepaid and guaranteed savings programs offer the advantage of keeping up with inflation of college expenses, no matter how high those costs may go. A risk-tolerant saver may be more attracted to the savings program while a risk-averse saver may be more attracted to the prepaid or guaranteed savings program.

Here are some of the major differences between programs:

1) Prepaid programs (with the possible exception of the unit-type or guaranteed savings programs) are currently at a disadvantage when applying for federal financial aid programs. The financial need of a family, as established by formula, is reduced dollar-for-dollar by amounts being paid for through the program. With a savings program, under current rules, the account value is generally considered an asset of the parent (a maximum of 5.6 percent of the account value is deemed available to pay for the cost of attendance) or other account owner. See chapter 4.

2) Many prepaid programs have a specified enrollment period each year. Prepayment contracts must be purchased during the enrollment period, and the price of a contract is adjusted each year when the new enrollment period begins. Savings programs do not have restricted enrollment periods and accept new accounts and contributions at any time.

3) Almost all state-sponsored prepaid programs require that either the account owner or the beneficiary meet state residency requirements. The majority of savings programs, however, are open to residents of any state. Any family considering investing in a 529 plan should evaluate the program in the state where the donor lives, the state where the designated beneficiary lives, and any state with a 529 plan that does not have residency requirements.

4) Most prepayment contracts are of limited duration. For example, the program may specify that the contract will be terminated, and a refund made, if the benefits are not used within 10 years after the beneficiary's

normal college matriculation date. Most savings programs, however, have no program-imposed limit on account duration and can remain open indefinitely as long as there is a designated beneficiary on the account.

5) Most contract-type and voucher-type prepaid programs provide only for undergraduate tuition and fees, while savings programs and unit-type prepaid programs can generally be used for any costs that meet the definition of "qualified higher education expense" under Code Section 529, including graduate school. This can be a significant limitation for students at most public institutions where tuition and fees comprise less than 50 percent of the student's total cost of attendance. However, nothing prevents a family from combining participation in a prepaid program with participation in a savings program.

6) All 529 plans allow withdrawals to pay for out-of-state colleges and universities. However, contract-type prepaid programs are generally designed for the child who eventually will be enrolling at an in-state public institution. For the beneficiary of a prepayment contract who attends an in-state private school, or an out-of-state school, the contract benefits must be valued before payments can be made. Many programs compute a value by applying the weighted-average, credit-hour value of in-state public universities. However, some prepaid programs compute a value by adding a low fixed rate of interest to the original contributions into the account. Also, most of these programs will limit the benefits paid to private and out-of-state institutions to the lesser of actual tuition and fees or the value of in-state tuition and fees. This means that a participant who moves out-of-state and then attends a public university in the new state will not receive a refund if the new state has lower in-state tuition than the old state. In this situation, the contract owner should evaluate if the best option is simply to cancel the contract and obtain a refund. The choice of college is not an issue in most savings and unit-type prepaid programs because beneficiaries receive the same return whether they attend an in-state public, in-state private, or out-of-state school.

7) Even if the beneficiary of a contract-type prepaid program chooses to enroll in an in-state public institution, the investment return will often depend on the institution attended and the number of credit hours taken. A student attending the most expensive public university in the state and

taking the maximum number of credit hours covered under the contract receives a better deal than the student who attends the least expensive university or takes fewer credit hours than the contract promises to cover. In some states, the range of public tuition can be very wide. The ultimate choice of school does not affect the investment return in a savings or unit-type program.

8) Most prepaid programs make payments directly to the institution after receiving notice of pending tuition bills from the participant. Savings programs generally permit cash withdrawals by the account owner or beneficiary, and do not require documentation to substantiate the use of the withdrawn funds.

9) State-sponsored prepaid programs tend to have more transaction fees than savings programs. Perhaps this is because prepaid programs are more difficult to administer, or because they are operated by state agencies that are accustomed to imposing fees. All 529 plans will list the fees charged to participants, including fees for enrollment, annual maintenance, and change of beneficiary or account owner. Savings programs compete more directly with other investment alternatives available to the college saver, and seem more intent on keeping fees and transaction charges to a minimum.

10) Some prepaid programs require a minimum purchase of at least one semester's worth of tuition, but allow payments to be made over time. The installment payments include an interest component, although the full payments are credited to the investment in the account and none of the extra payment is treated as interest expense for income tax purposes. Savings programs do not work this way and simply credit the account whenever a contribution is received.

11) State-sponsored prepaid programs, including both the unit-type and guaranteed savings programs, make actuarial assumptions (otherwise known as educated guesses) about the future performance of the program trust fund. Relevant factors used to calculate the liability for future payouts include the investment return on fund assets, the tuition benefits to be paid by the program, and the expected number of refunds. The bull market of the 1990s enabled the older prepaid programs to build large fund surpluses. These surpluses were maintained as "reserves" against future investment shortfalls. (Some programs are permitted to allocate

excess reserves to participant accounts, while others are prohibited from doing so. Pennsylvania's TAP program made a $4.3 million allocation of surplus to participant accounts in 1998, and may do so again in the future if reserves grow beyond the amount necessary for program stability). In recent years, the combination of stock market losses and spiraling public tuition has led to program reserves drying up and balance sheets showing a deficit in nearly all programs as of the end of 2002. The financial situation has been particularly difficult for newer prepaid programs that never had a chance to build reserves in the 1990s bull market. Several states have closed off their prepaid programs to new enrollment, and will reopen only when financial conditions improve or when the programs can be restructured to minimize any risk of loss.

12) Some prepaid programs and unit-type programs are backed by the full faith and credit of their sponsoring states, providing a safety net for participants should the program run out of funds. A few programs do not enjoy this guarantee, but do offer some added safety under laws that require the state legislature to consider an appropriation to the program if it runs into financial difficulties. Still other programs have no backing or guarantees from the state whatsoever. Savings programs typically have no state guarantee, and should have no reason to need one.

It is reasonable to expect that over time we will see further blurring of the lines that distinguish prepaid and savings programs. We are already beginning to see savings programs offering some inflation-protection features normally associated with prepaid programs, including guaranteed investment options. At the same time, some prepaid programs are becoming more flexible and investment-oriented. It may be difficult to achieve, but there is no reason why the best features of each type of 529 plan cannot be successfully incorporated into a single program. In fact, the best defense the states have against the possible "federalization" of 529 plans is to do just that.

SIX

What to Look for in a 529 Plan: A Checklist

Beyond the basic characteristics of the two types of 529 plans described in the previous chapter, numerous differences exist in program design among the various programs operating today. The task of sorting through all the choices can be somewhat daunting. Just understanding how the 529 plan in your home state works is difficult enough; shopping among competing 529 plans becomes extremely confusing.

Your analysis should involve not only a comparison of each program's investments or tuition guarantees, but also many other aspects of the program. Your own family circumstances, investment objectives, risk tolerance, and financial knowledge will all play a large part in selecting an appropriate 529 plan. The "best" 529 plan for one family is not necessarily the best one for another.

How do you go about this selection process? This book and our companion Web site (www.savingforcollege.com) are certainly good first steps. Then be sure to obtain the program materials for your own state's 529 plan. Finally, request information from other programs that interest you and that will allow you to participate as a nonresident.

Many individual investors rely on a professional financial planner or investment adviser in developing, implementing, and monitoring an investment plan. Before 2001, few financial professionals had the knowledge, experience, and interest in 529 plans to be of much help to you in this regard. But over the past four years, professionals have awakened to the benefits of 529 plans for their clients, and many programs have been adapted for distribution through advisers.

Whether you use an investment adviser or search on your own, learn as much as you can about a 529 program before you invest. Here are the primary information sources that may or may not be included in the materials provided to you:

State statute. Every state with a 529 plan will have a law on the books authorizing the program. Sometimes, more than one section of the law is involved, e.g., when special state tax treatment is provided for participants in the 529 plan.

Program rules. Usually, a state agency or program board is charged with implementing and overseeing the operation of the program and acting as trustee. This agency develops the official rules of the program as allowed by the statute. These rules are extremely important because they contain the program's operational details. The rules are prone to frequent change, however, so it is important to be sure that you are reading the most current version.

Program description. Many programs provide an extensive explanatory booklet that describes their rules. This document also explains the tax treatment of 529 accounts and contains appropriate disclaimers.

Investment prospectuses. If a 529 savings program invests in mutual funds, it may send you the prospectuses for those funds—the same SEC-registered prospectuses that any investor would receive. The 529 plan itself is not required to produce a prospectus because securities laws treat interests in a 529 plan as "municipal securities" exempt from SEC registration requirements.

Program booklet. You will usually find an attractive, glossy marketing piece that contains pictures of cute children and summarizes the key advantages of the program. This is often presented in a helpful FAQ (frequently asked questions) format. An enrollment/application form is generally provided with the program booklet.

Web site. Every 529 plan has a Web site. The Internet has become an extremely important and useful way to convey information and is perfectly suited to these programs. The best Web sites will make available all the materials provided in the enrollment packet, plus links to other higher-education information: financial aid programs, colleges and universities, and college cost calculators. Many 529 plans now allow you to enroll on-line.

The remainder of this chapter describes many of the ways in which 529 plans may differ from one another, and suggests an approach for comparing the various programs. This approach takes the form of a three-step process:

Step 1: Eliminate any 529 plans that clearly fall outside your criteria for acceptability, as well as those that will not accept you (due to eligibility restrictions).

Step 2: For each program, ask yourself the question "How much will my invested dollar produce by the time my beneficiary is ready for college?" Your own investment objectives, future college plans, and risk tolerance will play a part here. Be sure to consider the level of fees and expenses, as well as any state-tax benefits offered (or forfeited) or other "perks" offered by the plans.

Step 3: Make your final selection based on a comparison of the restrictive features in the programs. For example, some programs permit your relatives to make contributions directly to your account, while other programs do not. This feature may or may not be important to you; that is up to you to determine. You should also note that you can sometimes nullify a restriction by using multiple 529 plans, or by rolling over to a less-restrictive 529 plan later on.

How much time will you need to complete this three-step process? It could be a lot, depending on how many possibilities you wish to explore. There are so many 529 plans to choose from and they differ in so many ways that your beneficiary could have completed college before you finally complete the exercise. That would not be a good thing. The tools available in this book, i.e., the checklist in this chapter, the program descriptions contained in Part II, and the online tools and information available at www.savingforcollege.com, can help shortcut the process.

Before making any final decisions, however, read and understand the official program materials of the programs you are most interested in. Contact the program administrators directly to obtain further explanation and clarification. For some important items (e.g., legal and tax questions), consider having a conversation with your attorney, accountant, or other professional adviser. The importance of a thorough due diligence process cannot be overstated because it can greatly reduce the chances of being surprised or disappointed later on.

The following checklist is presented in three sections. It is organized in this manner so that you may more easily identify the 529 plans most likely to meet your needs. Revisit this checklist occasionally, as 529 plans are constantly making changes (usually improvements) to their program rules and investment options.

Section 1: Conditional criteria

The first section describes "conditional criteria"—eligibility or use requirements that either the program or the investor may impose when determining program suitability. The importance of each of these criteria will depend on your particular circumstances.

1) Are there any state residency requirements?

Most 529 savings programs do not require that you or the designated beneficiary reside in the sponsoring state, but a few do. Conversely, most contract-type and unit-type prepaid programs restrict enrollment to persons who meet state residency requirements. Even here, however, there are exceptions. Alabama's prepaid program, for example, is fully open to nonresidents.

Often, a 529 plan with restrictions will permit enrollment if either the account owner or the beneficiary is a state resident at the time of enrollment. If you are establishing an account for a grandchild living in a different state, you may want to consider the program offered in the state where your grandchild resides.

Questions regarding residency can arise in certain situations. Is there a minimum period of residency? What happens if the eligible resident moves out-of-state after the account is opened? What happens if enrollment is contingent on the state residency of the beneficiary, and you later change the beneficiary to someone who is not a state resident? How are the residency restrictions applied to military personnel stationed in the state, or those originally from the state but now stationed elsewhere?

Some 529 plans that impose residency restrictions will accept non-residents who meet other conditions. For example, Pennsylvania will accept into its guaranteed savings program any nonresident whose place of employment is within Pennsylvania. Nevada's prepaid program allows a nonresident alumnus of a Nevada post-secondary institution to enroll.

2) What are the other eligibility requirements?

Many 529 plans require that the individual account owner be of legal age (e.g. 18). In addition, the program may be restricted to account owners who are U.S. citizens or resident aliens. The program may require that the beneficiary have (or obtain within a certain period of time) a Social Security number or a federal taxpayer identification number.

Most prepaid programs require that the beneficiary be below a certain age or grade level at the time of enrollment, making these programs unsuitable for older individuals who may be planning to attend college in the future.

3) Can the account owner and the beneficiary be the same person?

Although just about every 529 savings program permits you to establish an account for yourself, this may not always be feasible in programs that place age or grade limits on beneficiaries. Such restrictions are common in prepaid programs.

4) How does the program handle funds coming from an existing UTMA or UGMA investment account?

Many families have children with assets in a Uniform Transfers to Minors Act (UTMA) account or Uniform Gifts to Minors Act (UGMA) account. If you are the custodian of the account, and you wish to invest the child's assets in a 529 plan, you will need to determine if, and how, the program accommodates funds coming from UTMA/UGMA accounts. There are a few different ways this is being done.

+ The program (e.g. New York) will permit the minor child to establish an account in his or her own name. A parent or legal guardian must execute documents and authorize decisions with respect to the account until the minor reaches the age of majority.

+ The program will permit the account to be titled in the same way as any other account owned by the minor under the UTMA/UGMA. The custodian must notify the program administrator at the time the custodianship is terminated upon the child reaching legal age so that the account can be re-titled in the child's own name. The program generally prohibits a change in beneficiary, or any withdrawal that is not for the benefit of the minor, until the custodianship terminates.

+ The program will title the account in the name of the adult acting as custodian but will provide a "check box" to indicate that the source of funds is an existing UTMA/UGMA account. The account will be restricted as to beneficiary changes and withdrawals until the custodianship terminates.

+ The program will title the account in the name of the adult acting as custodian with no additional restrictions or requirements. The program administrator in this instance adopts the position that it is the custodian's legal responsibility to ensure that the account is handled in accordance within UTMA/UGMA laws.

5) Will the program accept a corporation or a trust as account owner?

A corporate-owned 529 account can provide unique benefits as part of a bonus plan or non-qualified deferred compensation plan. The trustee of an irrevocable trust may also be attracted to the investment and tax advantages of a 529 plan and wish to establish an account with the beneficiary of the trust named as beneficiary of the 529 account. The ability to name a trust as successor owner can be particularly important to an individual who establishes an account and wants to be sure that in the event of death the account is used in accordance with his or her wishes. Passing ownership directly to an individual successor owner may be viewed as too risky since control of those funds, including the power to make withdrawals, rests entirely with the new owner.

It is particularly important that anyone who wishes to establish a non-natural entity as owner or successor owner seek professional advice from an attorney and an accountant. Many legal and tax complications can arise in these situations.

6) Are interests in the 529 plan being sold through brokers?

If you rely on a financial adviser who earns commissions from the sale of investment products, chances are that the adviser will focus on 529 plans that pay a commission. This isn't necessarily bad. Adviser-sold programs tend to be well-structured and have flexible features. They have passed the scrutiny of your adviser's broker-dealer, who typically provides substantial education and technical and administrative support to the adviser.

On the other hand, if you wish to conduct all the research and analysis on your own, or if you use a fee-only rather than commission-based financial planner, you will probably be more inclined to look for non-broker (i.e. direct-sold) 529 plans. You will generally incur lower program expenses in direct-sold plans and your program selection will not be restricted to those that pay a commission. In some cases, a fee-only financial planner will be able to acquire shares in an adviser-sold program at net asset value, which means that the sales load is waived.

Note that many direct-sold programs are prohibited by law from providing investment advice to you because they are not offered through licensed securities representatives or registered investment advisers.

Several states make direct-sold programs available to residents but require that nonresidents go through a financial adviser or pay the higher cost associated with adviser-sold shares.

7) What is the minimum contribution?

The issue here is your ability to make at least the minimum required contribution to the 529 plan. Some programs have no minimum contributions while others have minimum contributions of $1,000 or more. Many savings programs waive the initial lump-sum minimum contribution if you commit to an automatic investment plan. Prepaid programs generally offer different tuition packages at different prices. Many of these programs permit a monthly payment plan, albeit at a higher total cost.

8) Does the program accept contributions through payroll deduction and/or electronic funds transfer from your checking or savings account?

To contribute through payroll deduction or electronic funds transfer, make sure the program you select will accommodate it. Even if a program accepts contributions through payroll deduction, your employer must be able to meet the requirements of the program in establishing the payroll deduction process.

Some programs now permit online enrollment and contributions under new "electronic signature" rules. This can be a welcome convenience and is likely to become commonplace in the future.

9) Will your use of the program create any state-level gift or inheritance tax concerns?

Only a handful of states levy a gift tax (Connecticut, Louisiana, North Carolina, and Tennessee), but if you live in one of them you need to consider whether your contributions to a 529 plan give rise to a taxable gift. States do not necessarily follow the federal gift tax rules and they may treat contributions to the in-state program differently from contributions to an out-of-state program.

Your participation in a state's 529 plan should not subject your estate to inheritance tax or probate in that state, but there may be exceptions to that rule. The disclosure statement for the North Carolina 529 savings programs, for example, cautions that accounts owned by non-residents may be subject to North Carolina inheritance tax. Consult your attorney.

10) Does the 529 program participate in any affinity programs?

Upromise, Inc. is a privately-owned company offering a consumer-rewards program that directs your purchase rebates from participating vendors into a 529 account. Membership is free (www.upromise.com). Upromise maintains agreements with selected 529 savings programs and facilitates the investment of your rebates into those programs. If you join Upromise, you may wish to consider opening a 529 account in one of those programs. Another popular affinity program with linkage to 529 plans is offered by Vesdia Corporation through its BabyMint web site (www.babymint.com) and other sites. Several credit cards offer cash-back rewards that can be automatically directed into one or more 529 plans. Participants in Pennsylvania's TAP 529 Plan are eligible for free scholarships at a number of private colleges through an arrangement with SAGE Scholars (www.sagescholars.com).

11) Does the program place any restrictions on your ownership rights or give any of these rights to the beneficiary?

Most 529 plans permit you as account owner to change the designated beneficiary, determine when and for what purpose distributions are made, and cancel the account and request a refund. Some programs do not. For example, Michigan's prepaid tuition program, the Michigan Education Trust, is irrevocable and generally prohibits any refunds until after the beneficiary reaches age 18. Ohio's CollegeAdvantage program also restricts withdrawals from its Guaranteed Savings Fund option before the beneficiary reaches age 18. Be aware of the possible implications of restrictions like these. In certain situations they may be viewed as attractive features. The placement of ownership rights may affect other aspects of participation in a 529 plan—financial aid treatment, creditor concerns, and treatment of the account when applying for Medicaid.

12) Is an account in the program protected from the claims of creditors under state law?

A program offering special asset protection for participant accounts under state law may appeal to individuals with creditor concerns. Several programs offer this protection, although the degree of protection may vary. For instance, an account in New York's College Savings Program is entirely exempt if the account owner is also the beneficiary and a minor, but a maximum $10,000 is exempt if the account owner is anyone else. If you are participating in a 529 plan outside your own state, discuss with an attorney how the asset protection provided by that state applies to creditor actions in your own state.

13) Can a non-owner make contributions to an account in the program?

To establish an account that other persons, including your relatives, can contribute to without opening their own accounts, the 529 plan must accommodate non-owner contributions. Some 529 plans indicate they will not accept contributions from anyone other than the account owner, presumably to avoid any issues with regard to ownership rights, potential state tax deductions, or gift tax uncertainties.

14) Does the program permit the account owner to designate a successor owner?

If you as account owner of a 529 plan were to die, your 529 account does not terminate. Instead, account ownership passes to a successor. Most programs make it easy for you to designate a successor owner at the time of enrollment, and permit you to submit a change in your designation at any time. If you do not designate a successor owner, the program will either automatically install a new owner at the time of your death, or pass ownership to your estate. If passed automatically, the chain of possible successors might start with the program beneficiary or your spouse, depending on the rules of the program.

15) How complete and accurate are the program disclosures?

The quality and quantity of program disclosures can vary widely among different 529 plans. Interests in a 529 savings program are "municipal fund securities" exempt from federal regulation; however, those distributed through broker-dealers must conform to the rules of the Municipal Securities Rulemaking Board, a self-regulatory organization responsible to the SEC. Some programs offer very extensive disclosures that answer most questions, while others are not nearly as complete. Some areas to check are the following: investment policies and historical investment results of underlying funds, processing of contributions, withdrawal and account-change requests, description of resident state tax rules, and fees and expenses. Prepaid programs can have a longer list. Check to see how current the program disclosures are and whether updated information is available on the official program Web site. You may also want to judge how knowledgeable and responsive the program call center is when you ask questions by telephone. If you are working with a financial adviser, be sure the adviser is willing and able to obtain education and technical support from the program manager and/or distributor.

16) How does the program report account activity to its participants?

Every 529 plan sends you a statement of your account at least annually, and many will send it more frequently. Perhaps you want online access to your account. Not all programs provide that. If you establish your account through a financial adviser, it is unlikely that the account will appear along with other investments on your monthly or quarterly statements. However, this may happen more frequently in the future as financial advisers and individual investors begin demanding it. You should also read and understand a program's privacy policy. This is usually not a concern and your account information should be exempt from any state "open document" laws (but ask if you are not sure).

Sometimes privacy concerns stem from the requirement that all accounts with the same beneficiary be aggregated when applying the program's contribution limit. You may become privy to what other family members or friends are contributing when several people are contributing to accounts for the same beneficiary. Some programs will even print the unused contribution limit on monthly or quarterly account statements. (Most families will not be too concerned about this issue and will probably appreciate staying informed about the unused contribution limit.)

17) Has the IRS "qualified" the program?

A formal determination of qualified status from the IRS, although not required as a condition for a state to offer a 529 plan, can provide added comfort that the program is structured in compliance with Section 529 of the Code. Several programs have already applied for and received favorable determinations. Others have applied and are still waiting. Some programs do not intend to apply for IRS determination and are willing to rely on the legal opinions of their attorneys.

18) Which educational expenses are covered by the program?

Contract-type prepaid programs describe the specific costs covered under the contract. If the prepaid program you are considering covers only tuition and fees, you may want to add a savings, unit-type prepaid, or guaranteed savings program for more extensive coverage.

Some contract-type prepaid programs will pay for expenses besides tuition and fees if the beneficiary receives a scholarship and in certain other circumstances.

Following the 2001 tax law changes, it is no longer up to the 529 program administrator to determine which expenses meet the definition of "qualified higher education expenses." It will be up to you to properly report qualifying expenses as part of the tax return preparation process.

19) How does the program handle rollovers?

This last item in section 1 may be one of the most important. Although federal tax law permits you to roll over your account without federal tax or penalty under certain conditions, the program itself is not required to accommodate this transaction. Section 3 alerts you to restrictions and other concerns that may exist in a program but that are avoidable when you have the ability to easily, without cost or penalty, and at any time, transfer any amount from that program to a different one (assuming you meet the federal conditions for a rollover). To the extent that your current program does not support this, the red flags that may pop up from your review of the items in section 3 could take on greater weight.

Most often it is matter of expense, as some programs charge a small fee or penalty on an outbound rollover. In prepaid programs, your decision to transfer to another program may require a full or partial cancellation of your contract and the financial consequences may be more significant. A small number of 529 plans may even restrict your ability to request a refund of any type unless your beneficiary has reached a certain age or you can convince the program administrator of your need for the funds.

A direct trustee-to-trustee rollover is the easiest to accomplish but not all 529 plans will do this for you. If not, it becomes a matter of withdrawing funds from your existing 529 account and re-contributing those funds within 60 days to a new 529 plan. In either case, you must comply with the rollover restrictions concerning a change of beneficiary to another family member, or the limits on same-beneficiary rollovers (see chapter 3).

Section 2: Investment suitability criteria

The second section of the checklist describes "investment suitability criteria"—an evaluation of the investment characteristics of the program to determine which programs best meet your college savings objectives. Note that questions 39 through 43 pertain only to prepaid programs.

20) Does the program offer a college-savings strategy consistent with your own objectives and preferences?

This is the essential issue for most investors. What do I get for the money I contribute? How will my investment perform? How much risk am I accepting? How does it compare to other 529 plans, and to other types of investments? You will need to carefully consider what happens to your money after it is contributed to the program, and make the decision to join only after you become comfortable with its investment approach.

21) Does the program provide a "guarantee" that your investment will keep up with the increasing costs of college?

A "yes" answer is the hallmark of a prepaid program or guaranteed savings program, while a "no" answer indicates a savings program. Special considerations relating to prepaid programs and guaranteed savings programs are grouped below in questions 39 through 43. A savings program will not promise that your account will keep pace with any measure of increasing college costs (with very limited exceptions, such as Alaska's program that offers an option guaranteeing a minimum return equivalent to tuition increases at the University of Alaska, but only for beneficiaries who end up attending the University of Alaska). You have the potential to do better than the college cost inflation rate, but you also have the risk of seeing your account lag behind college costs.

22) Does the savings program offer an "age-based" asset allocation strategy, a menu of "static" portfolios, or both?

An age-based strategy is one in which your account is automatically moved to a more conservative asset allocation over time. Typically, the age of your beneficiary will determine the portfolio in the program into which your contributions are initially placed, although it is now common that a program will base the initial portfolio on the expected number of years to enrollment rather than age, or will simply allow you to choose your starting point from any of the program's age-based portfolios.

The idea of an age-based asset allocation strategy is that you will want to be more aggressively invested when your investment time horizon is long (e.g. for a young child), so your account will be invested primarily in stock funds. Over time, your account will gradually be shifted out of stock funds and into fixed-income and/or money market funds; it finally comes to rest in the most conservative age-based portfolio until withdrawn.

Savings programs manipulate asset allocations by means of two different mechanisms. One is by establishing a series of portfolios where each portfolio has a target asset allocation among stock, bond, and money market funds that generally does not change over time. Your account is transferred ("migrated") from one portfolio to the next at scheduled intervals. The second approach is to assign your account to a portfolio targeted to a particular year of use. Instead of moving your account from one portfolio to the next, the manager adjusts the underlying investments of the portfolio to achieve new asset allocation targets over time. Only when the target year of use is reached is the account transferred to a final "resting" portfolio.

Is one approach better than the other? Not necessarily. The first approach, in which your account is transferred among increasingly conservative portfolios, is more mechanistic yet more disciplined. You will know "going in" how your account is to be allocated among stocks, bonds, and money market funds at any point in the future. The second approach is less mechanistic and gives the portfolio investment manager a greater amount of discretion in adjusting the asset allocation for changing market conditions.

A "static" option in a savings program is one in which your portfolio's targeted asset allocation does not change over time. It can be a 100 percent equity option, a 100 percent fixed-income option, or a pre-determined blend of different asset classes. Most 529 savings programs with static options currently design each portfolio as a "fund of funds," using a mix of underlying mutual funds. An increasing number of programs now offer individual-fund portfolios in addition to blended-fund options and other options.

23) Does the program offer a principal-protected option?

If you have no tolerance for downside risk with the principal portion of your account, consider a savings program with an interest-bearing investment option that protects your principal. In fact, the unsteady performance of the stock market over the last few years has caused many states to re-evaluate their program investments and to add a "safe" option if none existed previously.

The amount of interest you earn may or may not match increasing college costs. A money market fund consists of short-term securities and is designed to maintain a level unit price, although its dividend/interest payout can swing dramatically over a short period of time. Some programs (including most of the programs managed by TIAA-CREF) are now offering "guaranteed" options that guarantee not only principal but a minimum level of interest as well (e.g., 3 percent). They declare an interest-crediting rate on a periodic basis and are backed by a "funding agreement" with a life insurance company. Another variation being introduced into the 529 marketplace is the "stable value" investment. This is a product that seeks to combine the stable share pricing of a money market fund with the higher returns of a bond fund. By leveling the yields of its underlying fixed-income securities, it also produces less variability in overall yield.

Some of the "prepaid tuition" programs can also be viewed as guaranteed principal-plus-interest investments, except that their yield is pegged to tuition increases. For example, the College Savings Bank makes its FDIC-insured CollegeSure® CD available through the Arizona and Montana programs. The interest rate is based each year on the increase in a national index of private college costs, less a 3 percent margin, with a minimum annual rate of 2 percent. Several of the contract-type prepaid programs permit you to cancel your contract and receive your payments back along with some amount of interest.

24) What are the other characteristics of the underlying securities in the options available under a savings program?

This book does not purport to provide a technical analysis of investments. However, you should attempt to determine the investment fundamentals of portfolios in a 529 plan (or rely on a professional who can) and see that it fits well with your other investments (retirement accounts, etc.). Ask the following questions:

+ How is the portfolio allocated among stocks, bonds, and money market funds?
+ How much of the portfolio is invested in international stocks, junk bonds, large-cap, medium-cap, and small-cap stocks?
+ Who manages the underlying mutual funds?
+ What are the track records of those funds?
+ Does the program require that you develop your own "portfolio" by allocating your contributions among individual mutual funds (or permit you to do so)?

Some 529 savings programs invest in mutual funds from one particular fund family (typically an affiliate of the 529 program manager), while others are "multi-manager," incorporating funds from two or more separate fund families. Under either model, the investment history of most 529 plans has not been long enough to make conclusive comparisons, although a detailed analysis of various portfolios can yield useful information. Many 529 plans now post 529 portfolio performance on their Web sites with the information updated either daily, monthly, or quarterly.

25) Does the program permit contributions to be allocated among multiple options?

If the answer is "no," you will have to open separate accounts for the same beneficiary if you wish to use more than one investment option.

26) Does the program permit you to switch between investment options as described in IRS Notice 2001–55?

Before the IRS issued Notice 2001–55 in September 2001, you were not permitted to move your 529 account from one investment option in the program to another. Now you may do so, program-permitting, but only once in any calendar year or whenever a change of beneficiary occurs. Nearly all 529 savings programs appear to have implemented this new flexibility.

27) How quickly does the program invest your contribution?

Not all 529 plans possess the administrative capabilities to ensure that your contribution is invested within a day or two of when your check is received. This can be of particular concern at certain times during the year, most notably late December when a large inflow of contributions can overwhelm processing capacities. The day on which your contribution is processed can also depend on the method you use in making your contribution. For example, it may take longer to process an initial contribution using an electronic funds transfer from your bank account than one made by check.

A delay means that you will not have the benefit (or possible detriment) of market activity during that time. A program that is not managed by an outside investment firm may lack the administrative resources needed to process investments on a daily basis. For example, the Virginia Education Savings Trust places contributions into portfolios twice each month. The program uses the earnings from a 14 to 28 day "float" of your investment to help offset program expenses.

28) How are earnings in the portfolio credited to your account?

The vast majority of savings programs use daily valuation. You own "shares" of the program trust fund and the price of those shares will reflect the daily share prices of the underlying funds, along with any investment earnings and program expenses posted to the trust fund. A small number of programs use balance-forward accounting instead of daily valuation. For example, in the Utah 529 plan, the expenses of the program trust are allocated to participant accounts at the end of each quarter based on average account balances of all accounts in the trust fund.

29) Does the program charge an enrollment fee?

Some 529 plans charge enrollment fees and others do not. Sometimes the enrollment fee is waived, or the amount reduced, in particular circumstances (e.g., for state residents or during special promotions). If you open multiple accounts for the same beneficiary, or for beneficiaries in the same family, the program may offer a discount off normal enrollment fees. Because it is a fixed charge, the effect of any enrollment fee on your overall return will depend on how much money you invest in the program.

If you are enrolling in a 529 plan through a financial adviser receiving commissions, there may be a sales charge or "load" depending on which "class" of shares you choose to acquire. The upfront load may be as little as one percent or as much as 5.75 percent of your contribution.

30) Does the program charge an annual account maintenance fee?

An account maintenance fee is a fixed-dollar amount charged against your account on a quarterly, semi-annual, or annual basis. These fees can vary from $5 to $50 per year. In some programs, the account maintenance fee is waived if you have a specified account balance or commit to an automatic investment plan.

31) What is the program's expense ratio?

The expense ratio of a savings program typically consists of two components. The first is the total of any asset-based fees charged against the value of the program fund by the outside program manager and/or state agency in charge of administering the 529 plan. The second consists of the expenses of the underlying mutual funds, which can range from very low-cost index funds to relatively high-cost international equity or other specialized sector funds. In some savings programs there is a third source of expense—certain administrative costs charged to the program fund, such as the cost of an annual audit—although these expenses tend to have a relatively small impact.

Some program managers include, or "wrap," the underlying fund expenses in the fees they charge to the 529 plan. The advantage to this approach is that it presents a simple and easy-to-understand fee structure, and there is no incentive for the program manager to select mutual funds with high underlying fees. A possible disadvantage is that the investor with a conservative asset allocation will be paying the same expense as the investor with an aggressive asset allocation, despite the fact that bond and money market funds generally have much lower expense ratios than stock funds.

Asset-based expenses in non-broker savings programs range from as little as one-quarter of one percent (0.25%) to as much as two percent. Considering the valuable tax benefits available with a 529 plan, and the special effort required to design, market, and administer a plan, the total fixed-dollar and asset-based expenses associated with most programs are very reasonable.

Programs distributed through financial advisers will charge additional asset-based fees that compensate the adviser. An example of this would be a program that charges an extra quarter-percent annual fee for "A shares" (along with an upfront sales load), an extra nine-tenths of one percent annual fee for "B shares" that convert to lower-cost A shares after six years and do not incur a sales load, and an extra six-tenths of one percent annual fee for "C shares" that do not convert and do not incur a sales load. Actual expenses vary among programs.

32) Are there charges for other transactions?

Some programs may impose a charge on beneficiary changes, account owner changes, rollovers, and certain other requests.

33) Can you claim a state income tax deduction for any or all of your contributions to the program?

Twenty-five states, and the District of Columbia, allow you to claim a state income tax deduction or credit for some or all of your contributions to the state's own 529 plan. Depending on your state income tax bracket and any limits placed on the deduction, this can be a very powerful incentive for choosing your own state's program.

Be sure you understand how the tax deduction in your state, if any, is regulated. Here are some important questions:

+ If the contributor is not the same as the account owner, which person claims the deduction?
+ Is the amount of deduction capped? If so, is the maximum deduction computed per contributor, per tax return, per beneficiary, or per account?
+ Can contributions in excess of any annual deduction limit be carried forward to future tax years?
+ Can you claim a deduction for an account you establish for yourself? Or does the beneficiary have to be your dependent?

If your state offers a state income tax deduction, you should recognize the circumstances under which you may be required to "recapture" the tax deduction in a future year. Most states require that you recapture prior deductions if you take a non-qualified withdrawal, and some states will apply the recapture to outbound rollovers as well. If you can claim a deduction for only a portion of your contributions, you may want to understand the ordering rules for recapture if only a portion of your account is withdrawn for non-qualified purposes. You may find, however, that your state has not yet fully explained how recapture applies in all situations.

34) Does the program offer any other financial incentives?

In lieu of a state income tax deduction, Minnesota and Maine offer a partial match for contributions made by low-income and moderate-income residents into their respective savings plans. Louisiana, Michigan and Rhode Island offer both a partial match for contributions and a limited state income tax deduction. New Jersey provides a first-year scholarship of as much as $1,500 to beneficiaries that attend a New Jersey public or private university. Utah has a separate endowment fund with earnings that are credited to the accounts of participants in its "Option 1." Kentucky guarantees that beneficiaries of accounts with at least $2,400 and open at least eight years can claim resident status for Kentucky public school tuition pricing no matter where they end up residing. Several states disregard balances in their own 529 plans when determining student eligibility for state-funded financial aid programs.

These are all examples of how states are working to make their programs as attractive as possible.

35) How will an account in the program affect the beneficiary's eligibility for need-based financial aid?

As things now stand, there can be a significant difference in the student's eligibility for need-based financial aid depending on which type of 529 plan—prepaid or savings—is being used. See chapters 4 and 5 for a discussion of this issue.

36) What is the term of the program manager?

The fact that a particular financial services firm has been selected to manage a 529 plan does not mean that the program will be using that manager forever. Management contracts are subject to terms of anywhere from two to 30 years. At the end of the initial program term, the contract may be extended or, under certain circumstances, the manager can be replaced. Naturally, in the event the manager is replaced, the program will probably look much different under the new manager. There are a few instances where this has occurred in the past, most notably in New York, where Upromise Investments replaced TIAA-CREF as program manager in 2003.

Besides manager changes, many other aspects of a program are subject to change at any time. Thus far, nearly all changes we have witnessed have benefited participants, but there is no guarantee that it will always be that way.

37) How popular is the program?

As a general rule, you want to join a 529 plan that has proven to be popular with others, or at least one that has the prospect of becoming popular. Level of assets in the program can be an indicator of popularity, although you need to consider several factors: how long the program has been around in its current form; restrictions on participation such as state residency, age, etc.; population of the sponsoring state; and whether the program is being distributed on a nationwide basis through financial advisers.

Programs must attract a sufficient level of assets in order to generate the revenues needed to pay for administration, investment management, and oversight. If the program is unable to achieve critical size, it becomes more likely that changes will be made, and these changes can be dramatic. While a replacement or addition of a program manager or changes to the investment offerings can be positive, other alterations, such as an increase in fees and expenses to cover the costs of operation, can be negative. The worst result is where the state, or the firm hired as program manager, loses its enthusiasm for the program and scales back its resources or the amount of attention it devotes.

Although it is impossible to establish a strict standard, any program at least two years old that has not yet attracted $50 million in assets can be considered small. A large 529 plan would be one with over $1 billion in assets. The largest prepaid program in the country is Florida's with approximately $3 billion. The largest savings program currently is Virginia's CollegeAmerica, managed by American Funds, with approximately $7 billion at the end of June 2004. Size does not correlate with investment performance. As mentioned above, the investment history of savings programs is still too short to make meaningful comparisons among most 529 plans.

Another way to gauge program popularity is to search for articles in the local and regional press. Often, the media are able to pick up on developments or concerns by keeping tabs with state and program officials. Sometimes the state's 529 plan becomes fodder in the political wrangling that characterizes many state legislatures and official offices.

38) Does the program rely on a state subsidy?

Most states expect their 529 programs to generate revenues sufficient to cover operating costs. A few states still find it necessary to subsidize program operations. A state subsidy to the program can help keep costs low for the participant, but budget cuts in the future may cause an increase in the fees charged to your account. Louisiana is a good example of a state that keeps fees low by paying its 529 plan administrative costs out of state coffers.

39) How much will your prepaid contract be worth at the college your beneficiary ultimately attends?

With the typical prepaid contract, the program will pay tuition and fees at any in-state public institution for the number of credit hours, semesters, or academic years that you purchase. Your investment "return" is determined in large part by the rate of future tuition increases at state schools. In many states, tuition levels are more sensitive to budgetary and political considerations than they are to increases in the cost of delivering education. In some states, there is a statutory cap on annual tuition increases.

Average in-state tuition levels are not the only factor. You will derive greater value from the contract if your beneficiary attends an expensive in-state public school than if he or she attends a less expensive school. In some states the range of costs can be wide. In some instances, if your beneficiary were to attend one of the least expensive state schools, you would be better off canceling the contract and receiving a refund.

Find out how the prepaid program will calculate benefits payable to a private or out-of-state school, in case your beneficiary does not attend a state school. The typical prepaid program will limit the amount paid to weighted average in-state tuition and fees.

40) How much will be refunded if you cancel your prepaid contract?

Will you receive the current tuition value of the contract, your payments along with interest, or only your payments without any interest? Is there a separate cancellation fee? In many states offering a prepaid program, the amount of refund will depend on the reason for cancellation. You are likely to receive more if your beneficiary dies, becomes disabled, or receives a scholarship. An "at-will" cancellation will result in the lowest refund.

When will the refund be paid? A cancellation of the contract may result in an immediate refund, or payments in installments, depending on the provisions of the contract.

41) How much does the prepaid contract cost?

Compare the price of the contract to the current tuition/fees at the institution your beneficiary is likely to attend. Is it the same, higher, or lower? Some prepaid programs and guaranteed savings programs, particularly the newer ones, are likely to charge more than the amount you would pay if your beneficiary were attending college this year. The "premium" is necessary for the program to cover administrative costs as well as to help build a reserve against potential shortfalls in the trust fund. A shortfall can occur if the program's obligation for future payments increases faster than the investment earnings in the trust. Any amount of premium reduces the overall return of your investment in the prepaid contract.

Older prepaid and guaranteed savings programs that built up their reserves during the 1990s may have less need to build an actuarial premium into their pricing. Some have been able to price their tuition packages very close to current levels, if not below.

The price may vary based on the age of your beneficiary. Prepaid programs with this feature offer a discount to younger beneficiaries because they provide the opportunity for higher and more predictable investment returns in the program trust fund.

Most prepaid programs permit you to pay for your contract in monthly installments. However, total payments under an installment payment plan will be higher than the amount you would pay in a lump sum. Check your rate of "interest" on the installment plan. Unless tuition prices increase more rapidly than the interest factor (often in the six percent to nine percent range) built into the installment contract, you are losing ground on each installment payment. Once you enter into an installment payment contract, you may be required to pay the total amount of installments even if you later decide to prepay with a lump sum payment. Be sure to check how flexible the program is in this regard. Also investigate the consequences of missing a scheduled payment.

Also check to see when your lump-sum payment or first installment payment is due. In some prepaid programs the payment deadline is several months after you enroll. If you decide to back out before the payment is due you will probably lose any enrollment fee paid.

42) Is the "tuition guarantee" backed by the full faith and credit of the state?

A full-faith-and-credit guarantee means the state is legally obligated to pay for the benefits promised by the prepaid program even if the program becomes insolvent. Such a guarantee can provide welcome assurances to the participant.

If a program is not backed by the state's full faith and credit guarantee, you run the risk that the program finds itself insolvent and provides less than full contract benefits to you or your beneficiary. Some prepaid programs do not have full-faith-and-credit backing, but do have a legislative guarantee that requires the state legislature to consider legislation that would appropriate funds for the program in the event the trust fund becomes insolvent.

The size of a program's reserve is important because it represents the "cushion" against future shortfalls caused when tuition increases outstrip investment earnings in the program trust fund. You can obtain this information from the annual financial statements made available by the program, although the financial position of the program may have changed substantially by the time the annual report is issued. The financial statements will also describe the types of investments being made by the trust, and the actuarial assumptions used in determining the obligation of the program to provide future benefits to participants. Many of the older prepaid programs were able to accumulate substantial reserves during the bull market of the 1990s; that is not the case for most of the newer prepaid programs.

43) Will the program allocate investment surpluses to participant accounts?

If a prepaid program manages to build up a large reserve through positive investment performance matched with modest tuition increases, will any of the surplus be used to increase benefits or reduce the cost for program participants? Some programs may indicate "yes," while others are prohibited from doing so by state law. The Pennsylvania TAP program actually allocated several millions of dollars of additional benefits to participant accounts at one point in its history. In the current general and higher-education economic climate, the chances of any program distributing this type of dividend in the near future appear slim.

Section 3: Manageable restrictions

The third section describes "manageable restrictions"—restrictions or hazards that may be evident in a program but can be avoided through a timely rollover to another 529 plan without those particular concerns. The ability to roll over your account means an unacceptable provision in any particular program should not necessarily eliminate it from contention. You simply have to manage the account and make the rollover at the appropriate time.

44) Are there any penalties or fees for withdrawing your money from the program?

Some programs may charge a fixed dollar fee (e.g., $50) on non-qualified withdrawals. Certain adviser-sold interests may incur a "contingent deferred sales charge" on non-qualified withdrawals within a specified period of time.

45) Are qualified withdrawals from the program exempt from your state's income tax?

Before 2002, several states provided an exemption from state income tax for qualified withdrawals from their own 529 plans; in only a few states was the exemption extended to withdrawals from other states' 529 plans as well. Beginning in 2002, however, withdrawals qualifying for federal tax exemption will also be exempt in many states, regardless of prior treatment. This is because the majority of states automatically conform to federal tax law changes.

Tax conformity is not universal, however, and a state may enact new laws to restrict exemption to withdrawals from its own 529 plan. Illinois has already done this. If your state taxes residents on qualified withdrawals from out-of-state 529 plans, you may still have the opportunity to take advantage of your state's income tax exemption if you roll over your balances in other 529 plans to your own state's program prior to withdrawal.

46) Are there any time or age limits on the use of the account?

If the 529 plan requires that the account be used by the time the beneficiary reaches age 30, for example, simply roll over the account to another state's program prior to reaching that point.

47) Is there a minimum time period before taking qualified or non-qualified withdrawals from your account?

Some programs impose a minimum holding period. New Mexico's 529 plan, for example, currently requires that a New Mexico resident have their account open 12 months before taking a qualified withdrawal.

48) Are there other withdrawal restrictions that can be avoided by rolling over to another 529 plan?

Here are some examples:

+ Your program has cumbersome substantiation requirements of education expenses that other 529 plans may not have.
+ Your program requires that the account owner be treated as the recipient of any undocumented withdrawals while other 529 plans give you the option of directing the withdrawal to your beneficiary (thereby shifting the income to a lower tax bracket).
+ Your program has a minimum withdrawal amount or limit on frequency of withdrawals that other programs do not have.

49) Will the program approve a request to transfer ownership of the account?

There are a number of reasons why you may decide you want to transfer ownership of your 529 account to someone else. One possibility is that an account you own may be subject to the claims of your creditors. Another possibility is that you do not want your account considered a countable asset for Medicaid purposes. Finally, you may at some point decide that you just do not want to be responsible for the management of the 529 account and would like someone else to handle it. The last two possibilities are particularly relevant for grandparents.

Some 529 plans do not approve requests for a transfer of ownership prior to your death or incapacity, or a court order in a divorce or other legal proceeding. To accomplish such a change, you would have to first roll over your account to another 529 plan that does permit owner transfers.

50) How much can be contributed to an account in the program?

One of the requirements for qualification under Section 529 is that the program establishes procedures so that participants do not contribute more than needed for the beneficiary's future qualified higher education expenses. These maximum contribution limits can vary significantly among 529 plans, with some savings programs below $250,000 per beneficiary and others above $300,000.

If you plan on making very large contributions, you should be sure to understand how the contribution limits are applied. In some savings programs, the limit refers to cumulative lifetime contributions. In others, it refers to the account balance which, when reached, triggers a stop on further contributions. Often the limit for your own account will be reduced once you begin taking qualified withdrawals. In no event will a contribution limit prevent your account from growing in value beyond that limit.

The IRS requires that all accounts in a state's programs with the same beneficiary be aggregated when applying the limit, without regard to the fact that there may be different account owners.

Many 529 plans will increase their contribution limits periodically as the cost of college attendance rises. But what do you do if the 529 plan you are interested in does not permit you to contribute as much as you think you should invest for your beneficiary's future higher education costs? The answer would be to open accounts in more than one program. The IRS does not require that a 529 plan consider balances in other states' programs when applying its limit. Although this may seem like an easy way to get around the individual state limits, exercise caution. You are looking for trouble if you open accounts in multiple programs simply as a way to shelter more assets than you can reasonably anticipate as the amount your beneficiary will need for college and graduate school.

A state that determines that you are intentionally exceeding your investment need for higher education costs will likely terminate your account and possibly charge extra penalties. The IRS may also look to challenge you.

SEVEN

Income Tax Planning with 529 Plans

nderstanding the federal income tax rules associated with a 529 plan is fairly straightforward. The three major income tax benefits—tax deferred growth, the tax exclusion for earnings withdrawn for qualified purposes, and the possible shifting of earnings to a low-income tax bracket when withdrawn for non-qualified purposes—are explained in detail in chapter 3. But once these basic federal income tax benefits of 529 plans are understood, the next step is to explore income tax planning opportunities associated with 529 plans. This chapter will help you do that. Below is a discussion of several income tax planning considerations related to 529 plans.

In which years should I take withdrawals from my 529 account?

Naturally, you should take withdrawals in years when the earnings are excluded and avoid taking withdrawals that generate taxable income. This is not as easy as it sounds. A lot will depend on when the beneficiary is attending college, the expenses that will be incurred, the amount of money in your 529 account, the amount of untaxed earnings in the account, your tax brackets, and the other tax benefits that may be available to you and your beneficiary. Fitting all the pieces together in one plan for an optimal tax result can be very challenging. Be sure to consider the following:

1) Hope and Lifetime Learning credits

Avoid using your 529 account to pay for 100 percent of qualifying college costs in a year when you or your beneficiary will be claiming one of these credits. Otherwise, as explained in chapter 3, claiming the credit will cause some portion of your 529 distribution to be subject to income tax (but not the 10 percent penalty tax). Instead, consider using other non–529 resources to pay for some of the expenses and spreading your 529 distributions between years to effectively capture qualified expenses above the amount of expenses that are applied to the credit. It is important to realize that the type of credit you claim can make a significant difference. In 2004, the Hope credit "consumes" up to $2,000 of tuition and related expenses while the Lifetime Learning credit consumes up to $10,000 of these expenses.

2) Above-the-line deduction for tuition and fees

The coordination rules here are different, but the result is similar. If you plan on claiming this deduction, realize that the pool of deductible expenses is reduced by the earnings portion of distributions from a 529 account attributable to tuition and related expenses. Some taxpayers will not be affected by this adjustment because they will incur enough in tuition to claim the maximum deduction ($4,000 in 2004 and 2005) even after the reduction for the distributed 529 earnings.

3) Sunset of 2001 EGTRRA changes in 2010

Unless the provisions of the 2001 Economic Growth and Tax Relief Reconciliation Act are extended or modified, the exclusion for qualified distributions from a 529 plan expires on December 31, 2010. The timing of distributions before or after that date will obviously make a difference.

However, it may not make much of a difference, since distributed earnings after 2010 will be taxable to the student and many students will be in a zero or very low tax bracket. In addition, the Hope or Lifetime Learning credits will be available to the eligible parent or student to offset or eliminate any tax caused by distributed 529 earnings.

4) Financial aid eligibility

Under current federal financial aid guidelines, a withdrawal from a 529 savings account that is tax-free for income tax purposes will also be excluded from a student's "expected family contribution" (see chapter 4). This favorable treatment could change in the future, either because the income tax exclusion disappears at the end of 2010, or because Congress and the U.S. Department of Education decide to change the rules. You may wish to take full advantage of the current treatment by withdrawing as much in tax-free 529 earnings as quickly as you can. If it turns out that withdrawals become a negative factor in financial aid eligibility you may want to alter your strategy. Since any income reported in the student's senior year of college will presumably have no impact on financial aid eligibility, it may make sense in those circumstances to target your 529 plan funding first to the senior year of college, and then work backwards to the freshman year.

How can I time the distributions from my 529 account when that will be my only source of funds for paying for college?

You should attempt to anticipate this situation when deciding how much to contribute to 529 plans. You may want to invest in a different vehicle (such as tax-efficient mutual funds) for the college expenses that will eventually be used towards the Hope or Lifetime Learning credits. Another option is to take out loans. Your ability to borrow funds in one year and repay in a later year offers the opportunity to time your 529 distributions for greatest effectiveness. Be aware, however, that the repayment of student loans is not included in the list of Section 529 qualified higher education expenses, so your use of the account for this purpose could result in additional tax and penalty.

How do distributions from a 529 plan affect my child's status as a dependent for tax purposes?

The use of a 529 plan may affect your ability to claim the beneficiary as a dependent on your tax return. To claim anyone as a dependent and take advantage of a $3,100 (in 2004) dependency exemption, certain tests must be met. One of these tests is the support test.[1]

The support test requires that you furnish more than one-half of the dependent's support during the year. It is not absolutely clear that withdrawals from a 529 account owned by you and used to pay for your child's college expenses will count as your support. If these withdrawals do not count as your support, you may fail the support test, precluding you from claiming the student as a dependent.

Failing the dependency tests can be advantageous, especially if you have high taxable income. The student will be able to claim his or her own personal exemption that may save more in taxes on the student's return than you give up in lost tax savings on your return. This occurs because the dependency exemption is phased out for high-income taxpayers. For 2004, the phase-out begins for married taxpayers filing jointly at an adjusted gross income of $214,050 and the exemption is phased out completely at an adjusted gross income of $336,550. The phase-out range for a single taxpayer is $142,700 to $265,200.

How will use of a 529 plan affect my state income taxes?

State tax planning can be important in getting the most tax benefits from a 529 plan. Several states provide an income tax deduction for all or a portion of your contributions to their 529 plans. If state deductions are available but are subject to a maximum annual amount, consider spreading out your contributions over two or more years rather than contributing one amount higher than the deduction limit. If you'd like to contribute more

---

1. The other tests are the relationship/household test, the citizenship test, the joint return test, and the gross income test. Usually the income from a 529 plan will not impact these tests if the dependent is your child under age 19, or between ages 19 and 23 and a full-time student for some part of each of five months during the year.

than the amount allowed as a deduction, and the program allows for it, consider first transferring the non-deductible portion of your contribution to other close relatives and asking them to make the contribution into an account for your child. Some of those contributors may get a tax break that would otherwise go unclaimed.

Most states allowing a deduction for contributions will require recapture of those deductions if non-qualified withdrawals are made in later years. This recapture will be in addition to the earnings portion of the non-qualified withdrawal reportable on the state return. Be sure to understand how the recapture rules work for the 529 plan in your state. For example, some states may require that a pro-rata amount of your deduction be recaptured anytime a non-qualified withdrawal is made, while others will recapture your deduction only after total non-qualified withdrawals exceed your non-deductible contributions into the 529 plan.

Many states have enacted legislation exempting qualified 529 distributions from state income tax, but in most cases the law applies only to distributions from a state's own 529 plan. In states that do not specifically exempt qualified distributions, the issue of taxability hinges on whether state tax law conforms to federal tax law. Conformity means that the computation of state taxable income begins with federal adjusted gross income or federal taxable income. Nearly every state now conforms; Alabama, Mississippi, and Pennsylvania do not. Illinois conforms for most items, but passed a law in 2002 that requires Illinois taxpayers to report distributed earnings from out-of-state 529 plans. Qualified distributions from either of Illinois' two 529 plans remain exempt from Illinois income tax.

In a state where qualified 529 distributions are exempt only by reason of conformity to federal tax law, the expiration of EGTRRA's federal tax exclusion in 2010 will cause distributions after 2010 to be taxed at the state level as well.

Are there any tax benefits in opening multiple accounts for my child?

Establishing multiple 529 accounts can provide you with an opportunity to control the amount and timing of distributed earnings. Of course, if all distributions are tax-free anyway, there is no strategic value in maintaining separate accounts. It is when a distribution produces taxable income (i.e. a non-qualified distribution), or when the earnings make a difference in the financial aid application, that this becomes important.

Each 529 account will have a different earnings ratio depending on its investment history, making it possible to take withdrawals on a selective basis. This strategy is similar to selecting certain mutual fund shares to sell based on their unrealized gains or losses. A 529 savings account established ten years prior to college is probably going to have a higher earnings ratio than an account established one year prior to college.

In years with sufficient qualified expenses, you would normally decide to withdraw from the account with the highest earnings ratio because the earnings will be excluded from taxable income. Withdrawals from the account with the lowest earnings ratio should be targeted for any years in which you decide to take a non-qualified withdrawal.

It may be possible to achieve this positioning by placing different types of investment into different accounts. For example, if you seek to diversify your college savings with a 50/50 blend of stocks and bonds, consider opening one 529 account with a 100 percent stock portfolio and a second 529 account with a 100 percent bond portfolio in a different 529 plan. Your two accounts will develop different earnings ratios as determined by their respective investment performance.

In a down market, the isolation of asset classes in separate accounts may produce the opportunity to claim a tax loss that might not exist with a single balanced account. You could liquidate the account showing a net loss while retaining the account showing a net gain. Chapter 12 explains how 529 losses may be deducted under certain conditions on your income tax return.

This strategy will not work for multiple accounts you maintain for the same beneficiary in one or more programs operated in one state. The IRS, under authority specifically provided by Section 529, requires that these accounts be aggregated in determining the earnings ratio (see chapter 3). The rule is confined to accounts with the same owner and beneficiary within one state's 529 plan, however, so the use of multiple states will still provide this opportunity, at least for now.

Should I borrow money now and invest it in a 529 plan?

It could make sense to fund a college savings account with borrowed money. The interest paid on the debt may produce an income tax deduction for you at a high tax bracket, while the 529 earnings may escape taxation altogether.

The tax law contains a prohibition against deducting interest on debt used to produce tax-exempt income. If you borrow money to invest in tax-free municipal bonds, for example, the interest expense on the loan is not deductible.[2] One question that becomes critical in the wake of the 2001 EGTRRA is whether the exclusion of qualified 529 distributions invokes the prohibition against deducting interest on borrowings. The answer appears to be "no," simply because the distributions are not, per-se, exempt. Unless certain hurdles are cleared the distributed earnings become taxable (and are scheduled to become taxable in any event for distributions after 2010). However, some caution is warranted; at publication date the IRS had not yet ruled on this specific issue.

Another question to be explored in considering whether to borrow is the character of the interest expense on the loan. If the interest were considered investment interest expense, it would be deductible as an itemized deduction, but only to the extent you have investment income. Any excess investment interest expense is carried forward indefinitely and deducted against investment income in future years.

It is somewhat doubtful that the use of debt to fund a 529 contribution could be considered a use for investment purposes, despite the fact that the debt proceeds are being deposited into an investment account with the 529 plan. The IRS might take the position that the debt was incurred for personal purposes, and not for investment purposes, because the contribution into the 529 plan is treated as a gift, and gifts are personal in nature. If this were the case, the interest on the debt would be classified as nondeductible personal interest.

In order to avoid the characterization problem, the best way to borrow for 529 funding purposes is with a home equity loan. Interest on

---

2. IRC Section 265(a)(2)

qualifying home-equity indebtedness of up to $100,000 is deductible on Schedule A of Form 1040, no matter what use is made of the borrowed funds. The home equity loan must be on a first or second home. The interest on home-equity indebtedness used for this purpose is not deductible for purposes of the alternative minimum tax (AMT), so be careful in determining the possible impact of the AMT.

Once you are comfortable that your interest can be deducted, calculate the after-tax interest rate on your loan. A taxpayer in a 30 percent tax bracket with a six percent interest loan is paying 4.2 percent interest after-tax (70 percent times six percent). The after-tax interest rate can then be compared to the expected return of your 529 account (assuming you can count on distributions being tax-free). An investment return above 4.2 percent in the above example means the investor is coming out ahead.

Of course, there may be many other things to think about before borrowing for this purpose. Cash flow impact is one. The loan will need to be paid back over time, while your investment presumably stays in the 529 plan until the college years. Impact on your borrowing ability for other purposes could be another consideration. And finally, there is the risk that the college savings account may not perform as well as originally anticipated, and the leveraging strategy could result in an overall loss.

What can I do if the beneficiary of my 529 account graduates from college and I still have money left in the account?

You can either withdraw the money, with the earnings portion of any withdrawal subject to federal income tax and the 10 percent penalty, or you can leave it in the account to continue growing tax-deferred. If you leave it in, you can keep the same beneficiary on the account (despite having graduated) or you can change the beneficiary to a qualifying family member.

Let's say that you no longer want to maintain the 529 account and would like the excess funds distributed to the account beneficiary. Make certain the withdrawn earnings are reported to the beneficiary (assuming the beneficiary is in a lower income tax bracket). If your 529 plan does not permit you to direct a non-qualified withdrawal to the account beneficiary, first roll over your account to a different 529 plan that does permit it.

Regardless of the recipient of a non-qualified withdrawal, the 10 percent federal penalty will be owed on the earnings portion of the withdrawal unless one of the penalty exceptions can be applied. Before EGTRRA, there appeared to be a way to avoid the 10 percent penalty imposed by the states on non-qualified withdrawals: by first replacing the original beneficiary with a dying family member, and then withdrawing the funds after the new beneficiary had died. This somewhat macabre technique will apparently no longer succeed since the penalty exception for death is now presented differently in the law. (Interestingly, substituting the beneficiary with a disabled relative still appears to fit within the penalty exception.)

Does a 529 account have to be for college?

The obvious attraction of tax-deferred earnings may cause some investors to consider putting money into a 529 savings plan account without actually intending to use the account to pay for higher education expenses. After all, if the account is later withdrawn, the added penalty is only 10 percent applied against the earnings portion of the withdrawal, and a few financial calculations may demonstrate that the tax deferral benefits can overcome the penalty after a certain number of years. The investor contemplating this action can either set up the account and name himself as beneficiary irrespective of his age (which many 529 plans permit), or he can name his child or other individual as beneficiary of the account but simply plan to revoke it in the future.

Naturally, this strategy would be viewed by many as an abuse of the tax laws. However, Section 529 does not contain any language that would put the individual investor at risk. Rather, the statute places the burden on the state by defining a 529 savings plan as one "under which a person may make contributions to an account which is established for the purpose of meeting the qualified higher education expenses of the designated beneficiary of the account." If investors establish accounts for a different purpose, namely the deferral of income, the tax-qualified status of the program may be in jeopardy. Some states, but certainly not all, have developed program rules that permit the program administrator to reject contributions or terminate accounts if it is determined that the account was established for a purpose other than the payment of the named beneficiary's qualified higher education expenses.

In any event, it would be difficult and perhaps unfair for a state program administrator to make this call. Many individuals are returning to school at a later age, even after retirement. And those who now have only a vague interest in returning to school may later decide to act on it once they have funds tucked away in a 529 plan account. However, be aware that the strategy of "overfunding" a 529 account can easily backfire. In a political environment that rewards taxable investors with low tax rates on capital gains and certain other types of investment income, the risk of having highly-taxed income and penalties on a future non-qualified 529 distribution can be too high, and should cause most individuals to limit their 529 contributions to truly-anticipated future college costs.

CHAPTER

EIGHT

Estate Planning with 529 Plans

The estate and gift tax rules surrounding 529 plans are unique and the planning considerations are anything but straightforward. In fact, the gift tax provisions contained in Section 529 fly in the face of the general gift tax rules contained elsewhere in the Internal Revenue Code.

The law provides that a contribution into a 529 plan after August 5, 1997 is treated as a completed gift from the donor to the account's designated beneficiary. Further, the gift is considered a gift of a "present interest" that qualifies for the $11,000 annual gift tax exclusion,[1] despite the fact that in nearly all 529 plans the designated beneficiary never has rights to the money. The portion of the contribution covered by the $11,000 annual gift tax exclusion is also excluded for purposes of the generation-skipping transfer tax.

Section 529 goes one step further and provides an election that allows the donor to treat a contribution of more than the $11,000 annual

---

1. The annual gift exclusion amount is adjusted for cost of living increases, in increments of $1,000. Prior to 2002, the annual gift exclusion amount was $10,000.

exclusion as occurring ratably over five years for gift tax purposes. This means you can contribute as much as $55,000 to the account of one designated beneficiary in a single year without creating a taxable gift, assuming you make no other gifts to that beneficiary during that five-year period. Although not contained in the statute, the IRS takes the position that if a contribution of more than $55,000 is made to a 529 plan, the averaging election applies only to the first $55,000 and the remainder is treated as a gift in the year of contribution. The five-year averaging election is made on the federal gift tax return, Form 709.

The value of the 529 account is excluded from your gross estate, with one possible exception. If you make the five-year election but then die before the first day of the fifth calendar year, a special rule applies. The portion of the contribution allocated to calendar years beginning after your death is included in your estate.

Besides the five-year averaging election, what is so unique about these rules?

The most startling aspect of the Section 529 gift and estate rules is that you can continue to exercise nearly complete control over your account. The account owner can change the designated beneficiary to another qualifying family member at will. Further, you will have the option to simply terminate the account and receive a refund of the account value, subject to income tax and a federal 10 percent additional tax on the earnings. While this rescission may defeat the purpose of removing value from an estate, it certainly provides the level of control and flexibility that many individuals seek when talking to advisers about gifting and other estate reduction programs.

If you change the designated beneficiary to a qualified family member, no further gift is involved, unless the new beneficiary belongs to a lower generation than the former beneficiary.[2] If the new designation crosses the generation boundary, the former beneficiary is treated as making a gift to the new beneficiary subject to all the normal gift tax rules. In this situation,

---

2. The rules for determining the assignment of generation to any particular individual are contained in IRC Section 2651.

the five-year averaging election can be made by the former beneficiary, if necessary, to minimize or avoid gift tax consequences.

Under usual estate and gift tax principles, the level of control enjoyed by the account owner would most assuredly cause the contribution to be treated as an incomplete gift and the value of the account to remain in his or her gross estate. In fact, this was precisely the treatment accorded contributions to a 529 plan from the time Section 529 was signed into law on August 20, 1996 until August 5, 1997, when it was amended by the Taxpayer Relief Act of 1997. During this time, a contribution made to a 529 plan was not treated as a gift. The subsequent withdrawal to pay for educational expenses was not treated as a gift either, because it was deemed to be a direct payment of tuition, and direct payments of tuition (and medical care) on behalf of another individual are not counted as gifts.[3]

How much can I remove from my estate by using a 529 plan?

Most 529 savings programs accept contributions of $250,000 or more for each child, grandchild, or other beneficiary. Contributions of this magnitude are likely to exceed the annual gift tax exclusions, even with the five-year election, and will result in a taxable gift. Your $1 million lifetime exemption for gifts can be employed to shelter such large contributions. Grandparents making substantial contributions for grandchildren must also consider the generation-skipping transfer (GST) tax. The GST exemption is $1,500,000 in 2004, increasing to $3.5 million by 2009.

Many donors, however, will attempt to stay within the amounts that can be contributed under the shelter of the $11,000 annual exclusion. This can still add up to a substantial sum. Consider the wealthy couple with four children. With each parent contributing $55,000 to the 529 plan account of each child, this couple can effectively remove $440,000 from their combined estates in one day without using up a single dollar of their lifetime gift exemptions. Not only is the value removed from their taxable estates, it is invested in a fund that should appreciate nicely over time

---

3. IRC Section 2503(e) describes the exclusion for certain transfers of educational and medical expenses.

without the drag of income taxes (because earnings are tax-deferred). And so the estate tax savings will grow even more substantially. That's effective estate planning!

Why should I contribute to a 529 plan when I can make direct tuition payments to reduce my estate?

A grandparent may be planning to make use of the unlimited gift tax exclusion under Internal Revenue Code Section 2503(e) for the direct payment of tuition to an educational institution. To the extent that tuition is paid with non-529 assets, the funds in a 529 plan may not be needed for college. Note, however, that the exclusion for direct payment of education expenses applies only to tuition, while a 529 plan may allow funding for all qualified higher education expenses.

There are other reasons to consider funding a 529 plan now even if you intend to make direct payments of tuition out of other funds in the future. For one thing, you may not live long enough to attend to the tuition payment in the future, and so the funds you intend to target for education funding become subject to tax in your estate. You may be better off by funding the 529 plan and removing mortality risk as a factor.

Furthermore, you may decide that there is little harm done by funding a 529 plan and later deciding to make direct tuition payments instead of taking withdrawals from the 529 plan. An over-funded 529 account can be redirected to another beneficiary in the family, or simply refunded subject to income tax and the 10 percent penalty.

What happens if I am making other direct gifts to the beneficiary?

Before funding a 529 account, be sure to count up your other annual-exclusion gifts to that beneficiary. These gifts reduce the amount of annual exclusion that you can apply to 529 contributions. For example, if you normally make a cash gift of $2,000 each year to your grandchild, you will have only $9,000 left in your annual exclusion. You should limit your 529 contribution under five-year averaging to $45,000 unless you are willing to exceed the exclusion amount and tap into your one million dollar lifetime exemption.

How do I make the five-year averaging election?

You are required to file Form 709 Gift (and Generation-Skipping Transfer) Tax Return in any year that you wish to make the five-year averaging election for your contributions to 529 plans. Form 709 is due on April 15, just like your federal income tax return, but is filed separate from your Form 1040. Make your election by checking Box B on Schedule A of Form 709. Attach an explanation to the return including the beneficiary's name, your total 529 contributions on behalf of the beneficiary, and the amount for which the election is made. (The election will apply to your total 529 contributions for that beneficiary except for the amount in excess of $55,000.)

You need only file Form 709 in the year of election. You will not have to file it for each subsequent year of the election period as long as you have no taxable gifts or generation-skipping transfers to report in those years.

If you and your spouse agree to split your gifts, one-half of your 529 plan contributions will be considered made by each of you. The five-year election would have to be on separate Forms 709 if applicable. Gift splitting can help keep your 529 contributions under the $11,000 annual exclusion amount (or the $55,000 five-year averaging maximum) when you and your spouse do not make equal 529 contributions or other gifts to individual donees. See the Form 709 instructions for information on the gift splitting election.

If my child's grandparent makes contributions to a 529 account on which I am account owner, who has made the gift to my child, the grandparent or me?

Although the IRS has not yet ruled on this particular question, the gift appears to be from the contributor—the grandparent in this case—to the designated beneficiary, even if the contributor is not the account owner. Because the contributor will not retain the rights of ownership in this situation, he or she should consider establishing his or her own account instead. Some grandparents do not desire ownership and prefer to leave responsibility for the 529 account to the beneficiary's parents. In fact, it may help prevent any future problems if eligibility for Medicaid ever becomes an issue. (In most states, 529 accounts are included in the account owner's assets when applying for Medicaid benefits.)

What happens if the designated beneficiary dies?

Most 529 plans provide that upon the beneficiary's death, the account owner can direct a distribution to the beneficiary's estate, or substitute a new qualifying family member for the deceased beneficiary and continue the account. If non-qualified distributions are made to the beneficiary's estate, or to a substitute beneficiary, the earnings will be taxable to that recipient but will escape the 10 percent penalty tax. Tax basis in the account is not "stepped up."

IRS proposed regulations suggest the value of the account is included in the deceased beneficiary's gross estate, despite the fact that he or she never had any control or ownership of that asset. Some tax attorneys argue that a beneficiary's gross estate should include the 529 account only where the beneficiary has rights of ownership, e.g. where the beneficiary is also the account owner. Most beneficiaries of 529 accounts are young family members with few assets, so the inclusion of the asset value in the estate would usually not create a tax problem.

Other issues to be resolved

There remain a number of other questions regarding the Section 529 gift and estate tax rules that are not adequately addressed by the IRS' 1998 proposed regulations. These include the following:

✦ What happens if the beneficiary is changed to a new non-family beneficiary? Although most 529 plans would not accept such a change request, if it were to occur anyway, would the deemed gift provisions under Section 529 still apply?

✦ What are the gift tax consequences when the account owner, rather than the beneficiary, receives a distribution out of a 529 account? Nothing in the proposed regulations suggests that the beneficiary reports a gift back to the account owner; nor does it appears that the initial gift, recorded at the time of contribution, is canceled or reversed. If the account owner were to take the refund proceeds and re-invest in another 529 account for the same beneficiary, assuming it is not a rollover, he or she has apparently made a second gift with essentially the same dollars.

✦ Is there a gift tax consequence to a transfer of account ownership? A literal reading of Section 529 indicates there is not. However, an estate reduction strategy involving the transfer of 529 account ownership, followed by a distribution to the new account owner, will be deemed abusive. See chapter 12 for more discussion.

✦ Assume a contributor dies after making the five-year averaging election, and is required to include a portion of the contributions in his or her gross estate. Can the marital deduction be applied to reduce the taxable estate if account ownership is left to the contributor's spouse?

NINE

529 Plans vs. Coverdell ESAs

The Coverdell education savings account, known until mid–2001 as the Education IRA, was spawned by the same 1997 tax law that gave birth to the Roth IRA, the Hope and Lifetime Learning credits, and the deduction for student loan interest. The Coverdell ESA is a direct competitor to the 529 plan, because each provides families of the college-bound with an opportunity for tax-free earnings.

The "old" Education IRA was not easy to recommend. Its biggest problem was the lack of compatibility with the Hope and Lifetime Learning credits. Families were required to forego the tax exclusion on qualified withdrawals if they wanted to claim either of the credits. There were other problems, too. The Education IRA created a recordkeeping burden, exposed the child to potential excise taxes in any year contributions were made to a 529 plan and an Education IRA, and could severely impact eligibility for federal financial aid. Considering that annual aggregate contributions to all Education IRAs for the same child were limited to $500, the potential tax savings could not easily overcome these disadvantages.

The "new" Coverdell ESA offers improved features. The 2001 EGTRRA increased the annual contribution limit from $500 to $2,000 and now permits coordination, rather than mutual exclusion, between the Coverdell ESA, the 529 plan, and the Hope and Lifetime Learning credits. In addition, elementary and secondary school expenses were added to the list of qualified education expenses (the late Senator Paul Coverdell was a leading proponent of the K–12 provision).

What is a Coverdell education savings account?

A Coverdell education savings account is a trust or custodial account created exclusively to pay the qualified education expenses of a named beneficiary. Many banks, savings and loan associations, brokerage firms and mutual fund companies now offer Coverdell ESAs in addition to traditional IRAs and Roth IRAs. However, a Coverdell ESA does not require that the contributor have earned income, and does not impact your ability to contribute to a traditional or Roth IRA. Annual contributions to Coverdell ESAs may not exceed $2,000 per designated beneficiary and, unless the child has "special needs," may not be made after the beneficiary reaches age 18. The $2,000 contribution limit is applied on a calendar-year basis across all Coverdell ESAs for the same child. You have until April 15 to make contributions counted towards the previous year's $2,000 limit.

Any individual, including your child, can contribute to a Coverdell ESA as long as the contributor's modified adjusted gross income (MAGI)[1] is less than $110,000 ($220,000 if filing a joint return). An individual's ability to contribute up to $2,000 for any child is reduced on a ratable basis as the contributor's modified AGI goes above $95,000, and is phased out completely at $110,000 (for joint filers the phase-out range is $190,000 to $220,000). If you are above the income limits, there is nothing to prevent you from making a gift to someone else—probably the child—who is within the limits, followed by a contribution of your gifted funds into the

---

1. MAGI means the adjusted gross income increased by certain exclusions relating to income earned abroad or received from certain American territories or possessions.

Coverdell ESA. A corporation that makes contributions to a Coverdell ESA is not subject to the income limits.

What is the federal income tax treatment of a Coverdell ESA?

Although your contributions to a Coverdell ESA are not tax-deductible, any withdrawals from the account are exempt from federal tax to the extent the beneficiary incurs qualified education expenses during the year. Qualified education expenses include qualified higher education expenses (QHEE) and qualified elementary and secondary education expenses (QESEE). See chapter 3 for the definition of QHEE. QHEE must be reduced by any other tax-free educational benefits, including scholarship and fellowship grants and employer-provided educational assistance.

The following three categories of elementary and secondary school expenses are included in QESEE:

1) tuition, fees, academic tutoring, special needs services in the case of a special needs beneficiary, books, supplies, and other equipment which are incurred in connection with the enrollment or attendance of the designated beneficiary
2) room and board, uniforms, transportation, and supplementary items and services (including extended day programs) which are required or provided by the school in connection with such enrollment or attendance
3) any computer technology or equipment or Internet access and related services, if such technology, equipment, or services are to be used by the beneficiary and the beneficiary's family during any of the years the beneficiary is in school

If a withdrawal is made from a Coverdell ESA in excess of the amount of qualified education expenses for the year, the earnings portion of the excess withdrawal is includable in the beneficiary's gross income, and an additional 10 percent penalty tax is imposed on the earnings. The earnings portion is computed by the beneficiary in the same manner that a 529 plan administrator computes the earnings portion of a 529 account distribution (see chapter 3). IRS Publication 970 (downloadable at www.irs.gov) contains complete instructions for computing the earnings portion of withdrawals and maintaining a record of the tax basis of the account. In 2003, the IRS changed the form used for reporting Coverdell ESA withdrawals from 1099-R to 1099-Q, and proposed that the Coverdell ESA provider, rather than the individual taxpayer, keep track of tax basis and report the earnings portion of a distribution. However, in Notice 2003-53, the IRS gave Coverdell administrators a reprieve by permitting Forms 1099-Q to be filed showing only gross distributions and the value of the account, and not requiring a breakdown between earnings and basis. At the time this book went to press, the 2004 reporting requirements had not yet been released.

The 10 percent penalty tax is computed on Form 5329 and paid with the beneficiary's federal income tax return. Exceptions to the penalty exist for withdrawals made on account of the beneficiary's death, disability, or receipt of a tax-free scholarship (to the extent of the scholarship value).

Check with your state concerning the state tax treatment of distributions from a Coverdell ESA. A state is not required to follow the federal rules described above, although nearly every state does so.

What is the federal gift and estate tax treatment of a Coverdell ESA?

Just like contributions to a 529 account, your contributions to a Coverdell ESA are considered completed gifts from you to the beneficiary and qualify for the annual $11,000 gift tax exclusion. However, the five-year averaging election does not apply to Coverdell contributions.

What happens if the account is not spent by the time the beneficiary graduates from college?

Any balance left in a Coverdell ESA when the beneficiary turns age 30 must be distributed within 30 days. The earnings portion is subject to income tax and the 10 percent penalty tax. (The age limit does not apply to "special needs beneficiaries.") Subject to the policies of the financial institution serving as trustee or custodian of the Coverdell ESA, a change in designated beneficiary may be made before then without incurring tax or penalty, as long as the new beneficiary is a member of the family. The definition of "member of the family" follows the definition contained in Section 529 (see chapter 3). A new beneficiary must be under age 30. A rollover of a withdrawal from a Coverdell ESA within 60 days into another Coverdell ESA for the beneficiary or member of the beneficiary's family under the age of 30 is permitted, but only once in a 12-month period.

A balance in a Coverdell ESA may also be withdrawn tax-free and penalty-free in a year when equal or greater contributions are made to a 529 plan for the same beneficiary. This option provides you with significant flexibility if you start out investing with a Coverdell ESA and later decide that you are better off in a 529 plan. It can also extend the deferral of earnings beyond age 30.

Who makes the decisions about investments, withdrawals, and beneficiary changes in a Coverdell ESA?

These aspects are governed by the adoption agreement used by the Coverdell ESA trustee or custodian. The IRS has made available two "model" agreements for use by financial institutions, Form 5305-EA for custodial accounts and Form 5305-E for trust accounts. Since the Coverdell ESA is established for a minor, a "responsible individual" must be named to the account. Forms 5305-EA and 5305-E generally specify that the responsible individual must be the beneficiary's parent or legal guardian (presumably to guard against multiple account contributions that exceed the $2,000 annual limit). However, the custodian or trustee may establish policies that permit someone else to be the responsible person.

The contributor who opens the account makes the initial investment selection and names the responsible individual. He or she also indicates whether the responsible individual is permitted to change the designated beneficiary to another qualifying family member, and whether control of the account passes to the beneficiary when he or she reaches the legal age of majority. After the account is established, the responsible individual makes decisions as to investments, withdrawals, and beneficiary changes.

Which is better—the 529 plan or the Coverdell education savings account?

Any family saving for a child's college education must decide whether their first $2,000 of savings goes into a 529 plan or to a Coverdell ESA (forgetting about other investment options for now). Beyond $2,000 in annual contributions, the Coverdell ESA is not an option. For a parent or other relative who is not eligible to contribute to a Coverdell ESA because of the income limits, it still appears possible to arrange the contribution by first gifting the money to the child (or to anyone else with income below the limits). Factors to consider include the following:

- ✦ K through 12 expenses. A Coverdell ESA can be withdrawn tax-free for qualifying elementary and secondary school expenses while a 529 account cannot be used for that purpose without incurring tax and a 10 percent penalty on the earnings. A family planning to send a child to a private school may find this feature of the Coverdell ESA to be very attractive. Even for children who will be attending public grade schools, the ability to use the Coverdell ESA for home computer purchases and certain other expenses may be seen as a significant advantage. Anyone home schooling his or her children must be careful; some states do not recognize this type of education as a "school." Legislation is being considered in Congress that would specifically include home schools.
- ✦ Investment options. The financial institution that serves as custodian or trustee of a Coverdell ESA can offer the same types of investments found in individual retirement accounts (IRA), including self-directed investment accounts. Contributions may not be invested in life insurance. The menu of investment options available through 529 plans is more limited.

+ Fees and expenses. Because Coverdell ESAs generally require less effort to administer, expenses are usually lower than with an equivalent amount invested in a 529 plan. Fees can vary significantly from one sponsor to another, however.

+ Account ownership. With most 529 plans, you remain the owner of the account and can revoke it at any time. That is not the case with Coverdell ESAs. Distributions from a Coverdell ESA are typically paid directly to the beneficiary or to a guardian on behalf of the beneficiary, and should not revert to the contributor or responsible individual. If the beneficiary of a Coverdell ESA dies, the account must be paid out to the beneficiary's estate unless another qualifying family member is substituted as beneficiary.

+ Financial aid. Until recently, a Coverdell ESA was considered the student's asset in determining eligibility for federal financial aid, and therefore was assessed at a 35 percent rate. This gave the 529 savings program an advantage for many families, since the value of a parent-owned 529 account is assessed at a maximum 5.6 percent rate. In January 2004, the U.S. Department of Education released a letter stating that a Coverdell ESA owned by a parent would receive the same federal financial aid treatment as a 529 account owned by a parent. Although the new position does not seem to have sound underpinnings—a Coverdell ESA is not "owned" by a parent in the same way a 529 account is—it should still be accepted as good news by college-bound families considering this particular investment option.

+ State tax benefits. Your state may offer you a state income tax deduction for some or even all of your contributions to its 529 plan. States generally do not permit a deduction for Coverdell contributions. If you live in a state with an income tax or a tax on dividends and interest, find out how withdrawals from a Coverdell ESA are treated, and how the treatment compares to distributions from a 529 plan. Many states conform to federal tax treatment for both programs, but that is not necessarily the case in your state.

+ Deduction for tuition and fees. Section 222 of the Internal Revenue Code, as enacted, favors the 529 plan in describing how distributions interact with the above-the-line deduction for tuition and fees. The IRS appears to have liberalized this provision, however, and based on Publication 970 and the instructions to 2003 Form 1040, Coverdell ESAs and 529 plans are treated no differently for this purpose.

+ Excise tax. If contributions to all Coverdell ESAs for a child exceed $2,000 in a year—or are made after the child reaches age 18 or by a taxpayer who is not eligible based on modified adjusted gross income—the excess contributions are subject to a 6 percent excise tax for each year until corrected. The excise tax is computed on Form 5329 and is filed alone or, if the child is required to file an income tax return, with the child's Form 1040. An excess contribution can be corrected for the year in which it arises by removing the contribution, along with all earnings attributable to the contribution, by May 31 of the year following the year of contribution. The earnings portion of a corrective withdrawal is subject to tax on the child's tax return for the taxable year for which the contribution was made, but the 10 percent penalty is not imposed. An uncorrected excess contribution will be treated as a new contribution in the following year. With a 529 plan, the investor need not worry about federal penalties on excess contributions. Rather, the programs themselves will establish and monitor contribution limits. Any contributions beyond those limits will not be accepted by the 529 plan, or will be returned when discovered, but in any event will not be subject to penalty.

+ Tax reporting. Before 2002, reporting distributions from a 529 plan on your tax return was much easier than reporting Coverdell withdrawals. The 529 plan administrator withheld any penalties and determined how much, if any, of your 529 account distribution was reportable as taxable income. Starting in 2002, the differences started to disappear. With both types of savings programs, the taxpayer now self-assesses the 10 percent penalty, if necessary, and maintains records of qualifying expenses in the event of an IRS audit. The only remaining difference is that a 529 plan will keep track of your basis and compute the earnings portion of distributions. With a Coverdell ESA, you may need to keep track of basis yourself. The IRS has proposed a change that would require Coverdell ESA administrators to keep track of basis, but administrators will face a problem in obtaining enough information to make an accurate basis determination in many cases.

+ Asset protection. Assets in Coverdell ESAs may be better protected from creditors than assets in 529 accounts. Speak to your attorney about the laws in your state, and if you invest in an out-of-state 529 plan, how any special protections in that state might apply to you.

+ Sunset of EGTRRA changes. The provisions of the 2001 EGTRRA expire on December 31, 2010. If not extended or otherwise modified through future tax law changes, we revert to pre-2002 treatment of 529 plans and Coverdell ESAs on January 1, 2011. The risk associated with the sunset provision seems to favor the Coverdell ESA over the 529 plan for an equivalent amount of contributions, because qualified withdrawals from a Coverdell ESA were tax free before 2002 while qualified distributions from a 529 plan were not tax free. Note, however, that before 2002 a tax-free withdrawal from a Coverdell ESA eliminated the possibility of claiming the potentially more valuable Hope or Lifetime Learning credit for the student's expenses. Many families would elect to pay tax on the Coverdell ESA withdrawals in order to claim the credit, placing Coverdell ESA withdrawals in about the same position as 529 plan distributions.

+ Transfer of assets. You can transfer assets from a Coverdell ESA to a 529 account tax-free as long as there is room for contributions under the limits of the 529 plan. However, it does not work the other way around. You may even plan for future Coverdell-to-529 transfers from the outset. For example, in order to maximize state tax benefits in a state that offers a limited annual deduction for contributions to its 529 plan, you may decide to "park" your savings beyond the deduction amount in a Coverdell ESA until a later year when the transfer of those savings into the 529 plan will yield a state tax deduction. Note that the untaxed earnings portion of the Coverdell ESA withdrawal will be recorded as earnings in your 529 account and reported as such when future distributions are made from the 529 plan. You will be required to provide the 529 plan administrator with documentation that shows the earnings portion of the Coverdell ESA withdrawal.

Can I regain direct ownership of the assets in my child's Coverdell ESA by transferring these assets to my 529 account, as long as I name my child the beneficiary of the 529 account?

Although you satisfy the literal requirements for a tax-free and penalty-free transfer, you may be violating state laws that would protect the ownership rights of your child in the Coverdell ESA. This situation is similar to assets that are owned by a minor through a custodial arrangement (UTMA or UGMA). Seek the advice of your attorney in this situation as you may be required by law to establish the 529 account in such a way as to protect the minor's ownership rights.

TEN

529 Plans vs. Qualified Savings Bonds

Under certain conditions, an owner of U.S. savings bonds may redeem those bonds and exclude the interest from income if the proceeds are used for qualified higher education expenses. These rules are contained in Section 135 of the Internal Revenue Code. Series EE bonds issued after 1989, including "Patriot Bonds" and all Series I bonds, purchased by an individual who is at least 24 years old before the bond's issue date, may qualify for the exclusion. These eligible bonds are sometimes referred to as education savings bonds.

Savings bonds are attractive to many savers because they are backed by the full faith and credit of the U.S. government, their interest is exempt from state and local income taxes, and they are easy to purchase. Applications are available through most banks, and bonds can be purchased directly over the Internet (www.savingsbonds.gov). They are issued in face values as low as $25.

A Series EE bond issued today will earn interest at the rate of 90 percent of the average yield on marketable Treasury securities with five-year maturities, adjusted every six months. They are issued at a 50 percent discount to face value, so a $50 bond costs $25. Accrued interest is added to the value of the bond and it is guaranteed to reach face value no later than 17 years after issuance.

Series I bonds (known simply as I Bonds) were first issued in September 1998 and are sold at face value, not at a discount. Interest is composed of a fixed rate of return plus a variable semiannual inflation rate based on the Consumer Price Index. The 30-year fixed rate on I Bonds issued between May 1, 2004 and October 31, 2004 is 1.00 percent. These particular bonds have an initial composite annual earnings rate of 3.39 percent, to adjust on November 1, 2004 for a new inflation figure.

Series EE and I bonds earn interest for up to 30 years and are redeemable after twelve months, although you forfeit three months of interest if you redeem a bond within five years of its issuance.

In order to exclude any bond interest under the Section 135 education exclusion, your income must be below a certain level in the year of redemption. In 2004, the exclusion is phased out for joint filers and surviving spouses with modified adjusted gross income between $89,750 and $119,750. The phase-out range for single taxpayers is $59,850 to $74,850. (Married taxpayers filing separate returns do not qualify for the exclusion.) These limitations are adjusted each year for inflation. Note that your income, for purposes of the limitation, includes the entire amount of interest on redeemed savings bonds without regard to the potential exclusion.

For many taxpayers, it will be difficult to predict future income levels at the time of a bond purchase, so the bond owner may end up not being able to take the tax break anticipated at purchase. The rule requiring that you be at least 24 years old is designed to prevent you from effectively avoiding the income limitation through issuance of bonds directly in your child's name.

The entire amount of bond redemption proceeds is compared to qualified higher education expenses in determining the amount of interest excluded from your gross income. If the redemption proceeds exceed qualifying expenses, the amount of excludable interest is reduced pro rata. The exclusion is figured on Form 8815, which is filed with your federal income tax return for the year you redeem the bonds.

"Qualified higher educational expenses" are defined differently for the bond income exclusion than for 529 plans and Coverdell education savings accounts. For the bond income exclusion, qualified higher education expenses include only tuition and fees for the bond owner or the bond owner's spouse or dependent. (A grandparent will usually not be able to take advantage of the exclusion.) They also include contributions made to a 529 plan or Coverdell education savings account that names you, your spouse or your dependent as beneficiary. Qualified expenses exclude any costs for sports, games, or hobbies, unless they are incurred as part of a degree program. Total qualified expenses are also reduced by the amount used in determining the Hope credit or Lifetime Learning credit, tax-exempt scholarships, 529 plan distributions, and withdrawals from a Coverdell ESA.

Qualified distributions from a 529 plan or Coverdell ESA can also impact your ability to take advantage of the education bond exclusion if the distributions cause your beneficiary to fail the support test for tax dependency. Chapter 7 discusses this issue with respect to 529 plans. (Coverdell ESA withdrawals are clearly included in the student's self-support.) If your child no longer qualifies as a dependent, your redemption of savings bonds to pay for the child's college expenses will be taxable.

For the college saver who appreciates the investment characteristics of savings bonds, this set of rules makes planning interesting, to say the least. And to use the bonds in conjunction with a 529 plan is particularly challenging. After reducing your child's total tuition and related expenses by your 529 distributions and Coverdell withdrawals, there will likely be little, if any, qualified expenses to use against bond redemption proceeds. And apparently, 529 plan distributions cannot be targeted to non-tuition, qualified higher education expenses, such as room and board, leaving the tuition and fees for use against bond redemption proceeds. The law does not allow you to apply 529 plan distributions on a selective basis for the purpose of calculating the bond income exclusion.

Which is better for college savings—savings bonds or a 529 plan?

If you have to choose, the 529 plan will be the preferred vehicle for many, although a number of variables should be considered. Certainly, your anticipated future income level is an important factor because the tax break on savings bond redemptions is lost for higher income taxpayers. If you own savings bonds but never find a way to fit within the education exclusion, the interest will be taxed to you at your rate when you redeem the bonds. Your income level will not prevent you from taking advantage of the tax exclusion on 529 plan distributions. Even if qualified distributions after 2010 become taxable, due to the sunset of EGTRRA, the tax will be figured at the student's tax rate, not yours. State and local income taxes can also make a difference; interest on savings bonds will always be exempt, which is not necessarily the case with qualifying distributions from 529 plans.

Another obvious consideration is the gross investment return available from a U.S. savings bond versus a 529 plan. Over a long investment horizon, a 529 savings account invested in a portfolio of equity and debt securities is likely to outperform a savings bond. But the level of market risk is higher, too, so a conservative investor may be more attracted to savings bonds no matter how long the targeted investment horizon is. However, a conservative investor could also choose a 529 savings plan with an option that guarantees principal and interest.

A 529 prepaid program will outperform a savings bond if the value of benefits under the contract, based on future tuition increases, exceeds the interest earnings on the bond. Recent history has shown tuition inflation on average to be significantly higher than increases in the Consumer Price Index. Whether the interest premium on savings bonds (such as the 1.00 percent fixed rate on I Bonds purchased from May 2004 through October 2004) can close the tuition inflation gap is a question that has no certain answer.

Yet another variable is the amount of money you have available for investment. A 529 savings program can be used for certain educational expenses, such as room and board, that savings bonds cannot cover under the education exclusion.

I already have a significant investment in eligible U.S. savings bonds, but I am interested in 529 plans too. What are my options?

Since it is difficult to effectively combine the tax exclusion for savings bonds with other education tax incentives, you need to decide whether the bond education exclusion is your best bet. Fortunately, you may not need to make this decision now. The tax law permits you to claim the exclusion in any year that contributions are made to a 529 plan or Coverdell education savings account that names you, your spouse, or your dependent as beneficiary. In essence, the contribution to a 529 plan or ESA constitutes a qualifying expense for purposes of the education savings bond exclusion.

The ability to make this transfer out of savings bonds without triggering tax provides a wonderful degree of flexibility. In fact, you may decide to purchase qualifying savings bonds with the intent of making this transfer in a future year. It is important to remember, however, that you must satisfy the income requirements in the year of redemption in order to take advantage of the opportunity.

Here are some situations in which the transfer should be considered:

+ You currently own qualifying U.S. savings bonds and your income is within the limits this year. But the bonds are targeted for college expenses in a future year, and your income may be too high in that year. By redeeming the bonds now and transferring the proceeds into a 529 plan or Coverdell ESA, you succeed in "locking in" the tax exclusion on bond interest no matter what your income level is in the future. Note, however, that the untaxed interest will incur not only income tax but the 10 percent penalty as well if a non-qualified withdrawal is made in the future. (You will be required to provide the 529 plan administrator with documentation that shows the untaxed interest in any year bond redemption proceeds are transferred to your 529 account.) The strategy may also backfire if qualified 529 withdrawals are made after the tax exclusion sunsets in 2010.

+ Rather than being unsure of your income in a future year, you may be unsure of your ability to claim your child as a dependent under the various dependency tests. You may decide to make the transfer from savings bonds to a 529 plan this year while your child is still a dependent. It will not matter for

Section 529 distribution purposes whether or not the beneficiary is a dependent.

✦ You intend to use your qualifying savings bonds to pay college expenses for a currently enrolled child. Even though your income is within the bond exclusion limits, you discover that you will not be able to take full advantage of the exclusion because you lack sufficient qualified expenses. This can easily occur, for instance, when the tuition is counted toward the Hope or Lifetime Learning credit, or when it is reduced by qualified distributions from a 529 plan or Coverdell ESA. You will save taxes by first directing the bond redemption proceeds to a 529 plan or Coverdell ESA and then taking distributions for college expenses. Section 529 plan and Coverdell ESA withdrawals can be used to pay for certain expenses (i.e. room and board, books, supplies, and equipment) that are not considered qualified expenses under the Section 135 education savings bond exclusion.

✦ Now that Coverdell ESAs can be used for certain elementary and secondary school expenses, the conversion of U.S. savings bonds for this purpose could also make sense.

I am a grandparent who owns post–1989 savings bonds and I would like to use these bonds to pay for my grandchild's college costs. Can I take advantage of the education bond exclusion?

Unfortunately, unless your grandchild is also your dependent you do not qualify for the Section 135 education savings bond exclusion. You will have to report the interest income on your tax return in the year you redeem the bonds even if you use the proceeds to fund a 529 plan or Coverdell ESA for the grandchild. However, there may be a loophole. You can establish a 529 account and name yourself as beneficiary. Then, cash in your bonds tax-free by funding the 529 account. Later on, you can change the beneficiary of the 529 account to your grandchild. Be sure to discuss this strategy with your own tax professional before attempting it.

Why should I worry about qualifying for the education bond exclusion when I can avoid tax by purchasing the bonds in my child's name and reporting the accrued interest on her tax return each year?

This alternative strategy can work well. Assuming your child can effectively shelter the annual bond interest accrual with her $800 standard deduction, choosing to report the interest each year can produce the best after-tax returns regardless of your circumstances in the year of redemption. Take care that this election, which applies to all future years unless you request permission from the IRS to change, does not backfire in the event your child is under the age of 14 and earns total investment income above the "kiddie tax" trigger (currently $1,600). For more information see IRS Publication 550, available online at www.irs.gov.

Also be sure to consider other aspects of placing investments in the name of your child, such as gift tax consequences and student financial aid impact.

Some parents who otherwise qualify for the education bond exclusion discover too late that the savings bonds were originally issued in the child's name, violating the requirement that the bonds be issued to an individual at least 24 years old. If they do not elect annual reporting of interest, the entire amount of accrued interest is taxable to the child upon redemption. It may be possible, however, to re-register the bonds in the name of the parent. Go to www.savingsbonds.gov for more information about correcting mistakes in the registration of your bonds.

ELEVEN

529 Plans vs. Other Investment Alternatives

Many different strategies and financial products are available to the family seeking to save for future college costs. Besides 529 plans, Coverdell education savings accounts, and U.S. savings bonds, a number of other investment choices and forms of ownership have become popular over the years. While these alternatives may not be directly or exclusively geared to college savings, they are easily adapted for this purpose. This chapter will discuss several of these options in comparison to the 529 plan.

IRA Withdrawals Used for Higher Education Expenses

Before the Taxpayer Relief Act of 1997, an IRA withdrawal taken before the owner turned 59½ years of age and used to pay for education expenses would incur a 10 percent penalty on premature distributions. The changes in the Taxpayer Relief Act of 1997 now allow a premature IRA withdrawal to be taken without penalty if used to pay for qualified higher education expenses of the taxpayer or the taxpayer's spouse, child, or grandchild. Qualified higher education expenses are reduced by the proceeds from the tax-free redemption of qualified U.S. savings bonds.

This can certainly be helpful. Many individuals have assets in individual retirement accounts and it is nice to know that those assets are accessible not only for retirement, but also in the event they are needed for college expenses. Note, however, that any *earnings* in a traditional IRA will still be taxable when withdrawn for college. The *principal* portion will also be taxable to the extent you claimed a deduction for contributions to the IRA.

A Roth IRA can be more effective than a traditional IRA when tapped for college expenses. Like a traditional IRA, the earnings portion of a premature Roth IRA distribution for qualified higher education expenses will still be subject to income tax. But Roth IRA distributions are first considered a return of principal; earnings come out only after the principal is exhausted. A viable strategy is to withdraw principal for college expenses and leave the earnings to grow in the Roth IRA. Once you turn 59½ (and assuming the Roth IRA is at least five years old), you can withdraw earnings at any time and exclude the earnings from tax.

Which investment vehicle should I use—an IRA or a 529 plan?

For many people, the answer would be the IRA, and more specifically, the Roth IRA. The Roth IRA offers federal income tax benefits equivalent to the 529 plan (and perhaps even better after 2010 if the Section 529 exclusion expires). In addition, the Roth IRA withdrawn in retirement can be used for any purpose without negative consequences, whereas the 529 plan is restricted to qualified higher education expenses. Consider also that for many people the objective of funding retirement is a higher priority than funding college. Borrowing is almost always an option for college expenses but not for retirees with inadequate financial resources.

So why not forget about the 529 plan and just concentrate on using the Roth IRA? If you are not already contributing the maximum amount to a Roth IRA, perhaps you should. But the Roth IRA is subject to income limitations, just like the Coverdell ESA. Furthermore, the annual contribution limit in 2004 is only $3,000 ($3,500 under a catch-up provision for those age 50 and above). It also requires that you have earned income of at least the amount of the contribution.

For federal financial aid purposes, an IRA or Roth IRA is a mixed blessing. The IRA balance will not be counted as part of the expected family contribution. But if IRA withdrawals are taken during the year, the financial aid application requires that any untaxed principal, in addition to taxable earnings that show up on the Form 1040, be added to the student's or parents' income in the calculation.

You will probably find that the IRA is not the total solution to saving for your child's college expenses. Even if it were large enough to cover the cost, tapping it for college means it will not be there for your retirement. A 529 plan will probably still provide the best means to save for the largest portion of future college expenses.

How about my employer's 401(k) plan? Should I redirect any of the savings that come out of my pay to a 529 plan instead?

Unlike an IRA, a 401(k) cannot be tapped directly for college expenses before you retire. If the plan permits you to take a loan, you could use the loan proceeds to pay college expenses, but the loan must be repaid.

Using a 401(k) will depend on your own particular circumstances. As discussed above, the importance of saving for retirement may turn out to be your overriding concern and you will want to maximize any opportunity you have to contribute to qualified retirement plans. An analysis of your current and projected future tax situation can also help in your decision. With a 401(k) you are making "pre-tax" contributions—i.e. you receive an upfront tax break on your contributions—but you pay income tax down the road on the full amount of each distribution. Contributions to a 529 plan are made with after-tax dollars, and the contribution portion of each distribution always comes out tax-free.

If your state offers a tax deduction for contributions into its 529 plan, you may decide that is reason enough to direct some dollars into that program. However, in most cases it will be unwise to do so if it means you will be giving up an employer match of your 401(k) contributions.

Tax-Exempt and Tax-Deferred Securities

Traditional investment planning for college-bound families often includes the transfer of income-producing assets from parent to child in order to take advantage of the child's low tax bracket. When the child is under 14, this planning must consider ways to avoid the "kiddie tax." Assuming the child has no earned income, up to $1,600 (in 2004) of investment income can be received by the child at low cost ($800 is sheltered by the standard deduction and the next $800 is taxed at the 10 percent tax rate), while investment income above $1,600 will be taxed at the parents' top marginal tax rate. One strategy often employed by families facing the kiddie tax will be to have the child under 14 invest in tax-exempt municipal bonds or tax-deferred U.S. savings bonds. The investment choices will broaden in the year the child turns 14 because income at that time will be taxed entirely at the child's tax rate. For children owning U.S. savings bonds, choosing to recognize interest income each year as it accrues may be beneficial if (1) the child is under 14 and does not have enough income to trigger the kiddie tax, or (2) if the child is 14 or older and can recognize the annual interest accrual at a lower tax rate than in the year the bonds will be redeemed.

Of course, investment assets in the child's name may not be recommended if financial aid eligibility is a consideration, recognizing that a child's assets are assessed at a much higher rate than parents' assets in calculating the expected family contribution to college costs. Families in this position may consider investing in annuity contracts or life insurance because these assets are generally not assessable in the financial aid calculation.

Life insurance has attractive tax features, including tax-deferred build-up of value and tax-free death benefits. Universal life insurance policies can work especially well as a college savings vehicle. They are flexible and allow parents to adjust the level of premium payments, borrow against cash value, and make partial withdrawals. A related product, variable universal life, allows the policy owner to select the underlying investments from a menu of mutual funds and provides more upside potential in the cash value build-up. If a cash-value policy is used as a college savings vehicle, it is important to start early in the child's life to allow time for the policy to build in value. A careful review of the prospectus is necessary to understand all costs and restrictions.

Annuities are insurance products sometimes chided for their low investment return as affected by mortality and expense charges, as well as for the penalties charged on withdrawal or surrender in the first five to ten years. There is an additional problem for most college parents in that annuity payments received prior to the age of 59½ will not only incur income tax but a 10 percent federal excise tax. A 529 plan will generally provide a better tax outcome when used for college expenses.

Treasury Inflation-Indexed Securities

The U.S. Treasury is promoting its 10-year inflation bonds (sometimes known as TIPS) as an appropriate investment for college savings. These bonds are sold in $1,000 denominations and the principal value is adjusted upwards each year for inflation as measured by the CPI. The bond's redemption value after 10 years includes the annual inflation adjustments. The coupon rate paid on these bonds is lower than a comparable-term regular Treasury bond, but the rate is applied to the inflation-adjusted value, so the interest paid to the bondholder increases each year. Even if you are satisfied with the yield, the tax treatment of these bonds is a disadvantage. Investors must pay federal tax each year not only on the interest payments, but also on the value increase from the inflation adjustment.

The inflation protection offered by TIPS and the tax advantages of a 529 plan might seem like an attractive combination for the safety-conscious investor interested in hedging tuition inflation. In fact, 529 savings programs in a few states now offer investment options featuring TIPS.

Zero Coupon and College Savings Bonds

Zero coupon bonds are bonds that do not pay interest but are issued at a discount to face value. The size of the discount determines the effective interest rate on the bond if held to maturity. Zero coupon bonds can be useful for college saving because maturities can be matched to the college years, and holders do not have to deal with the reinvestment of interest (unlike interest-paying bonds). The price of a zero coupon bond sold prior to maturity is affected not only by the amount of unearned interest, but also by market conditions at the time of sale. In a period of rising interest rates, the relative value of the bond will decrease.

There are several types of zero coupon bonds, each with unique tax and investment characteristics. Zero Coupon Treasury bonds are U.S. Treasury bonds or notes that have been stripped of their coupons and sold at a discount to face value. Corporations issue zero coupon bonds that provide a higher return on investment because they are subject to the risk of default (principal and earned discount could be lost). Banks may issue zero coupon certificates of deposit that are FDIC-insured (up to $100,000).

Most zero coupon alternatives, including those mentioned above, suffer a disadvantage: although you don't receive the interest until redemption, you are required to report each year's earned discount in taxable income. Zero coupon municipal bonds do not present this problem because their interest is tax-exempt for federal and state purposes (except for the individual who has to pay state tax on an out-of-state bond).

Several states have issued bonds that are specifically targeted to families saving for college. These are essentially zero coupon municipal bonds although they are often given the name of college savings bonds, baccalaureate bonds, or something similar. The most significant disadvantage of this investment option is that municipal bonds generally yield less than taxable bonds and may not keep pace with rising college costs. States that have issued these types of bonds include Arkansas, Connecticut, Hawaii, Illinois, Massachusetts, Michigan, Minnesota, New Hampshire, Ohio, Rhode Island, Tennessee, Virginia, and Washington. There will likely be less activity in this area in the future due to the increasing use of 529 plans.

Mutual Funds

Five main advantages are commonly cited for the use of taxable mutual funds, as opposed to 529 plans, for college savings. They are (1) potential for superior investment performance, (2) ability to direct the investments, (3) low tax rates on capital gains and dividends, (4) lower fees and expenses, and (5) ability to use the investment for any purpose without penalty. Each of these factors is examined below.

The first supposed advantage, potential for superior investment performance, is valid only when comparing taxable mutual funds to the prepaid variety of 529 plan. The 529 savings programs provide the college saver with returns directly linked to the investments in the 529 portfolios, and these investments are often the same equity mutual funds that would be attractive to the non–529 college saver. In fact, they may be even better. Taxable mutual funds are sometimes deliberately managed to achieve a "tax-efficient" result, creating a risk that investment decisions are based on tax considerations. The manager of a 529 savings program has no reason to be concerned with the tax consequences of investment activity and can focus entirely on making the best investment decisions within its asset guidelines and investment policy.

The second noted advantage of taxable mutual funds, the ability to direct investments among different funds at the discretion of the owner, will never be totally matched by 529 plans absent a change to the law. By definition, a 529 plan cannot allow the account owner to direct the investments. In actuality, the increasing number of 529 savings programs, the ever-expanding menu of investment options available, and the conditional ability to change your investment option or roll over your account to another state's program, together provide as much flexibility as most investors will ever need.

Several 529 savings programs have recently introduced or announced a lineup of single mutual funds available to participants. An investor will be able to customize 529 portfolios using one or more of these mutual funds, if desired, and reallocate balances between the funds at least once every year.[1] This innovation injects a new dimension of self-direction to the 529 realm, enabling the investor to concentrate his or her savings in sectors that are not widely available through the traditional portfolio options, such as small cap funds or international stock funds.

Perhaps more relevant, however, is the question of whether your ability to direct investments is an advantage or a disadvantage. The majority of 529 savings programs still utilize professional money managers and large financial services companies to determine the mix of investments that will produce the best balance of risk and return for any particular beneficiary's college savings. Is it likely that the self-directed account will perform better over the relevant time period? That is a question that investors are going to have to answer themselves, perhaps with the help of their professional advisers.

Many experts who have studied this issue as it relates to self-directed 401(k) accounts would answer "no" to that question. The "age-based" portfolios available through many 529 plans may be an advantage because they prevent the novice investor from doing damage to his or her own savings. Of course, the age-based approach does not produce an asset allocation and investment approach that takes into account all the other components of your financial situation. A professional investment adviser or financial planner can provide valuable services even if you select the age-based option, and should be able to incorporate the 529 investment into your total financial picture in an effective way.

The third perceived advantage of taxable mutual funds, low tax rates on capital gains and dividends, will generally not stand up to close scrutiny, particularly if we assume that qualified distributions from a 529 plan

---

1. See chapter 3 for a discussion of the investment flexibility now permitted under IRS Notice 2001-55.

will remain free from federal taxes after 2010. A 2003 study published by the TIAA-CREF Institute compared after-tax accumulations of an investment in a 529 plan and a portfolio of equivalent investments (stock mutual funds) in a taxable account.[2] Assuming the investor is in the 25% federal tax bracket and a 6% state tax bracket, and that the expenses are the same under both alternatives, the study found that the 529 investor winds up with 12.2 percent more after 18 years than the mutual fund investor.

But what about the expenses in a 529 plan (the fourth objection listed above)? Most 529 plans charge management fees and/or account maintenance fees and these charges will reduce your overall investment return. The TIAA-CREF Institute study included a second set of calculations which assumed 529 plan expenses 0.47% higher than taxable mutual fund expenses. The result: the advantage of the 529 plans over the 18-year investment horizon was reduced from 12.2 percent to 8.0 percent.

Placing taxable mutual funds in your child's name under the UTMA or UGMA may offer the best answer. According to the TIAA-CREF Institute study, the combination of lower tax rates (the child is assumed to be in the 10% federal tax bracket and a 1.5% state tax bracket in the study), and lower expenses outside of a 529 plan, resulted in a higher accumulation in the UTMA/UGMA. However, an outright gift to your child may not be desirable (see the discussion below). Also, the study found that the advantage of a state income tax deduction in certain 529 plans can overcome the disadvantage of 529 program expenses.

The fifth objection is the flexibility to use mutual funds for any purpose. An investor withdrawing funds from a 529 plan for a purpose other than college suffers the consequence of reporting the earnings as ordinary income and paying an additional 10 percent penalty tax. In most cases, the investor would have been better off using taxable mutual funds. The risk of winding up in this situation should be assessed prior to making the decision to use a 529 plan. If you do use a 529 plan, and ultimately find yourself in the position of withdrawing funds that will not be used for college, you should consider the option of directing the withdrawal to your child, not to yourself, to lessen the tax cost.

---

2. TIAA-CREF Institute, *The 2003 Tax Law's Impact on College Savings Plans*, Quarterly (Summer 2003)

Uniform Gifts or Transfers to Minors Act

The Uniform Gifts to Minors Act (UGMA), adopted in some form in all 50 states, allows assets to be transferred to a custodian for the benefit of a minor child. The child receives direct ownership of the assets upon reaching the age of majority (18 or 21) as determined under state law. The Uniform Transfers to Minors Act (UTMA), a more recent alternative to the UGMA, and available in nearly all states, works in essentially the same manner. The UTMA account is preferable in several respects, because it may stay open for a longer period of time (up to age 25 in some states), and because it can hold certain types of assets, such as real estate interests, that the UGMA account cannot. UGMA/UTMA accounts do not provide the level of control available to the donor in a 529 plan, where assets may be kept out of the hands of the beneficiary indefinitely.

Dividends, interest, or capital gains realized in an UGMA/UTMA account will be taxed to the minor beneficiary and are subject to the "kiddie tax" if the child is under age 14. However, the donor, not the child, will recognize the income from an UGMA/UTMA account if it is used to satisfy the donor's legal obligation to support the minor. Payment of college expenses could in some instances constitute the legal obligation of the donor/parent, shifting the income burden back to the parent.

You also need to be careful about the estate tax treatment of UGMA/UTMA accounts. While a contribution to a 529 plan is removed from your gross estate (subject to partial add-back if you die in the five-year period after making the gift-tax averaging election), UGMA/UTMA transfers will be included in your gross estate if you die while serving as custodian. To avoid this risk, name someone else (perhaps your spouse) as custodian at the time the account is established and relinquish your control over its management.

Can I transfer my child's existing UGMA/UTMA assets into a 529 plan?

Yes, if you are custodian and decide that a 529 plan is a better way to save, you can liquidate the current investments and reinvest the proceeds in a 529 plan. The sale of investments may generate a tax on capital gains. See checklist item #4 in chapter 6 for a description of the different ways 529 plans accommodate contributions from an existing UGMA/UTMA account. Ultimately, it is your responsibility as custodian to comply with state law in handling UGMA/UTMA funds. Some parents will be disappointed to learn that a transfer of assets to a 529 plan will not result in a transfer of ownership rights from the minor to the parent. The minor will assume direct ownership of the 529 account at the age of majority or other age established under the law. For this reason, consider spending down current UGMA/UTMA assets for the benefit of the minor, and replacing those funds by contributing your own money into a 529 plan. If you do have a 529 account for a minor under UGMA/UTMA, establish a different account for any of your own funds.

Irrevocable Trust

A gift to an irrevocable trust allows you to maintain some level of control over the assets by dictating the terms of the trust agreement. The trust agreement could provide that your beneficiaries will receive trust corpus and income only under certain conditions. However, there are several problems with this approach. Any income retained in the trust is taxed not to you or to the trust beneficiary, but to the trust itself, at tax brackets that escalate very quickly. Also, your transfer to the trust is considered a gift of a "future interest," and does not qualify for the $11,000 annual gift tax exclusion.

You can deal with the gift tax problem by establishing a "Crummey" trust. A Crummey power allows the beneficiary to withdraw the current year's gift within a limited time period (often 30 days following the contribution of funds to the trust). The beneficiary is not expected to exercise this right. When properly drafted and executed, the transfer of property to a Crummey trust qualifies for the $11,000 annual gift tax exclusion as a gift of a present interest. Income generated by the trust may be taxed to the trust, to the beneficiary with Crummey withdrawal rights, or to the distributee of the income, depending on the circumstances.

A 529 plan offers the asset control that individuals establishing Crummey trusts are attempting to achieve, without all the complications. A Crummey trust can invest in life insurance policies, however, which is not possible with 529 plans.

Section 2503(c) Minor's Trust

Another way to qualify the gift-in-trust for the $11,000 annual gift tax exclusion is to establish the trust under Internal Revenue Code Section 2503(c). The so-called "minor's trust" provides the trustee total discretion to expend trust corpus and income for the benefit of the minor before he or she turns 21; the beneficiary receives any remaining balance upon reaching age 21. The estate tax and income tax consequences are variable depending on a number of factors. Section 529 plans are better than Section 2503(c) trusts for most college savers.

Section 2503(b) Income Trust

This trust requires all income to be distributed at least annually. The "income interest" will qualify for the $11,000 annual gift tax exclusion as a gift of a present interest, valued under IRS tables, while the "remainder interest" is a gift of a future interest. There is no requirement that the trust terminate when the beneficiary turns 21. Again, the 529 plan is superior to the 2503(b) trust in that the entire interest may be retained in the 529 plan until you decide to withdraw it, the earnings are tax-deferred and potentially tax free, and the entire contribution (not just the income interest) qualifies for the annual gift tax exclusion.

Family Partnership

A family partnership or family limited liability company can be formed to hold securities and other investments that may be targeted for college savings or any other purpose. This can be a very useful tool for transferring assets to the next generation and can provide a way to shift income, reduce a large estate, and even provide some level of creditor protection. For gift and estate tax purposes, a valuation discount may be available for the fractional partnership interest gifted to the child. This may of course be challenged by the IRS, which demands a "business purpose" for the partnership and has a particular problem with family partnerships consisting only of marketable securities and no other business assets. In addition to all the potential tax advantages of a family partnership, you can also maintain effective control of the portion of the assets that are gifted away by giving away limited partnership interests and retaining the general partnership interest. The general partner has the authority to make decisions for the partnership, including the timing and amount of distributions to the partners.

The disadvantage of family partnerships is that they must be carefully crafted and they require significant effort for annual recordkeeping and tax reporting. In addition, the Internal Revenue Code contains certain income tax provisions targeted directly at family partnerships. A full explanation of the advantages and disadvantages of a family partnership is beyond the scope of this book and anyone interested in this option should consult an attorney. Due to the expense of setting up and maintaining family partnerships, they are usually only recommended when significant assets are at stake. A 529 plan, on the other hand, is a much simpler and much less expensive way to set up a college savings program for your family.

TWELVE

Managing Your 529 Account

Aparent—let's call him John—decides to use a 529 plan but wants to keep it as simple as possible. He begins by establishing an investment account, or purchasing a prepaid tuition contract, for each of his children in his own state's 529 plan. As the years go by, he pays little attention to the accounts, confident they will be there to help pay for whatever colleges his children decide to attend. When the college bills finally roll in, John taps the entire value of each account or contract for that purpose.

For John, as well as for many others, this uncomplicated approach will produce the desired results, and even the most restrictive 529 plan can be an appropriate choice. Realize, however, that federal tax law offers a significant degree of flexibility to those utilizing 529 plans as a savings vehicle. From a planning perspective, this flexibility can be extremely attractive. It means that you are not locked into the decisions made when the account is first established. As circumstances change, you can make adjustments to ensure that the benefits of your college savings accounts are maximized.

Most 529 plans allow you to change some aspect of your account. Well-timed changes can save federal and state income taxes, estate taxes, and generation-skipping transfer taxes, and can enhance eligibility for federal financial aid as well. Even if you change nothing substantial, you may still have to make some decisions along the way in order to take full advantage of 529 plans.

The flexibility allowed under federal tax law is not fully incorporated into all 529 plans. As demonstrated in chapter 6, some programs may significantly limit your maneuverability. Understand these limitations before making contributions. This factor can influence your choice of program.

Basic Account Management

Let's assume that you have decided which 529 plan to use. You used the checklist in chapter 6 or sought the guidance of your financial planner. You read through the official program materials and understand how the program works. If it is a savings program with different investment options, you have selected the option, or combination of options, that seems best. What else do you need to think about? There are at least three questions you face between now and the time your child graduates from college.

1) When should you make your contributions?

It may not be wise to throw every penny into your chosen 529 plan (or plans) at your first opportunity. You can do better by timing your contributions to obtain the most benefit from your investment and save as much in taxes as possible. Here are some reasons why:

+ Capital gains tax. If you liquidate other investments to fund your 529 account, carefully consider the tax consequences. Properly timing the sale can make a difference in how much income tax you pay.

✦ State tax benefits. If your state offers an income tax deduction for your contributions, or perhaps a matching grant, consider how the timing of your contributions can affect the benefit you receive. For instance, if you live in a state like New York that offers a limited deduction for your contributions to its 529 plan, with no carryover of excess contributions, you may want to spread your contributions over more than one year to capture a greater tax benefit.

✦ Gift tax. If you want to contribute more than $11,000 for a single beneficiary, or if you are making other gifts to that individual, be careful to formulate a gifting strategy. One of your objectives may be to stay within the $11,000 annual gift tax exclusion. Careful use of the five-year averaging election will help you do this. If it is already late in the year, consider making your $11,000 contribution this year, and waiting until the beginning of next year before contributing another $55,000 under the five-year averaging election. This way you have funded your account with $66,000 in gift-tax-free contributions rather than $55,000. (However, you will have consumed your annual gift exclusions going into year six rather than year five.)

✦ Account expenses. Consider how the timing of your contributions might affect your overall program cost. Some 529 savings programs waive annual account maintenance fees if you sign up for automatic deposits from your checking or savings account, or if you maintain a minimum account balance. With prepaid programs, the price of your contract can vary significantly based on the age of your child. By purchasing a contract this year, you may get better pricing. In some cases, you may be better off waiting until next year if you can determine that the price will not increase by much and you can set the money aside in an interest-earning account in the meantime. In many prepaid programs, you will also need to decide whether to purchase a higher-priced contract under an installment payment plan (total payments will be more than the lump-sum cost of the contract), or a lower-priced contract now with the intent to buy additional semesters or tuition units in future years.

✦ Market risk. Investing in a 529 savings program is similar to investing in mutual funds. Although the concepts of modern portfolio theory are beyond the scope of this book, some experts recommend "dollar cost averaging" as a way to manage the risk of a volatile stock market. This involves making contributions at regular intervals. (A number of 529 plans now offer a dollar-cost-averaging mechanism that allows the investor to preprogram the movement of a large initial contribution into equity-based options over time.) Remember also that your college savings accounts are probably just one piece of your total investment "pie" and that you should be balancing your asset allocation across all investments. If you do not feel comfortable managing your own investments, seek the help of an investment professional.

2) When should you take distributions to pay for college costs?

In a 529 prepaid program you may not have a great deal of flexibility in the timing of your benefits because payout procedures are probably standardized. But this does not mean that you should forget entirely about timing opportunities. The date that the program makes payments to your child's school will determine the year in which the expenses are considered paid under any other tax provisions including the Hope credit, the Lifetime Learning credit, and the above-the-line Section 222 deduction for higher education expenses. A payment of second-semester bills in January rather than December can make a significant difference in your tax liability.

With the 529 savings programs, and with most of the unit-type prepaid or guaranteed savings programs, you will have much more latitude in the timing of distributions. It is up to you to decide how to allocate your account between academic years, and when to request distributions. It appears under the current tax rules that you must carefully coordinate any cash withdrawals from your 529 savings account to fall within the same calendar year as your payment of qualifying expenses. To determine the tax consequences of your withdrawals, you will need to compare the beneficiary's total qualified expenses to total 529 withdrawals. If you pay for college costs this year, but receive your 529 plan distribution next year, you may find that you have a tax problem. The IRS may eventually develop new rules that permit some crossover in matching expenses with cash withdrawals, but any such rules would add to your recordkeeping burdens.

Keep in mind that the coordination of various tax incentives for higher education can make for very complex planning. As an example, consider that Section 529 qualified higher education expenses are reduced by expenses used to determine a Hope or Lifetime Learning credit. Since a Hope credit is calculated on up to $2,000 in qualified expenses, but a Lifetime Learning credit is calculated on as much as $10,000 in qualified expenses, you may find that it is better to target the 529 withdrawals to the Hope credit years rather than to the Lifetime Learning credit years. See chapter 7 for a more extensive discussion of income tax planning considerations.

3) When should you take a non-qualified withdrawal?

Consider taking a non-qualified withdrawal whenever the tax and financial aid consequences will turn out better for you than the use of your account for qualified higher education expenses. Because you will be subject to income tax and a 10 percent penalty, this tactic is not often recommended, but here are some possible scenarios where a non-qualified withdrawal may be beneficial:

+ In many prepaid programs, the value of the contract for beneficiaries attending college out-of-state is limited to actual tuition
at the institution being attended. A beneficiary who is enrolled in
the prepaid program but later moves and becomes a resident of
another state may find that public university tuition in the new
state is lower than tuition in the old state. In this situation, canceling the contract might be better than using it to pay tuition at the
lower rate.

✦ A refund of the account might make sense when its use for qualified expenses would severely impact a financial aid award. You will not necessarily know this until your child is close to college age and you assess the prospects for financial aid.

✦ If your account has lost value—the balance is less than cumulative net contributions—a termination and liquidation of the account may produce an income tax benefit. The loss is deductible on your tax return as a miscellaneous itemized deduction. Discuss this strategy this with a tax professional before claiming such a deduction. Many taxpayers will be unable to gain any tax relief from miscellaneous itemized deductions because of the 2 percent-of-adjusted-gross-income floor, or because of the alternative minimum tax.

If a non-qualified distribution produces an unwanted result, and you have no immediate need for the funds, consider leaving the account alone (if permitted under the rules of the 529 plan). An account in a 529 savings program will continue to grow tax-deferred until you decide to take distributions, and that can be many years down the road.

Managing Multiple Accounts

Here are several reasons to think about opening multiple accounts for the same beneficiary:

1) *To gain state tax deductions.* If you live in Virginia, multiple accounts for the same beneficiary may lead to a larger tax deduction than just one account. If you live in any other state that offers a deduction for contributions, but places an annual cap on the amount of deduction, be sure to study the tax rules to determine if you are maximizing the benefit.

2) *To diversify your investments.* While some savings programs give you ample opportunity to diversify your investments within one account by spreading your contribution among different investment options,

others require that you establish multiple accounts to use more than one of the available investment options. Further diversification can be achieved by establishing accounts in different 529 plans.

3) *To combine a prepaid program with a savings program.* Because prepaid programs typically cover tuition and fees only, it is becoming more common to combine prepaid and savings programs as a way to save for all qualified higher education expenses.

4) *To contribute more than the individual state contribution limit.* If the 529 plan you've chosen has a contribution cap of $250,000 and you have $280,000 to invest, you would have to open accounts in multiple states. But do not attempt to use multiple states as a way to deposit more than you can reasonably justify as necessary for your beneficiary's higher education expenses.

5) *To take advantage of a limited benefit.* Some states provide a tax deduction, or a partial match, for your contribution, subject to a dollar limit. While the incentive may persuade you to direct your first dollars into that program, you may decide to use a different 529 plan for contributions beyond the amount that secures the maximum benefit.

6) *To start the clock running.* Even if a particular 529 plan is not your first choice, you may want to open a small account in it if there are any benefits that require a minimum period of participation. For example, a couple of 529 plans require that your account be open for a minimum period of time before taking qualified withdrawals. Or perhaps your state offers a program that allows your beneficiary to "vest" as a state resident for purposes of paying tuition at the state's public institutions. This can be a valuable benefit if your family moves out of state and sends a child back to a public university in that state.

7) *To reduce income taxes.* See chapter 7 for a discussion of how multiple accounts can be used to your advantage by permitting selective withdrawals based on each account's "earnings ratio."

Multiple accounts can mean multiple fees, however, and also can mean that you may not be able to achieve the breakpoints where your fees are reduced or eliminated. Multiple accounts will also result in more statements and other collateral material coming your way from the programs.

Account Management Beyond the Basics

Advanced account management involves making changes to your account after you have established it. There are three basic categories of change, any one of which should be considered in the appropriate circumstances:

1) *Changing the designated beneficiary.* A beneficiary change can be made in most 529 plans simply by filling out a change form and submitting it to the plan administrator. Sometimes a fee will be charged. To avoid termination of the original account, and the triggering of income tax and penalty, the new beneficiary must qualify under the Section 529 definition of "member of the family" (see chapter 3). As an alternative to a complete change of beneficiary, the owner may be able to accomplish a partial change by establishing another account for the new beneficiary and transferring some funds from the first account to the second through a rollover.

2) *Changing the account owner.* Many 529 plans allow the original account owner to transfer ownership of an account to someone else. These programs generally do not require that the new account owner be a member of the family or have any other specific relationship to the original owner. Other programs do not accept a request to change account owner prior to the original owner's death or incapacity, while still others spell out procedures in limited circumstances, such as when the account owner and spouse are separated or divorced. For the most part, a change in account ownership is a tax-neutral event. However, this is an area that invites IRS scrutiny and can create tax uncertainties, especially when questions surrounding the generation-skipping transfer tax arise, or where a non-individual account owner is involved (some states allow corporations, trusts, and other entities to be account owners).

3) *Transferring balances between 529 plans.* Section 529 allows a tax-free rollover from one state's 529 plan to another state's any time the beneficiary of the account is changed to a new beneficiary who is a member of the family of the old beneficiary. In addition, a same-beneficiary rollover can be transacted once in any 12-month period. It is important that you understand a 529 plan's rollover rules before you make a contribution, because you will want to know whether you can move the account

easily and inexpensively to another state if the original investment loses its appeal.

The following strategies exemplify the use of rollovers.

Change strategy #1: For the undecided investor

Let's say you are attracted to the tax advantages and investment approach of a 529 plan, but have no specific plans to use your savings for your own or someone else's education. You, your children, your grandchildren, or some other family member might need education funds in the future, but you do not want to irrevocably commit your savings to that purpose. Think about establishing an account and naming yourself as beneficiary. If you later decide to fund a relative's college or graduate-school education, you can then change the beneficiary designation to that relative.

> *Example:* Joyce is a 50-year old grandmother with $20,000 invested in bank certificates of deposit. She is already funding her 401(k) account and Roth IRA to the maximum extent allowable, and has substantial assets in those retirement plans. Joyce decides to open an account in a 529 savings plan using the $20,000 received when her CDs mature. She names herself as beneficiary of the account, with the idea of taking post-graduate classes in the future, although having no specific plans to do so. Joyce has successfully converted taxable CD interest income into a tax-deferred savings vehicle. Ten years later, Joyce retires with substantial assets in her retirement accounts and decides to change her 529 account beneficiary designation from herself to her grandson, who is now 11 years old. She makes the five-year averaging election so that the value of the gift (now $55,000) does not consume any of her $1 million lifetime gift exemption. The account will continue to grow tax-deferred until the grandson uses the funds for college. If distributions are used before 2011, they will be tax free. If they are used after 2010 and the EGTRRA tax exclusion is not extended, distributed earnings will be taxable to the student.

Alternatively, Joyce can name her grandson as initial beneficiary of the account even if she thinks she may need the account for herself in the future. She can always request a non-qualified withdrawal from the account, subject to income tax and penalty. The advantage of this approach is that the value of the account is removed from her taxable estate now, along with any future earnings and appreciation. If she does, in fact, request a non-qualified withdrawal in the future, the amount of the withdrawal will come back into her estate.

With her substantial assets and a desire to shelter as much income from tax as possible, Joyce may want to establish two sizable accounts: one for herself and another for her grandson. She can, for example, contribute $55,000 in 2004 to a 529 plan for her grandson and make the five-year averaging election for gift tax purposes. Instead of waiting until 2009 to make an additional gift-tax-free contribution to that account, she establishes a second account with herself as beneficiary. Joyce's contributions to this account can now grow tax deferred and in 2009 she can simply change the beneficiary to her grandson and shelter another $55,000 (or more, if inflation adjustments cause the annual exclusion to be increased) from gift tax.

The 529 plan administrators can refuse to accept Joyce's contributions or terminate the account if they determine that Joyce does not intend to use the account to pay the higher education expenses of the named beneficiary (whether it is her grandson or herself).

Change strategy #2: For the family that may qualify for financial aid

Chapter 4 describes how an interest in a 529 plan may impact the student's eligibility for financial aid. Let's say you have purchased a contract in your state's prepaid program and discover as your child prepares to enter college that the tuition benefits paid by the program will reduce a need-based grant on a dollar-for-dollar basis. As mentioned above, you may find you are better off by canceling the contract and receiving a refund.

An even better answer might be a rollover of your account from the prepaid program to a savings program. Under current federal aid methodology, the savings account may result in a better financial aid package. Some states, like Virginia, offer both a prepaid and a savings program and will facilitate the transfer of accounts between the programs without any loss in accrued value.

Finally, if there are younger children in the family, you may want to consider changing the beneficiary designation on your 529 account to a younger child. Assuming you can finance the older child's college education from other resources, including the financial aid package, you at least are able to delay the consequences to a future year.

> *Example:* The Quigleys have 529 savings accounts for their four children. When the eldest child, Jackie, begins her senior year of high school, the parents investigate her eligibility for federal financial aid. They discover that Jackie's 529 account will negatively impact her chances for a scholarship, grant, or tuition discount. The Quigleys change the designated beneficiary on Jackie's account to a younger child in the family. After Jackie has submitted her aid application for her final year of college, her parents may decide to transfer 529 assets back to her to pay for the remaining balance (as long as doing this will not cause an adjustment to her award). This exercise may be repeated for each child in the family as he or she nears college age.

A word of caution to those who own 529 accounts for the student's siblings: It is not entirely clear that you can exclude the value of sibling 529 accounts when reporting parents' assets on the Free Application for Federal Student Aid (FAFSA). Although the U.S. Department of Education does not appear to require inclusion, some financial aid administrators will take these accounts into consideration when developing the aid package. Institution-funded grants and scholarships may also be impacted.

Change strategy #3: For those in states offering benefits to college savers

If you have more to invest than your state allows as an income tax deduction, and you do not want to delay any contributions to a future year, consider parking the excess in another state's 529 plan. Roll over the assets to your home-state program in a later year to claim additional state tax deductions. Unless your state restricts the deduction to "virgin" contributions (apparently the case, at least to some degree, in Colorado, Illinois, Maryland, and Rhode Island) your state won't care that the assets are being rolled over from another 529 plan.

You can also avoid "wasting" the in-state benefits of a large contribution by gifting a portion of your contribution to someone else on the understanding that the money will be contributed to an account for your designated beneficiaries. For example, you may be able to secure additional state tax deductions for your own parents by gifting cash to them to establish 529 accounts for your children. You run the risk that your parents, who now control the account, will use the money for something other than educating your children (unless they transfer account ownership back to you). Be sure to consider any gift-tax consequences.

There may be a way to invest with an out-of-state 529 plan and still take advantage of your state's tax deduction. This involves a rollover to the out-of-state program after first establishing an in-state account (and claiming the deduction for your contributions to it). It is important that you check to see if your state requires "recapture" of your deduction on a rollover to another state's program.

Besides maximizing any state benefits on your contributions, you should also look for state tax exemption on qualified distributions. Let's assume your state imposes income tax on the earnings distributed from out-of-state 529 plans, but provides an exemption for qualified distributions from its own 529 plan. You can consider a rollover from the out-of-state program to the in-state program any time prior to using the account for qualified expenses.

Planning for state income tax savings can be an uncertain exercise, particularly where 529 plans are concerned. Obtain the advice of a tax professional in your state.

Avoid Abusive Change Strategies in Estate Tax Planning

The estate and gift tax rules surrounding 529 plans offer unique opportunities to reduce the gross estate of someone attempting to shift assets to a lower generation. They also give rise to strategies that some individuals believe will allow for a large tax-free intergenerational transfer of wealth that cannot be accomplished through traditional gifting techniques. These strategies pose a challenge to the IRS as it attempts to regulate the use of Section 529, and they pose a risk to taxpayers who use them without adequately considering the consequences of an IRS challenge. For example, consider the following "loophole":

> *Example:* John wants to contribute $220,000 to a 529 plan for his son Freddy while avoiding gift taxes. He can only contribute $55,000 this year under the five-year averaging election without causing a taxable gift. However, John also has three nieces, so he decides to establish three accounts with a $55,000 contribution for each niece. The five-year election shelters these contributions from gift tax. John figures that he can change the beneficiary to his son whenever he wants without triggering further gift tax consequences. The 2001 EGTRRA amended the Section 529 definition of "member of the family" to include first cousins, so John's change of beneficiary qualifies as a rollover. Because the cousins are the same generation as his son, there is no deemed gift from any of the nieces to Freddy (see chapter 9).

This maneuver is an end run around the annual gift tax exclusion limits, and the IRS will probably not be happy if it finds out about it. But how can this apparent abuse be distinguished from a situation where John truly intends to help fund the future college expenses of his nieces, and only because of unforeseeable circumstances does he find it necessary to later change the beneficiary to his own son?

There are similar "opportunities" to leverage the annual exclusion through other family members. For instance, John conceivably could have

THE BEST WAY TO SAVE FOR COLLEGE

established 529 accounts for his own five brothers and their wives using the available annual exclusions to place hundreds of thousands of dollars into tax-deferred investment accounts, removing these assets from his estate without incurring gift tax. The substitution of his son as designated beneficiary on these accounts would be deemed a gift from these extended family members to John's son due to the difference in generations, but annual gift exclusions could again be deployed to avoid gift tax consequences.

To carry this to its absurd conclusion, consider how you might try to create a tax problem for your most-despised relative.

Example: Ed never forgave his brother Sean for taking, and then losing, his baseball card collection 40 years ago and now sees an opportunity to make him pay for it. Ed contributes $55,000 to a 529 plan, designating brother Sean as the account beneficiary and electing five-year averaging to avoid any gift tax consequences. As owner of the account, Ed then changes the beneficiary from Sean to his own son, Kyle. Sean is never aware of his brother's actions, which according to Section 529 create a gift from Sean to his nephew Kyle (Kyle belongs to a lower generation than Sean). Sean understandably fails to make the five-year averaging election, and so has unwittingly made a taxable gift that utilizes part of his $1 million lifetime exemption. Ed lets Sean know about this after it is too late to do anything about it, and Sean realizes that he has now lost some of his lifetime exemption, or even worse, has failed to report a taxable gift requiring payment of gift taxes, interest, and possible penalties.

Although the literal reading of the statute appears to demand this result, and donative intent is not required for the federal gift tax to apply, it seems unlikely that an unsuspecting donor could actually be assessed gift tax by the IRS. Perhaps the final regulations under Section 529 should require that the original intended beneficiary "accept" the designation before the gift of a 529 contribution can be considered "completed." Rules similar to the qualified disclaimer provisions of the Internal Revenue Code could accomplish this. In the above example, Sean would have had the opportunity to smell the trap and refuse the position of designated beneficiary.

A change of account owner can also be an opportunity for abuse. Many 529 plans allow you to transfer your account to someone else. The mere act of transferring ownership appears to have no federal income tax or gift tax consequences. This follows the logic of Section 529, provided the 529 account is ultimately expended for the beneficiary's qualified higher education expenses. But what happens if the new account owner revokes the account? Is there a gift tax consequence? If the answer is no, then the opportunity presents itself to transfer wealth without making a gift.

> *Example:* Shirley is a wealthy grandmother making maximum annual exclusion gifts to her son Todd and her grandson Timmy. Todd is wealthy in his own right and making his own annual exclusion gifts to Timmy. To bypass Todd's generation and get more of the family wealth to her grandson, Shirley establishes a 529 account for Todd, using the money she normally gifts directly to him. Shirley then transfers ownership of the 529 account to Timmy so Timmy becomes the account owner with his father as beneficiary. Timmy simply revokes the account and receives the money without any gift tax (although generation-skipping transfer tax may still be a concern).

An often-heard phrase is "if it's too good to be true, then it probably is." Section 529 of the Internal Revenue Code challenges that notion, especially in the area of estate and gift taxes. There is no question that the law provides unique benefits that are counterintuitive to anyone familiar with the "normal" estate and gift tax rules. The best advice, however, is to stay within reasonable bounds and remember that 529 plans are intended to be a tax-advantaged college savings vehicle, not a tax shelter.

State by State Comparisons

This Section contains a brief description of each state's 529 plan as of the date this book went to press. Although substantial effort has been made to be as accurate as possible in these descriptions, they are not a substitute for your thorough review of the materials available from the particular program being considered, including enrollment materials, the application form, and the master contract. These descriptions have not been approved or verified by program officials.

Note that many states with existing programs are contemplating or are in the process of making changes to their 529 plans. Please visit the Web site at www.savingforcollege.com to find out about these changes.

However, before describing the state programs, we first describe the only non-state sponsored 529 plan. Independent 529 Plan is a private-college prepaid tuition program authorized under the 2001 tax law changes.

SOURCE: PRIVATE COLLEGES

PROGRAM NAME:	Independent 529 Plan
529 TYPE:	Institutional prepaid contract
SPONSOR:	Tuition Plan Consortium LLC, a non-profit membership organization comprised of participating colleges and universities
PROGRAM MANAGER:	TIAA-CREF Tuition Financing, Inc.
INITIAL YEAR OF OPERATION:	2003
TELEPHONE:	1–888–718–7878
INTERNET:	www.independent529plan.org

Who can purchase Tuition Certificates? Individuals 18 years and older, UTMA/UGMA custodians, and legal entities.

Enrollment period: Open year-round

Time or age limitations on beneficiary or on use of benefits: A minimum of 36 months must lapse between the initial purchase date of a Tuition Certificate and its first redemption. A Tuition Certificate must be used by the 30th anniversary of its purchase or it will be canceled for the refund amount.

Contract benefits: A Tuition Certificate may be redeemed for a predetermined percentage of tuition and mandatory fees at any of approximately 240 participating private colleges around the country. The particular college to be attended does not have to be identified at the time of certificate purchase. For students who end up attending a non-participating institution, Tuition Certificates can be canceled for the refund amount.

Contract options: A Tuition Certificate is issued for each program year based on all payments made for the beneficiary during that program year. Total Tuition Certificates may not exceed five years of undergraduate tuition and mandatory fees at a participating institution.

Costs: There is no enrollment fee. The minimum purchase is $500, or $25 per month, and the maximum purchase is five years of full-time tuition and mandatory fees at the highest-cost participating institution. For each program year (July 1 to June 30), payments into the program purchase a Tuition Certificate representing a percentage of future tuition and mandatory fees at any one of the participating private colleges. The percentage will vary for each school, depending on its current tuition rate and certificate discount rate. Each college must offer a discount of at least 0.50% per year off current tuition cost, and the value of the certificate discount compounds between the time of purchase and the time of certificate redemption.

Cancellation provisions: Tuition Certificates can be canceled at any time following the first anniversary of the initial payment for the certificate. The refund amount will be the amount paid for Tuition Certificates adjusted by the net investment performance of the program trust, subject to a maximum annual return of 2% and a maximum annual loss of 2%.

Contract changes: The program accepts requests to change beneficiary and name a successor owner. Transfer of account ownership is not permitted. There are no special provisions concerning rollovers to another 529 plan (refund provisions would apply).

Program backing: Tuition Certificates are not backed by any guarantees. However, each participating institution makes a binding commitment to accept such certificates in payment of tuition and mandatory fees. Payments received by the program are pooled in a trust fund, with investments managed by TIAA-CREF.

Special considerations:

- Independent 529 Plan continually recruits new colleges into the program, and any college coming in must agree to accept Tuition Certificates from existing participants.

STATE: **ALABAMA**

PROGRAM NAME:	Prepaid Affordable College Tuition (PACT) Program
529 TYPE:	Prepaid contract
STATE AGENCY:	Board of Trustees of the Trust Fund, chaired by the State Treasurer
INITIAL YEAR OF OPERATION:	1990
TELEPHONE:	1–800–252–7228
INTERNET:	www.treasury.state.al.us

Who can purchase a contract? Individuals 19 years old and older or represented by a guardian or custodian, and approved legal entities. There are no Alabama residency requirements.

Enrollment period: August and September each year

Time or age limitations on beneficiary or on use of benefits: The beneficiary must be in the 9th grade or below at the time of program enrollment. Contract benefits must be used within 10 years after the beneficiary's projected college entrance date.

Contract benefits: The contract pays undergraduate tuition and mandatory fees for up to 135 semester hours at any Alabama public college or university. The value derived from the contract will depend in part on the selection of institution and number of credit hours taken, because public institutions in Alabama have different tuition and fee levels. If the beneficiary decides to attend a private college in Alabama or an out-of-state college, PACT will pay an amount up to, but not more than, the weighted average tuition and mandatory fees charged at Alabama public four-year institutions. There is a $25 out-of-state school transfer fee charged each academic period. If the beneficiary receives a scholarship or grant, the amount that PACT pays to the institution can be applied to room and board, books, or supplies.

Contract option: A four-year (maximum 135 semester hours) contract is offered.

Costs: There is a one-time $100 enrollment fee. For the August and September 2004 enrollment period, the lump-sum price for a student in the ninth grade was $21,670. Prices were discounted for younger beneficiaries to as low as $18,168 for an infant. The contract price may also be paid in 60 monthly installments or over an extended period through the year of projected enrollment. Monthly payments are computed to include an effective annual 7%–8% cost for making payments over time.

Cancellation provisions: Cancellation of the contract results in a refund of contract payments (less a cancellation fee of $75), plus interest. The rate of interest applied is the average passbook savings interest rate at the five largest Alabama banking institutions, but not greater than 5%, as computed for each year. The program may, at its discretion, pay the refund in installments, rather than in a lump sum. The cancellation fee is waived if the beneficiary has died or become disabled.

Contract changes: The program accepts requests to change beneficiary, and transfer contract ownership. There are no special provisions concerning rollovers to another 529 plan (cancellation provisions would apply).

State backing: Contracts are not backed by the full faith and credit of the state of Alabama. The trustee invests program assets with the goal of creating a reserve to protect against shortfalls in the program fund.

Special considerations:
- Under state law, qualified distributions from this program are exempt from Alabama state income tax. Distributions from other state 529 plans may subject an Alabama resident to Alabama state tax, as Alabama currently does not conform to federal tax treatment of qualified distributions.

STATE: ALABAMA

PROGRAM NAME:	Higher Education 529 Fund
529 TYPE:	Savings
STATE AGENCY:	Board of Trustees of the Trust Fund, chaired by the State Treasurer
PROGRAM MANAGER:	Van Kampen Asset Management Inc.
INITIAL YEAR OF OPERATION:	2002
TELEPHONE:	1–866–529–2228
INTERNET:	www.treasury.state.al.us (direct-sold)
	www.vankampen.com (advisor-sold)

Who can purchase a contract? U.S. citizens and residents 19 years and older, corporations, trusts, estates, and state/local government agencies. This program is distributed both direct and through brokers. Anyone who does not meet Alabama's residency requirements must open their account through a broker.

Time or age limitations on beneficiary or on use of account assets: None

Age-based investment options: The Years to Enrollment option offers five distinct time horizons with up to three risk tolerance levels: Aggressive, Moderate, and Conservative. Contributions are placed into the portfolio corresponding to the option selected and the number of years to expected enrollment, and later reassigned to more conservative portfolios as the beneficiary approaches college.

Static investment options: Select among three blended-fund portfolios (100% equity, 100% bond, and 100% money market and short term securities) and eight individual-fund portfolios within four asset classes (stock and bond, domestic stock, global and international, and bond).

Underlying investments: Mutual funds from Van Kampen

Fees and expenses: A $10 annual account maintenance fee ($25 for Alabama nonresidents) on accounts with $25,000 or less, and underlying fund expenses recently ranging from approximately 0.59% to 1.75% (portfolio weighted average). In addition, accounts opened through a broker are subject to one of three alternative broker expense structures that will determine any initial sales charge, contingent deferred sales charge, and/or additional asset-based fees. There is no enrollment fee.

Maximum contributions: Accepts contributions until all Alabama account balances for the same beneficiary reach $300,000.

Minimum initial contribution: $250 per portfolio for Alabama residents and $1,000 for all others ($25 per month with automatic investment).

Account changes: The program accepts requests to change beneficiary, transfer account ownership, name a successor owner, and transact rollovers and investment changes that meet the requirements of federal tax law and IRS regulations.

Special considerations:

- Distributions from this program, and from other state 529 plans, may subject an Alabama resident to Alabama state tax as Alabama currently does not conform to federal tax treatment of qualified distributions.
- There is pending legislation that, if passed, would exempt qualified distributions from this program from Alabama state income tax for Alabama residents.

STATE: **ALASKA**

PROGRAM NAME:	University of Alaska College Savings Plan
529 TYPE:	Savings
STATE AGENCY:	Education Trust of Alaska
PROGRAM MANAGER:	T. Rowe Price Associates, Inc.
INITIAL YEAR OF OPERATION:	2001
TELEPHONE:	1–866–277–1005
INTERNET:	www.uacollegesavings.com

Who can purchase a contract? U.S. citizens and resident aliens with a valid Social Security number or federal taxpayer identification number, UTMA/UGMA custodians, and legal entities. Not available through brokers.

Time or age limitations on beneficiary or on use of account assets: None

Age-based investment options: The Enrollment-Based Portfolios contain eight portfolios of underlying funds, ranging from 100% equity to 20% equity. Contributions are placed into the portfolio corresponding to the number of years to expected enrollment based on the age of the beneficiary or as selected by the account owner. Seven portfolios shift to a more conservative investment allocation over time, eventually transferring to the College portfolio.

Static investment options: Select among five portfolios: the Equity Portfolio (100% stocks), the Fixed Income Portfolio (100% bonds), the Balanced Portfolio (60% stocks and 40% bonds), the Preservation Portfolio (100% bonds and money market with an insurance wrapper), and the ACT portfolio (mix of stock, bond, and money market funds).

Underlying investments: Mutual funds from T. Rowe Price

Fees and expenses: $30 annual account maintenance fee on accounts less than $25,000 (waived where the owner has at least $75,000 invested in the program for multiple beneficiaries, for accounts enrolled in an automatic investment or payroll deduction plan, and for accounts with an investment in the ACT portfolio), 0.30% annualized program management fee charged against the value of the account (no management fee for ACT), and underlying fund expenses recently ranging from approximately 0.45% to 0.80%. There is no enrollment fee.

Maximum contributions: Accepts contributions until all Alaska account balances for the same beneficiary reach $250,000.

Minimum initial contribution: $250, or $50 per month

Account changes: The program accepts requests to change beneficiary, transfer account ownership, name a successor owner, and transact rollovers and investment changes that meet the requirements of federal tax law and IRS regulations.

Special considerations:
- The ACT portfolio carries a guarantee by the Education Trust of Alaska that the earnings rate will keep pace with tuition inflation at the University of Alaska to the extent that account assets are used to pay for tuition at the University of Alaska.
- Contributions can be made by Alaska residents to any portfolio in the plan directly through the annual Alaska Permanent Fund Dividend.
- There are no state income tax incentives because Alaska does not have a personal income tax.
- Under Alaska law, an account is exempt from a claim by the account holder's or the beneficiary's creditors and is not subject to involuntary transfer or alienation (with an exception relating to certain valid child support orders).

STATE: **ALASKA**

PROGRAM NAME: T. Rowe Price College Savings Plan
529 TYPE: Savings
STATE AGENCY: Education Trust of Alaska
PROGRAM MANAGER: T. Rowe Price Associates, Inc.
INITIAL YEAR OF OPERATION: 2001
TELEPHONE: 1–800–369–3641
INTERNET: www.troweprice.com/collegesavings

Who can purchase a contract? U.S. citizens and resident aliens with a valid Social Security number or federal taxpayer identification number, UTMA/UGMA custodians, and legal entities. Not available through brokers.

Time or age limitations on beneficiary or on use of account assets: None

Age-based investment options: The Enrollment-Based Portfolios contain eight portfolios of underlying funds, ranging from 100% equity to 20% equity. Contributions are placed into the portfolio corresponding to the number of years to expected enrollment based on the age of the beneficiary or as selected by the account owner. Seven portfolios shift to a more conservative investment allocation over time, eventually transferring to the College portfolio.

Static investment options: Select among four portfolios: the Equity Portfolio (100% stocks), the Fixed Income Portfolio (100% bonds), the Balanced Portfolio (60% stocks and 40% bonds), and the Preservation Portfolio (100% bonds and money market with an insurance wrapper).

Underlying investments: Mutual funds from T. Rowe Price

Fees and expenses: $30 annual account maintenance fee on accounts less than $25,000 (waived where the owner has at least $75,000 invested in the program for multiple beneficiaries, and for accounts enrolled in an automatic investment or payroll deduction plan), 0.30% annualized program management fee charged against the value of the account, and underlying fund expenses recently ranging from approximately 0.45% to 0.80%. There is no enrollment fee.

Maximum contributions: Accepts contributions until all Alaska account balances for the same beneficiary reach $250,000.

Minimum initial contribution: $250, or $50 per month

Account changes: The program accepts requests to change beneficiary, transfer account ownership, name a successor owner, and transact rollovers and investment changes that meet the requirements of federal tax law and IRS regulations.

Special considerations:
- There are no state income tax incentives because Alaska does not have a personal income tax.
- Under Alaska law, an account is exempt from a claim by the account holder's or the beneficiary's creditors and is not subject to involuntary transfer or alienation (with an exception relating to certain valid child support orders).

STATE: ALASKA

PROGRAM NAME:	John Hancock Freedom 529
529 TYPE:	Savings
STATE AGENCY:	Education Trust of Alaska
PROGRAM MANAGER:	T. Rowe Price Associates, Inc.
DISTRIBUTION PARTNER:	Manulife Financial Securities, LLC
INITIAL YEAR OF OPERATION:	2001
TELEPHONE:	1–866–222–7498
INTERNET:	www.johnhancockfreedom529.com

Who can purchase a contract? U.S. citizens and resident aliens with a valid Social Security number or federal taxpayer identification number, UTMA/UGMA custodians, and legal entities. This program is distributed through brokers.

Time or age limitations on beneficiary or on use of account assets: None

Age-based investment options: The Enrollment-Based Portfolios contain six multi-managed portfolios of underlying funds, ranging from 100% equity to 20% equity. Contributions are placed into the portfolio corresponding to the number of years to expected enrollment based on the age of the beneficiary or as selected by the account owner. Five portfolios shift to a more conservative investment allocation over time, eventually transferring to the College portfolio.

Static investment options: Select among three blended-fund portfolios (Future Trends Portfolio, Equity Portfolio, and Fixed Income Portfolio), a money market portfolio, and eight individual-fund portfolios. A dollar-cost averaging option provides for automatic monthly reallocations.

Underlying investments: Mutual funds managed by American, Davis, Fidelity, Franklin Templeton, John Hancock, Oppenheimer, PIMCO, and T. Rowe Price.

Fees and expenses: $30 annual account maintenance fee on accounts less than $25,000 (waived for accounts enrolled in an automatic investment plan), 0.75% (Class A shares, and Class B shares in year 7 and after) or 1.65% (Class B shares in years 1 through 6 and Class C shares) annualized program management fee charged against the value of the account, and underlying fund expenses recently ranging from approximately 0.55% to 1.32%. In addition, contributions may be subject to initial or contingent deferred sales charges depending on share class. The Money Market Portfolio is offered without a sales charge and is subject to an annual program management fee of 0.75%. There is no enrollment fee.

Maximum contributions: Accepts contributions until all Alaska account balances for the same beneficiary reach $250,000.

Minimum initial contribution: $1,000, or $50 per month, per portfolio

Account changes: The program accepts requests to change beneficiary, transfer account ownership, name a successor owner, and transact rollovers and investment changes that meet the requirements of federal tax law and IRS regulations.

Special considerations:

- There are no state income tax incentives because Alaska does not have a personal income tax.
- Under Alaska law, an account is exempt from a claim by the account holder's or the beneficiary's creditors and is not subject to involuntary transfer or alienation (with an exception relating to certain valid child support orders).

STATE: ARIZONA

PROGRAM NAME:	Arizona Family College Savings Program (College Savings Bank)
529 TYPE:	Savings
STATE AGENCY:	Arizona Commission for Post-Secondary Education
PROGRAM MANAGER:	College Savings Bank
INITIAL YEAR OF OPERATION:	1999
TELEPHONE:	1–800–888–2723
INTERNET:	http://arizona.collegesavings.com

Who can purchase a contract? U.S. citizens, UTMA/UGMA custodians, trusts, state/local government agencies, and 501(c)(3) organizations. Not available through brokers.

Time or age limitations on beneficiary or on use of account assets: The underlying investments are certificates of deposit (CDs) with maturities ranging from one to twenty-five years, timed to mature in the years the beneficiary attends college and/or graduate school. The CDs are subject to early redemption penalties ranging from 1% to 10% of principal for withdrawals prior to maturity.

Age-based investment options: None

Static investment option: Funds are invested in CollegeSure® Certificates of Deposit, a product of College Savings Bank.

Underlying investments: CollegeSure® CDs issued after August 1, 2003 earn interest at a variable rate pegged to a tuition inflation index, less a 3% margin, not to fall below 2%. The tuition index is the College Board's Independent College 500® Index measuring one full year of average tuition, fees, and room and board at four-year private colleges. The interest rate adjusts each July 31.

Fees and expenses: There are no enrollment or account maintenance fees.

Maximum contributions: Accepts contributions until all Arizona account balances for the same beneficiary reach $275,000.

Minimum initial contribution: $250 lump sum, $100 per month with automatic investments, or $25 per pay period with payroll deduction.

Account changes: The program accepts requests to change beneficiary, transfer account ownership (but only to the beneficiary, or to the owner's spouse as part of a divorce proceeding), and name a successor owner. The Commission has not ruled on whether a qualifying rollover to another 529 plan will be assessed a 10% penalty on earnings.

Special considerations:

- Principal and interest are backed by the full faith and credit of the U.S. Government up to $100,000 per depositor.
- Under state law, qualified distributions from this program and all other 529 plans are exempt from Arizona state income tax.
- The value of the account will not be counted in determining eligibility and need for student financial aid programs provided by the state of Arizona.
- The account is established as a revocable trust with spendthrift provisions, providing additional protection from creditors.

STATE: **ARIZONA**

PROGRAM NAME:	Arizona Family College Savings Program (SM&R)
529 TYPE:	Savings
STATE AGENCY:	Arizona Commission for Post-Secondary Education
PROGRAM MANAGER:	Securities Management and Research, Inc.
INITIAL YEAR OF OPERATION:	1999
TELEPHONE:	1–888–66–READY (1–888–667–3239)
INTERNET:	www.smrinvest.com/college

Who can purchase a contract? U.S. citizens, UTMA/UGMA custodians, trusts, state/local governments, and 501(c)(3) organizations. This program is distributed both direct and through brokers.

Time or age limitations on beneficiary or on use of account assets: None

Age-based investment options: None

Static investment options: Select among ten SM&R mutual funds ranging from technology to money market.

Underlying investments: SM&R mutual funds, including SM&R Alger funds.

Fees and expenses: $10 enrollment fee per mutual fund and underlying fund expenses recently ranging from approximately 0.49% to 1.29% for the fixed income funds and from 1.30% to 2.10% for the equity funds. In addition, accounts opened through a broker are subject to one of two alternative broker expense structures that will determine any initial sales charge, contingent deferred sales charge, and/or additional asset-based fees. There is no account maintenance fee.

Maximum contributions: Accepts contributions until all Arizona account balances for the same beneficiary reach $275,000.

Minimum initial contribution: $20 to $500 per mutual fund depending on fund and frequency of contribution.

Account changes: The program accepts requests to change beneficiary, transfer account ownership, name a successor owner, and transact rollovers and investment changes that meet the requirements of federal tax law and IRS regulations.

Special considerations:

- Under state law, qualified distributions from this program and all other 529 plans are exempt from Arizona state income tax.

- The value of the account will not be counted in determining eligibility and need for student financial aid programs provided by the state of Arizona.

STATE:	**ARIZONA**

PROGRAM NAME:	Waddell & Reed InvestEd Plan
529 TYPE:	Savings
STATE AGENCY:	Arizona Commission for Post-Secondary Education
PROGRAM MANAGER:	Waddell & Reed
INITIAL YEAR OF OPERATION:	2001
TELEPHONE:	1–888–WADDELL (1–888–923–3355)
INTERNET:	www.waddell.com

Who can purchase a contract? U.S. citizens and resident aliens with a valid federal tax-payer identification number, UTMA/UGMA custodians, trusts, state/local government agencies, and 501(c)(3) organizations. This program is distributed through Waddell & Reed advisors or Legend advisors.

Time or age limitations on beneficiary or on use of account assets: None

Age-based investment option: Contributions are placed into one of three portfolios—Growth (ages 0–8), Balanced (ages 9–15), or Conservative (ages 16 and up)—corresponding to the beneficiary's age, and later reassigned to more conservative portfolios as the beneficiary reaches certain ages.

Static investment options: Select among three portfolios: Growth, Balanced, or Conservative. Each portfolio invests in six or seven underlying mutual funds.

Underlying investments: Waddell & Reed Advisors Funds

Fees and expenses: $10 enrollment fee. Total annual expenses, including underlying fund expenses, distribution fees, and other expenses, range from 1.68% to 1.83% for Class A shares and from 2.43% to 2.62% for Class B and C shares. These figures are net of a 0.30% fee waiver through April 30, 2005. In addition, initial and deferred sales charges may apply depending on share class. There is no account maintenance fee.

Maximum contributions: Accepts contributions until all Arizona account balances for the same beneficiary reach $275,000.

Minimum initial contribution: $500 lump-sum, $50 per month with automatic contributions, or $25 per payroll with payroll deduction.

Account changes: The program accepts requests to change beneficiary, transfer account ownership, name a successor owner, and transact rollovers and investment changes that meet the requirements of federal tax law and IRS regulations.

Special considerations:
- Under state law, qualified distributions from this program and all other 529 plans are exempt from Arizona state income tax.
- The value of the account will not be counted in determining eligibility and need for student financial aid programs provided by the state of Arizona.

STATE: ARIZONA

PROGRAM NAME:	Pacific Funds 529 College Savings Plan (Arizona)
529 TYPE:	Savings
STATE AGENCY:	Arizona Commission for Post-Secondary Education
PROGRAM MANAGER:	Pacific Life
INITIAL YEAR OF OPERATION:	2003
TELEPHONE:	1–800–722–2333
INTERNET:	www.collegesavings.PacificLife.com (AZ residents)
	www.PacificLife.com (nonresidents)

Who can purchase a contract? Individuals (including joint ownership with spouse), UTMA/UGMA custodians, state/local government agencies, and 501(c)(3) organizations. This program is distributed both direct and through brokers. Anyone who does not meet Arizona's residency requirements must open their account through a broker.

Time or age limitations on beneficiary or on use of account assets: None

Age-based investment options: None

Static investment option: Select among five fund-of-fund options and fifteen individual-fund options.

Underlying investments: Pacific Funds, including subadvised funds with AIM, Goldman Sachs, Invesco, Janus, Lazard, MFS, PIMCO, Pacific Life, Putnam, Salomon Brothers, and Van Kampen.

Fees and expenses: $10 enrollment fee, (waived for Arizona residents purchasing direct), and underlying fund expenses which vary by fund and share class. In addition, accounts opened through a broker are subject to one of three alternative broker expense structures that will determine any initial sales charge, contingent deferred sales charge, and/or additional asset-based fees. There is no account maintenance fee.

Maximum contributions: Accepts contributions until all Arizona account balances for the same beneficiary reach $275,000.

Minimum initial contribution: $500 per fund, or $50 per fund per month

Account changes: The program accepts requests to change beneficiary, transfer account ownership (but only to beneficiary, to custodian of beneficiary, or to owner's spouse as part of a divorce proceeding), name a successor owner, and transact rollovers and investment changes that meet the requirements of federal tax law and IRS regulations.

Special considerations:

- Under state law, qualified distributions from this program and all other 529 plans are exempt from Arizona state income tax.
- Accounts are subject to spendthrift provisions, providing additional protection from creditors.
- The value of the account will not be counted in determining eligibility and need for student financial aid programs provided by the state of Arizona.

STATE:	**ARKANSAS**
PROGRAM NAME:	GIFT College Investing Plan
529 TYPE:	Savings
STATE AGENCY:	Committee composed of the Director of the Department of Higher Education, the Executive Director of the Arkansas Teacher Retirement System, and the Treasurer of State
PROGRAM MANAGER:	Mercury Advisors
DISTRIBUTION PARTNER:	Franklin Templeton Investments
INITIAL YEAR OF OPERATION:	1999
TELEPHONE:	1–877–615–4116
INTERNET:	www.thegiftplan.com

Who can purchase a contract? Individuals, UTMA/UGMA custodians, and legal entities. This program is distributed both direct and through brokers. Anyone who does not meet Arkansas residency requirements must open their account through a broker.

Time or age limitations on beneficiary or on use of account assets: None

Age-based investment option: The Age-Tailored Active Allocation Option contains nine portfolios of underlying mutual funds. Contributions are placed into the portfolio corresponding to the beneficiary's age, or as selected by the account owner, and later reassigned to more conservative portfolios as the beneficiary approaches college.

Static investment options: Select among four portfolios: Growth (100% equity), Growth and Income (75% equity), Balanced (50% equity) and Fixed-Income.

Underlying investments: Mutual funds from Merrill Lynch Investment Managers and Franklin Templeton.

Fees and expenses: $25 annual account maintenance fee on accounts less than $20,000 (waived for Arkansas residents), 0.55% annualized program management fee charged against the value of the account, and underlying fund expenses recently ranging from approximately 0.83% to 1.33% (portfolio weighted average). In addition, accounts opened through a broker are subject to one of three alternative broker expense structures that will determine any initial sales charge, contingent deferred sales charge, and/or additional asset-based fees. There is no enrollment fee.

Maximum contributions: Accepts contributions until all Arkansas account balances for the same beneficiary reach $245,000.

Minimum initial contribution: $250 for Arkansas residents; $1,000 for nonresidents.

Account changes: The program accepts requests to change beneficiary, transfer account ownership, name a successor owner, and transact rollovers and investment changes that meet the requirements of federal tax law and IRS regulations.

Special considerations:

- Under state law, qualified distributions from this program and all other 529 plans are exempt from Arkansas state income tax.
- An account, or any legal or beneficial interest in an account, shall not be subject to attachment, levy, or execution by any creditor of an account owner or designated beneficiary.

STATE: **CALIFORNIA**

PROGRAM NAME:	Golden State ScholarShare College Savings Trust
529 TYPE:	Savings
STATE AGENCY:	ScholarShare Investment Board
PROGRAM MANAGER:	TIAA-CREF Tuition Financing, Inc.
INITIAL YEAR OF OPERATION:	1999
TELEPHONE:	1–877–728–4338
INTERNET:	www.scholarshare.com

Who can purchase a contract? Individuals living in the U.S. who have reached the age of majority, emancipated minors, UTMA/UGMA custodians, and legal entities. Not available through brokers.

Time or age limitations on beneficiary or on use of account assets: None

Age-based investment options: Choose between two schedules: the Age-Based Asset Allocation Option and the Aggressive Age-Based Allocation Option. Contributions are placed into one of 11 age bands corresponding to the beneficiary's age and selected schedule. The portfolios automatically shift to a more conservative investment allocation over time.

Static investment options: Select among three portfolios: the 100% Equity Option (80% domestic equity and 20% international equity), the 100% Social Choice Equity Option, and the Guaranteed Option. The Guaranteed Option is invested in an instrument that guarantees principal and a minimum 3% annual rate of interest (actual rate is declared quarterly).

Underlying investments: TIAA-CREF institutional mutual funds; the Guaranteed Option consists of a funding agreement issued by TIAA-CREF Life Insurance Company.

Fees and expenses: 0.70% annualized program management fee charged against the value of the account (none for the Guaranteed Option), which includes the expenses of the underlying mutual funds. The ScholarShare Investment Board also charges an administrative fee of up to 0.10% annually. There are no enrollment or account maintenance fees.

Maximum contributions: Accepts contributions until all California account balances for the same beneficiary reach $275,000.

Minimum initial contribution: $25, or $15 with payroll deduction

Account changes: The program accepts requests to change beneficiary, transfer account ownership, name a successor owner, and transact rollovers and investment changes that meet the requirements of federal tax law and IRS regulations.

Special considerations:

- California does not specifically provide that qualified distributions are exempt from state income tax, but its tax law generally conforms to federal tax law and so any qualified distributions that are exempt from federal income tax are also exempt from California income tax.
- For California residents, a 2.5% California additional tax on earnings is imposed on non-qualified withdrawals from this program and any other 529 plan.

STATE:	**COLORADO**
PROGRAM NAME:	Prepaid Tuition Fund
529 TYPE:	Prepaid unit
STATE AGENCY:	CollegeInvest, a division of the Colorado Department of Higher Education
INITIAL YEAR OF OPERATION:	1997
TELEPHONE:	1–800–448–2424
INTERNET:	www.collegeinvest.org

Please note: This program is closed to new investments and had no plans to re-open at the time this book went to press.

STATE:	**COLORADO**
PROGRAM NAME:	Scholars Choice College Savings Program
529 TYPE:	Savings
STATE AGENCY:	CollegeInvest, a division of the Colorado Department of Higher Education
PROGRAM MANAGER:	Citigroup Asset Management
INITIAL YEAR OF OPERATION:	1999
TELEPHONE:	1–888–5–SCHOLAR (1–888–572–4652)
INTERNET:	www.scholars-choice.com

Who can purchase a contract? U.S. residents, UTMA/UGMA custodians, and legal entities. Although this program has in the past been distributed both direct and through brokers, recent program changes restrict participation to brokered accounts beginning in November 2004.

Time or age limitations on beneficiary or on use of account assets: None

Age-based investment options: The Age-Based and Years to Enrollment options contain up to seven portfolios of underlying mutual funds. Contributions are placed into the portfolio corresponding to the beneficiary's age, or number of years to expected enrollment, and later reassigned to more conservative portfolios as the beneficiary approaches college.

Static investment options: Select among five portfolios: the Balanced 50/50 Option (50% equity and 50% fixed income), the All Equity Option, the All Fixed Income Option, the Equity 80% Option, and the Fixed Income 80% Option.

Underlying investments: Mutual funds managed by Salomon Brothers, Smith Barney, American Funds, and MFS.

Fees and expenses: $20 annual account maintenance fee on accounts less than $2,500 (waived for Colorado residents). For direct-sold accounts, there is a 0.99% to 1.09% annualized program management fee charged against the value of the account, which includes the expenses of the underlying mutual funds. For broker-sold accounts, there are underlying fund expenses recently ranging from approximately 0.50% to 0.79% (portfolio weighted average). In addition, accounts opened through a broker are subject to one of three alternative broker expense structures that will determine any initial sales charge, contingent deferred sales charge, and/or additional asset-based fees. There is no enrollment fee.

Maximum contributions: Accepts contributions until all Colorado account balances for the same beneficiary reach $280,000.

Minimum initial contribution: $25 (no minimum with payroll deduction)

Account changes: The program accepts requests to change beneficiary, transfer account ownership, name a successor owner, and transact rollovers and investment changes that meet the requirements of federal tax law and IRS regulations.

Special considerations:

- Contributions (excluding rollovers) are fully deductible in computing Colorado taxable income. Deductions may be subject to recapture if non-qualified withdrawals or rollovers to another state's 529 plan are made in a subsequent year.
- Under state law, qualified distributions from this program and all other 529 plans are exempt from Colorado state income tax.
- Moneys credited to or expended from the savings trust fund by or on behalf of an account owner, depositor, or designated beneficiary of a savings contract are exempt from all claims of creditors of the account owner, depositor, and designated beneficiary.

STATE: COLORADO

PROGRAM NAME:	Stable Value Plus College Savings Program
529 TYPE:	Savings
STATE AGENCY:	CollegeInvest, a division of the Colorado Department of Higher Education
PROGRAM MANAGER:	Travelers Insurance Company
INITIAL YEAR OF OPERATION:	2003
TELEPHONE:	1–800–448–2424
INTERNET:	www.collegeinvest.org

Who can purchase a contract? U.S. residents, UTMA/UGMA custodians, and legal entities. Not available through brokers.

Time or age limitations on beneficiary or on use of account assets: None

Age-based investment options: None

Static investment option: Funds are invested in a stable value investment under a funding agreement with Travelers Insurance Company. The interest rate is declared annually and is currently 4.05% (3.06% net of program fee) for the year ending December 31, 2004.

Fees and expenses: $20 enrollment fee (waived for accounts opened with a rollover from Colorado's Prepaid Tuition Fund or Scholars Choice programs), and 0.99% annualized program management fee charged against the value of the account, which includes the expenses of the underlying investment. There is no account maintenance fee.

Maximum contributions: Accepts contributions until all Colorado account balances for the same beneficiary reach $280,000.

Minimum initial contribution: $25

Account changes: The program accepts requests to change beneficiary, transfer account ownership, name a successor owner, and transact rollovers that meet the requirements of federal tax law and IRS regulations.

Special considerations:

- Colorado residents receive the same state income tax and creditor protection benefits described previously for the Scholars Choice College Savings Program.

STATE: **COLORADO**

PROGRAM NAME:	To be announced
529 TYPE:	Savings
STATE AGENCY:	CollegeInvest, a division of the Colorado Department of Higher Education
PROGRAM MANAGER:	Upromise Investments, Inc.
INVESTMENT MANAGER:	The Vanguard Group
INITIAL YEAR OF OPERATION:	Not yet open
TELEPHONE:	1–800–448–2424
INTERNET:	www.collegeinvest.org

CollegeInvest has announced plans to launch a new direct-sold 529 savings program to be managed by Upromise Investments, Inc. and The Vanguard Group. Accounts originally opened on a direct basis in the Scholars Choice program will be transferred to this new program when it begins operations.

STATE: **CONNECTICUT**

PROGRAM NAME:	Connecticut Higher Education Trust (CHET)
529 TYPE:	Savings
STATE AGENCY:	Connecticut State Treasurer
PROGRAM MANAGER:	TIAA-CREF Tuition Financing, Inc.
INITIAL YEAR OF OPERATION:	1997
TELEPHONE:	1–888–799–CHET (1–888–799–2438)
INTERNET:	www.aboutchet.com

Who can purchase a contract? U.S. citizens and resident aliens with a valid Social Security number or federal taxpayer identification number, UTMA/UGMA custodians, and legal entities. Not available through brokers.

Time or age limitations on beneficiary or on use of account assets: None

Age-based investment option: The Managed Allocation Option contains 10 portfolios of underlying funds. Contributions are placed into the portfolio corresponding to the age of the beneficiary. The portfolios shift to a more conservative investment allocation over time.

Static investment options: Select between two portfolios: the High Equity Option (80% equity and 20% fixed income and money market), and the Principal Plus Interest Option. The Principal Plus Interest Option is invested in an instrument that guarantees principal and a minimum 3% annual rate of interest (actual rate is declared quarterly).

Underlying investments: TIAA-CREF institutional mutual funds; the Principal Plus Interest Option consists of a funding agreement issued by TIAA-CREF Life Insurance Company

Fees and expenses: 0.57% annualized program management fee charged against the value of the account (none for the Principal Plus Interest Option), and the underlying fund expenses recently ranging from approximately 0.08% to 0.20% (portfolio weighted average, with the total of these two fees not to exceed 0.79%). The program trustee may be reimbursed up to 0.02% of average daily net assets annually for expenses. There are no enrollment or account maintenance fees.

Maximum contributions: Accepts contributions until all Connecticut account balances for the same beneficiary reach $235,000.

Minimum initial contribution: $25, or $15 with payroll deduction

Account changes: The program accepts requests to change beneficiary, transfer account ownership, name a successor owner, and transact rollovers and investment changes that meet the requirements of federal tax law and IRS regulations.

Special considerations:

- Under state law, qualified distributions from this program are exempt from Connecticut income tax. Because Connecticut tax law generally conforms to federal tax law, any qualified distributions from other 529 plans that are exempt from federal income tax are also exempt from Connecticut income tax.

STATE: DELAWARE

PROGRAM NAME:	Delaware College Investment Plan
529 TYPE:	Savings
STATE AGENCY:	Delaware College Investment Board
PROGRAM MANAGER:	Fidelity Investments
INITIAL YEAR OF OPERATION:	1998
TELEPHONE:	1–800–544–1655
INTERNET:	www.fidelity.com/delaware

Who can purchase a contract? U.S. citizens and resident aliens 18 years and older, UTMA/UGMA custodians, trusts, state/local government agencies, and 501(c)(3) organizations. Not available through brokers.

Time or age limitations on beneficiary or on use of account assets: None

Age-based investment option: The Age-Based Strategy contains eight portfolios of underlying funds. Contributions are placed into the portfolio corresponding to the age of the beneficiary or as determined by the account owner. Seven portfolios shift to a more conservative investment allocation over time, eventually transferring to the College portfolio.

Static investment options: Select among three portfolios: 100% equity, 70% equity, and conservative (100% fixed income and money market).

Underlying investments: Fidelity Investments mutual funds

Fees and expenses: $30 annual account maintenance fee on accounts under $25,000 (waived for accounts enrolled in the automatic investment plan), 0.30% annualized program management fee charged against the value of the account, and underlying fund expenses recently ranging from approximately 0.65% to 0.81% (portfolio weighted average). There is no enrollment fee.

Maximum contributions: Accepts contributions until all Delaware account balances for the same beneficiary reach $270,000.

Minimum initial contribution: $500, or $50 per month

Account changes: The program accepts requests to change beneficiary, name a successor owner, and transact rollovers and investment changes that meet the requirements of federal tax law and IRS regulations. Account ownership may not be transferred prior to the owner's death or incapacity.

Special considerations:

- Delaware does not specifically provide that qualified distributions are exempt from state income tax, but its tax law generally conforms to federal tax law and so any qualified distributions that are exempt from federal income tax are also exempt from Delaware income tax.

STATE: **DISTRICT OF COLUMBIA**

PROGRAM NAME:	DC College Savings Plan
529 TYPE:	Savings
STATE AGENCY:	District of Columbia College Savings Program Trust
PROGRAM MANAGER:	Calvert Asset Management Co., Inc.
INITIAL YEAR OF OPERATION:	2002
TELEPHONE:	1–800–987–4859 (DC residents); 1–800–368–2745 (nonresidents)
INTERNET:	www.DCCollegeSavings.com

Who can purchase a contract? U.S. citizens and resident aliens of legal age with a valid Social Security number or federal taxpayer identification number, UTMA/UGMA custodians, and legal entities. This program is distributed both direct and through brokers. Accounts opened by anyone who does not meet District of Columbia residency requirements will be subject to broker expenses.

Time or age limitations on beneficiary or on use of account assets: None

Age-based investment option: The Age-Based Option contains five portfolios of underlying funds. Contributions are placed into the portfolio corresponding to the beneficiary's age or as determined by the account owner, and later reassigned to more conservative portfolios as the beneficiary approaches college. Account owners have the option to freeze the account at a particular portfolio.

Static investment options: Select among six individual-fund portfolios (Income, Balanced, Equity Index, US Large Cap Equity, US Mid Cap Equity, and US Small Cap Equity), and the Stability of Principal Investment Option which guarantees principal and a minimum 3% annual rate of interest.

Underlying investments: Mutual funds managed by Calvert, MFS, Brown Capital, and State Street; the Stability of Principal Investment Option consists of a funding agreement with Acacia Life Insurance Company.

Fees and expenses: $25 enrollment fee (waived for DC residents), $30 annual account maintenance fee (reduced to $15 for DC residents), 0.15% annualized program management fee charged against the value of the account, and underlying fund expenses recently ranging from approximately 0.35% to 1.77% (none for the Stability of Principal Investment Option). In addition, accounts opened through a broker, and DC nonresident accounts opened directly, are subject to an initial sales charge except for contributions invested in the Stability of Principal Investment Option.

Maximum contributions: Accepts contributions until all DC account balances for the same beneficiary reach $260,000.

Minimum initial contribution: $100 lump sum, $25 per month with automatic investments, or $15 per payroll with payroll deduction.

Account changes: The program accepts requests to change beneficiary, transfer account ownership, name a successor owner, and transact rollovers and investment changes that meet the requirements of federal tax law and IRS regulations.

Special considerations:

- Up to $3,000 ($6,000 for married couples filing joint returns where both spouses are account owners) of total annual contributions may be deducted from DC taxable income each year. Rollover contributions or contributions made by someone other than the account owner are not eligible for the deduction. Contributions in excess of $3,000 may be carried forward and deducted for up to five additional years. Deductions may be subject to recapture if non-qualified withdrawals or rollovers within two years of opening an account to another state's 529 plan are made in a subsequent year.
- Under DC law, qualified distributions from this program are exempt from DC income tax. Because DC tax law generally conforms to federal tax law, any qualified distributions from other 529 plans that are exempt from federal income tax are also exempt from DC income tax.

STATE: **FLORIDA**

PROGRAM NAME:	Florida Prepaid College Plan
529 TYPE:	Prepaid contract
STATE AGENCY:	Florida Prepaid College Board
INITIAL YEAR OF OPERATION:	1987
TELEPHONE:	1–800–552–GRAD (1–800–552–4723)
INTERNET:	www.florida529plans.com

Who can purchase a contract? Individuals 18 years and older, and legal entities. The beneficiary must be a Florida resident or the child of a divorced parent who is a Florida resident.

Enrollment period: Early Fall through January of each year

Time or age limitations on beneficiary or on use of benefits: The beneficiary must be under 21 years of age and below the 12th grade at the time of program enrollment. Contract benefits must be used within 10 years after the projected college enrollment date; however, the contract owner may extend the benefits for an additional 10 years.

Contract benefits: The contract pays in-state undergraduate tuition at Florida public institutions, with optional plans that pay local fees and/or dormitory housing. If the beneficiary attends an accredited, not-for-profit, four-year, degree-granting independent college or university in Florida, or a qualified out-of-state college, the program will transfer an amount equal to current rates at public universities in Florida.

Contract options: There are three options. The Four-Year University Tuition Plan covers 120 semester credit hours at a public university in Florida. The 2 + 2 Tuition Plan covers 60 semester credit hours at a community college and 60 semester credit hours at a public university in Florida. The Two-Year Community College Tuition Plan covers 60 semester credit hours at a community college in Florida. The program also offers an optional dormitory plan and an optional local mandatory fee plan.

Costs: There is a one-time $50 enrollment fee. For the Fall 2003 enrollment period, lump-sum contract prices for a child in the 11th grade ranged from $3,374 for the two-year community college tuition plan to $10,186 for the four-year university tuition plan. Prices are discounted for younger beneficiaries. Contract payments may be made in a lump sum, 55 monthly installments, or in monthly installments until October of the scheduled enrollment year. Monthly installment payments are computed to include an additional cost for making payments over time.

Cancellation provisions: Contracts can be canceled at any time. The refund amount will be the payments made. For contracts less than two years old, the refund is reduced by a cancellation fee of the lesser of $50 or 50% of payments. In the case of death, disability, or receipt of scholarship, the cancellation fee will be waived, and the contract owner will be refunded an amount equal to the current rates at Florida public universities.

Contract changes: The program accepts requests to change beneficiary if transferred prior to matriculation, transfer contract ownership, and name a successor owner. There are no special provisions concerning rollovers to another 529 plan (cancellation provisions would apply).

State backing: The program is backed by the full faith and credit of the state of Florida. If the state of Florida terminates the program, all beneficiaries within five years of enrollment are guaranteed full contract benefits. Others are guaranteed to receive a refund of payments made into the program, plus interest.

Special considerations:

- The beneficiary will be eligible to attend Florida state universities and community colleges as a resident for tuition purposes even if he or she moves away from Florida prior to matriculation.

- Payments in the program are exempt from forfeiture under Florida law. This exemption may be recognized by a bankruptcy court if claimed by the debtor.
- There are no state income tax incentives because Florida does not have a personal income tax.

STATE: **FLORIDA**

PROGRAM NAME:	Florida College Investment Plan
529 TYPE:	Savings
STATE AGENCY AND PROGRAM MANAGER:	Florida Prepaid College Board
INITIAL YEAR OF OPERATION:	2002
TELEPHONE:	1–800–552–GRAD (1–800–552–4723)
INTERNET:	www.florida529plans.com

Who can purchase a contract? U.S. citizens and resident aliens 18 years and older, UTMA/UGMA custodians, and legal entities. Not available through brokers.

Time or age limitations on beneficiary or on use of account assets: None

Age-based investment option: The Age-Based / Years-To-Enrollment Option allocates the account between the Fixed Income option and the U.S. Equity option based on the age of the beneficiary or the number of years to enrollment. Contributions are placed into one of five bands, and later reassigned to more conservative bands as the beneficiary approaches college.

Static investment options: Select among four portfolios: Fixed Income, U.S. Equity, Balanced, and Money Market.

Underlying investments: Investment portfolios separately managed by U.S. Trust Company of New York, Trusco Capital Management, Deutsche Asset Management, and Northern Trust Investments.

Fees and expenses: $50 enrollment fee and 0.75% annualized program management fee charged against the value of the account, which includes the expenses of the investment managers. There is no account maintenance fee.

Maximum contributions: Accepts contributions until all Florida account balances for the same beneficiary reach $287,000.

Minimum initial contribution: $25, or $15 with automatic investment or payroll deduction; $250 minimum balance required within 24 months of establishing the account.

Account changes: The program accepts requests to change beneficiary, transfer account ownership, name a successor owner, and transact rollovers and investment changes that meet the requirements of federal tax law and IRS regulations.

Special considerations:

- There are no state income tax incentives because Florida does not have a personal income tax.
- Amounts paid into or out of the program by or on behalf of the account owner or the designated beneficiary are exempt from all claims of creditors.

STATE:	**GEORGIA**
PROGRAM NAME:	Georgia Higher Education Savings Plan
529 TYPE:	Savings
STATE AGENCY:	Board of Directors of the Georgia Higher Education Savings Plan
PROGRAM MANAGER:	TIAA-CREF Tuition Financing, Inc.
INITIAL YEAR OF OPERATION:	2002
TELEPHONE:	1–877–424–4377
INTERNET:	www.gacollegesavings.com

Who can purchase a contract? Individuals, UTMA/UGMA custodians, and legal entities. Not available through brokers.

Time or age limitations on beneficiary or on use of account assets: None. However, an account must be open for one year in order to avoid Georgia state income taxes on the earnings portion of a withdrawal.

Age-based investment options: The program offers a choice between two schedules: the Managed Allocation Option and the Aggressive Managed Allocation Option. Contributions are placed into the portfolio corresponding to the selected schedule and the age of the beneficiary. The portfolios shift to a more conservative investment allocation over time.

Static investment options: Select among three portfolios: the 100% Equity Option, the Balanced Option, and the Guaranteed Option. The Guaranteed Option is invested in an instrument that guarantees principal and a minimum 3% annual rate of interest (actual rate is declared quarterly).

Underlying investments: TIAA-CREF institutional mutual funds; the Guaranteed Option consists of a funding agreement issued by TIAA-CREF Life Insurance Company.

Fees and expenses: 0.85% annualized program management fee charged against the value of the account (none for the Guaranteed Option), which includes the expenses of the underlying mutual funds. There are no enrollment or account maintenance fees.

Maximum contributions: Accepts contributions until all Georgia account balances for the same beneficiary reach $235,000.

Minimum initial contribution: $25, or $15 with payroll deduction

Account changes: The program accepts requests to change beneficiary, transfer account ownership, name a successor owner, and transact rollovers and investment changes that meet the requirements of federal tax law and IRS regulations.

Special considerations:

- Contributions up to $2,000 per dependent beneficiary may be deducted from Georgia taxable income each year for parents or guardians who itemize on their federal tax return and have an adjusted gross income under $50,000 for single filers or $100,000 for joint filers. The maximum deduction allowable per beneficiary decreases by $400 for each $1,000 of federal adjusted gross income over the applicable limit. Deductions may be subject to recapture if non-qualified withdrawals are made in a subsequent year or if qualified withdrawals are made within one year of establishing the account.
- Under state law, qualified distributions from this program are exempt from Georgia income tax, except for withdrawals within one year of opening the account. Because Georgia tax law generally conforms to federal tax law, any qualified distributions from other 529 plans that are exempt from federal income tax are also exempt from Georgia income tax.
- The value of the account will not be counted in determining eligibility and need for student financial aid programs provided by the state of Georgia.

STATE: **HAWAII**

PROGRAM NAME:	TuitionEDGE
529 TYPE:	Savings
STATE AGENCY:	State of Hawaii College Savings Trust Fund
PROGRAM MANAGER:	Delaware Investments
INITIAL YEAR OF OPERATION:	2002
TELEPHONE:	1–866–529–3343
INTERNET:	www.tuitionedge.com

Who can purchase a contract? U.S. citizens and permanent residents who have reached the age of majority, UTMA/UGMA custodians, and legal entities. This program is distributed both direct and through brokers. Anyone who does not meet Hawaii's residency requirements must open their account through a broker.

Time or age limitations on beneficiary or on use of account assets: None

Age-based investment option: The Age-Based option contains seven portfolios of underlying investment strategies. Contributions are placed into the portfolio corresponding to the beneficiary's age, and later reassigned to more conservative portfolios as the beneficiary approaches college.

Static investment options: Select among four portfolios: Aggressive, Balanced, Conservative, and a Savings Account option with First Hawaiian Bank.

Underlying investments: Delaware Investment custom investment strategies

Fees and expenses: $25 annual account maintenance fee on accounts with $10,000 or less (waived for Hawaii residents), and 0.95% (none for the Savings Account option) annualized program management fee charged against the value of the account, which includes the expenses of the underlying investment strategies. There is no enrollment fee. In addition, accounts opened through a broker are subject to one of three alternative broker expense structures that will determine any initial sales charge, contingent deferred sales charge, and/or additional asset-based fees.

Maximum contributions: Accepts contributions until all Hawaii account balances for the same beneficiary reach $305,000.

Minimum initial contribution: $15 per investment option

Account changes: The program accepts requests to change beneficiary, transfer account ownership, name a successor owner, and transact rollovers and investment changes that meet the requirements of federal tax law and IRS regulations.

Special considerations:
- Hawaii does not specifically provide that qualified distributions are exempt from state income tax, but its tax law generally conforms to federal tax law and so any qualified distributions that are exempt from federal income tax are also exempt from Hawaii income tax.

STATE: **IDAHO**

PROGRAM NAME:	Idaho College Savings Program (IDeal)
529 TYPE:	Savings
STATE AGENCY:	Idaho College Savings Program Board
PROGRAM MANAGER:	TIAA-CREF Tuition Financing, Inc.
INITIAL YEAR OF OPERATION:	2001
TELEPHONE:	1–866–IDEALED (1–866–433–2533)
INTERNET:	www.idsaves.org

Who can purchase a contract? Individuals, UTMA/UGMA custodians, and legal entities. Not available through brokers.

Time or age limitations on beneficiary or on use of account assets: None

Age-based investment option: The Managed Allocation Option contains 11 portfolios of underlying mutual funds. Contributions are placed into the portfolio corresponding to the age of the beneficiary. The portfolios shift to a more conservative investment allocation over time.

Static investment options: Select between two portfolios: the 100% Equity Option (80% domestic equity and 20% international equity) and the Guaranteed Option. The Guaranteed Option is invested in an instrument that guarantees principal and a minimum 3% annual rate of interest (actual rate is declared quarterly).

Underlying investments: TIAA-CREF institutional mutual funds; the Guaranteed Option consists of a funding agreement issued by TIAA-CREF Life Insurance Company.

Fees and expenses: 0.70% annualized program management fee charged against the value of the account (none for the Guaranteed Option), and underlying fund expenses recently ranging from approximately 0.16% to 0.23% (portfolio weighted average). There are no enrollment or account maintenance fees.

Maximum contributions: Accepts contributions until all Idaho account balances for the same beneficiary reach $235,000.

Minimum initial contribution: $25, or $15 with payroll deduction

Account changes: The program accepts requests to change beneficiary, transfer account ownership, name a successor owner, and transact rollovers and investment changes that meet the requirements of federal tax law and IRS regulations.

Special considerations:

- Contributions of up to $4,000 annually per claimant ($8,000 for joint filers) may be deducted from Idaho taxable income.
- An Idaho taxpayer must include the entire amount of a non-qualified withdrawal in Idaho income, whether or not contributions were entirely deducted.
- Idaho does not specifically provide that qualified distributions are exempt from state income tax, but its tax law generally conforms to federal tax law and so any qualified distributions that are exempt from federal income tax are also exempt from Idaho income tax.

STATE: ILLINOIS

PROGRAM NAME:	College Illinois!
529 TYPE:	Prepaid contract
STATE AGENCY:	Illinois Student Assistance Commission
INITIAL YEAR OF OPERATION:	1998
TELEPHONE:	1–877–877–3724
INTERNET:	www.collegeillinois.com

Who can purchase a contract? U.S. residents 18 years and older, UTMA/UGMA custodians, and legal entities. The purchaser or beneficiary must be an Illinois resident for at least 12 months prior to program enrollment.

Enrollment period: Begins October 27, 2004 and ends March 31, 2005 (August 1, 2005 for newborns)

Time or age limitations on beneficiary or on use of benefits: The contract must be purchased at least three years before benefits can be used to pay for tuition and fees; beneficiary must begin using contract benefits within ten years of the projected college enrollment date and then has ten years to use all benefits.

Contract benefits: The contract pays in-state undergraduate tuition and mandatory fees at an Illinois public institution according to the plan and number of years selected. The value derived from the contract will depend in part on the selection of institution, because public institutions in Illinois have different tuition and fee levels. If the beneficiary decides to attend a private college in Illinois or an out-of-state college, the program will pay the equivalent value of the contract based on the average mean-weighted credit hour cost of in-state tuition and fees. A $15 fee will be deducted from the benefit for each different private or out-of-state institution the student attends. If the beneficiary receives a scholarship or grant, a semester-by-semester refund of the value of the benefits can be requested, or the benefits can be retained to pay for graduate school or continuing education.

Contract options: One to nine semesters at a public four-year university, one to four semesters at an Illinois community college, or a combination of four semesters at a community college and four semesters at a public university.

Costs: There is a one-time $85 enrollment fee (reduced to $50 for subsequent applications by the same purchaser). In the enrollment period that ended March 31, 2004, lump-sum contract prices for a child in the ninth grade or higher ranged from $1,206 for the one-semester community college plan to $33,983 for the nine-semester university plan. Prices are discounted for younger beneficiaries grouped in ranges by grade in school. Contract payments may be made in a lump sum, in monthly or annual installments, or by combination of down payment and monthly installments. Installment payments are computed to include an effective annual 8% cost for making payments over time along with a small account maintenance fee.

Cancellation provisions: The contract may be canceled at any time after three years for a refund of all contract payments, plus interest at 2% annually, less a cancellation fee of up to $100. Cancellation within three years does not return any interest. In the event of the beneficiary's death, disability, or receipt of scholarship, the refund is based on the average mean-weighted credit hour cost of in-state tuition and fees, and a cancellation fee is not assessed.

Contract changes: The program accepts requests to change beneficiary, transfer contract ownership, and name a successor owner. There are no special provisions concerning rollovers to another 529 plan (cancellation provisions would apply).

State backing: Contracts are not backed by the full faith and credit of the state of Illinois. If the program is discontinued, beneficiaries who are enrolled in college, or will be within five years, are entitled to all contract benefits; others will receive a return of contributions plus interest. The Governor and General Assembly must consider legislative appropriation of funds to the extent needed to cover program liabilities in the event the program is discontinued.

Special considerations:
- Under state law, qualified distributions from College Illinois! are exempt from Illinois state income tax. Distributions from other state 529 plans may subject an Illinois resident to Illinois state tax, as Illinois currently does not conform to federal tax treatment of qualified distributions.
- Beginning in 2005, payments into the program are deductible from Illinois income tax.

STATE: ILLINOIS

PROGRAM NAME:	Bright Start College Savings Program
529 TYPE:	Savings
STATE AGENCY:	Illinois State Treasurer
PROGRAM MANAGER:	Citigroup Asset Management
INITIAL YEAR OF OPERATION:	2000
TELEPHONE:	1–877–43–BRIGHT (1–877–432–7444)
INTERNET:	www.brightstartsavings.com

Who can purchase a contract? U.S. residents, UTMA/UGMA custodians, and legal entities. Accounts may be opened directly with the program or through participating financial
institutions and brokers.

Time or age limitations on beneficiary or on use of account assets: None

Age-based investment options: Choose between the Aged-Based Option or the Aged-
Based with Bank Deposits Option. Each contains six portfolios of underlying mutual and
money market funds. Contributions are placed into the portfolio corresponding to the
beneficiary's age, and later reassigned to more conservative portfolios as the beneficiary
approaches college. For accounts opened through participating Illinois banks, fully insured
or collateralized bank deposits are substituted for a portion of the fixed income and/or
money market funds.

Static investment options: Select among four portfolios: the Equity Portfolio, the Fixed
Income Portfolio, the Fixed-Income Portfolio with Bank Deposits, and the Principal Protection Income Portfolio. For accounts opened through participating Illinois banks, the only
option is the Fixed Income Portfolio with Bank Deposits.

Underlying investments: Mutual funds from Smith Barney, MFS, and Salomon Brothers,
and a stable value investment from Aegon; for accounts opened through participating Illinois banks, certificates of deposit comprise 50% of the Fixed Income Portfolio.

Fees and expenses: 0.99% annualized program management fee charged against the
value of the account, which includes the expenses of the underlying mutual funds. There
are no enrollment or account maintenance fees, except that accounts opened through a
participating financial institution may be charged up to $30 as a one-time processing fee.
Accounts may be opened through participating financial institutions, Salomon Smith Barney brokers and certain third-party selling agents without additional program expenses or
sales charges.

Maximum contributions: Accepts contributions until all Illinois account balances for the
same beneficiary reach $235,000.

Minimum initial contribution: $25 (no minimum with payroll deduction)

Account changes: The program accepts requests to change beneficiary, transfer account ownership, name a successor owner, and transact rollovers and investment changes that meet the requirements of federal tax law and IRS regulations.

Special considerations:

- All contributions in 2004, except for the earnings portion of a rollover from another 529 plan, are fully deductible in computing Illinois taxable income. Beginning in 2005, each contributor is limited to $10,000 in annual deductions.
- Under state law, qualified distributions from Bright Start are exempt from Illinois state income tax. Distributions from other state 529 plans may subject an Illinois resident to Illinois state tax, as Illinois currently does not conform to federal tax treatment of qualified distributions.

STATE: INDIANA

PROGRAM NAME:	CollegeChoice 529 Investment Plan
529 TYPE:	Savings
STATE AGENCY:	Indiana Education Savings Authority (IESA)
PROGRAM MANAGER:	One Group Investments
INITIAL YEAR OF OPERATION:	1997
TELEPHONE:	1–866–400–PLAN (1–866–400–7526)
INTERNET:	www.collegechoiceplan.com

Who can purchase a contract? Individuals 18 years and older, emancipated minors, UTMA/UGMA custodians, and legal entities. Direct enrollment is subject to broker expenses except that the initial sales charge is waived for Indiana residents who invest in the age-based option without the services of a financial advisor.

Time or age limitations on beneficiary or on use of account assets: None

Age-based investment option: The Age-Based Program contains five portfolios of underlying mutual funds. Contributions are placed into the portfolio corresponding to the beneficiary's age, and later reassigned to more conservative portfolios as the beneficiary approaches college.

Static investment options: Select among four blended-fund portfolios (Growth, Growth & Income, Balanced, and Conservative), and eight individual-fund portfolios.

Underlying investments: Mutual funds from One Group, plus single-fund portfolios offering the Fidelity Advisor Inflation-Protected Bond Fund, Templeton Foreign Fund, Massachusetts Investors Growth Fund, and the Royce Low-Priced Stock Fund.

Fees and expenses: Annual account maintenance fee of $30 for Indiana non-residents, $10 for Indiana residents, and $25 for accounts converted from the Indiana Family College Savings Plan regardless of residence (waived for accounts with balances of at least $25,000 or with automatic contributions), annual state authority fee of $10 for Indiana non-residents only, and underlying fund expenses recently ranging from approximately 0.35% to 1.49% (portfolio weighted average). In addition, except for accounts converted from the predecessor program (Indiana Family College Savings Plan) and other specified situations, accounts are subject to one of three alternative broker expense structures that will determine any initial sales charge, contingent deferred sales charge, and/or additional asset-based fees. Initial sales charges are waived for Indiana residents who invest in the age-based option without the services of a financial advisor. There is no enrollment fee.

Maximum contributions: Accepts contributions until all Indiana account balances for the same beneficiary reach $236,750.

Minimum initial contribution: $50

Account changes: The program accepts requests to change beneficiary (except that a new beneficiary under Fee Structure C must be less than 17 years old), transfer account ownership, name a successor owner, and transact rollovers and investment changes that meet the requirements of federal tax law and IRS regulations.

Special considerations:
- Under state law, qualified distributions from this program are exempt from Indiana income tax. Because Indiana tax law generally conforms to federal tax law, any qualified distributions from other 529 plans that are exempt from federal income tax are also exempt from Indiana income tax.
- The value of the account will not be counted in determining eligibility and need for student financial aid programs provided by the state of Indiana.

STATE: **IOWA**

PROGRAM NAME:	College Savings Iowa
529 TYPE:	Savings
STATE AGENCY:	State Treasurer of Iowa
PROGRAM MANAGERS:	Upromise Investments, Inc. and The Vanguard Group
INITIAL YEAR OF OPERATION:	1998
TELEPHONE:	1–888–672–9116
INTERNET:	www.collegesavingsiowa.com

Who can purchase a contract? U.S. residents 18 years and older, and UTMA/UGMA custodians. Not available through brokers.

Time or age limitations on beneficiary or on use of account assets: None

Age-based investment options: Choose one of four investment tracks that vary in the amount of equity risk assumed. Each track contains five portfolios of underlying investments. Contributions are placed into the portfolio corresponding to the selected track and beneficiary's age, and later reassigned to more conservative portfolios within that track as the beneficiary approaches college.

Static investment options: Select among eight options ranging from an aggressive growth portfolio to a money market portfolio.

Underlying investments: Index mutual funds and a money market fund from Vanguard Group.

Fees and expenses: 0.65% annualized program management fee charged against the value of the account, which includes the expenses of the underlying mutual funds. There are no enrollment or account maintenance fees.

Maximum contributions: Accepts contributions until all Iowa account balances for the same beneficiary reach $239,000.

Minimum initial contribution: $25

Account changes: The program accepts requests to change beneficiary, transfer account ownership, name a successor owner, and transact rollovers and investment changes that meet the requirements of federal tax law and IRS regulations.

Special considerations:

- Account owners may deduct a maximum of $2,290 (in 2004) in contributions each year, per beneficiary, from Iowa state income tax. Deductions may be subject to recapture if non-qualified withdrawals or rollovers to another state's 529 plan are made in a subsequent year.

- Under state law, qualified distributions from this program are exempt from Iowa income tax. Because Iowa tax law generally conforms to federal tax law, any qualified distributions from other 529 plans that are exempt from federal income tax are also exempt from Iowa income tax.

- The value of the account will not be counted in determining eligibility and need for student financial aid programs provided by the state of Iowa.

STATE: KANSAS

PROGRAM NAME:	Learning Quest Education Savings Program
529 TYPE:	Savings
STATE AGENCY:	Kansas State Treasurer
PROGRAM MANAGER:	American Century Investment Management, Inc.
INITIAL YEAR OF OPERATION:	2000
TELEPHONE:	1–800–579–2203 for direct sales
	1–877–882–6236 for broker sales
INTERNET:	www.learningquest.com

Who can purchase a contract? U.S. citizens and resident aliens, UTMA/UGMA custodians, and legal entities. This program is distributed both direct and through brokers.

Time or age limitations on beneficiary or on use of account assets: None

Age-based investment options: The program offers a choice among three investment tracks: Aggressive, Moderate and Conservative. Each track contains seven portfolios of underlying mutual funds. Contributions are placed into the portfolio corresponding to the selected track and the age of the beneficiary as determined by the account owner. Six portfolios shift to a more conservative investment allocation over time, eventually transferring to the Short-Term portfolio.

Static investment options: Select between a 100% equity option and a 100% money market option.

Underlying investments: American Century mutual funds

Fees and expenses: $27 annual account maintenance fee on accounts less than $25,000 (waived for Kansas residents), 0.39% annualized program management fee charged against the value of the account (none for the money market option), and underlying fund expenses recently ranging from approximately 0.47% to 1.00% (portfolio weighted average). There is no enrollment fee. In addition, accounts opened through a broker are subject to one of three alternative broker expense structures that will determine any initial sales charge, contingent deferred sales charge, and/or additional asset-based fees.

Maximum contributions: Accepts contributions until all Kansas account balances for the same beneficiary reach $235,000.

Minimum initial contribution: $2,500 or $50 per month ($500 or $25 per month for Kansas residents).

Account changes: The program accepts requests to change beneficiary, transfer account ownership, name a successor owner, and transact rollovers and investment changes that meet the requirements of federal tax law and IRS regulations.

Special considerations:

- Contributions (excluding rollovers) of up to $2,000 per beneficiary in 2004, increasing to $3,000 per beneficiary per year beginning in 2005, are deductible from Kansas adjusted gross income ($4,000 in 2004 if married, filing jointly, increasing to $6,000 in 2005). Deductions may be subject to recapture if non-qualified withdrawals are made in a subsequent year. Any withdrawals made within the first year of account establishment may be subject to recapture according to Kansas regulations.
- Kansas does not specifically provide that qualified distributions are exempt from state income tax, but its tax law generally conforms to federal tax law and so any qualified distributions that are exempt from federal income tax are also exempt from Kansas income tax.
- There is some creditor protection for accounts established for a beneficiary who is a lineal descendant (some exceptions may apply).

STATE: KANSAS

PROGRAM NAME:	Schwab 529 College Savings Plan
529 TYPE:	Savings
STATE AGENCY:	Kansas State Treasurer
PROGRAM MANAGER:	American Century Investment Management, Inc.
DISTIBUTION PARTNER:	Charles Schwab & Co., Inc.
INITIAL YEAR OF OPERATION:	2003
TELEPHONE:	1–800–435–4000
INTERNET:	www.schwab.com/529

Who can purchase a contract? U.S. citizens and resident aliens, UTMA/UGMA custodians, and legal entities. This program is distributed through Charles Schwab's independent advisors or can be purchased directly through Charles Schwab.

Time or age limitations on beneficiary or on use of account assets: None

Age-based investment options: The program offers a choice among four investment tracks: Aggressive, Moderately Aggressive, Moderately Conservative, and Conservative. Each track contains several portfolios of underlying mutual funds. Contributions are placed into the portfolio corresponding to the selected track and the age of the beneficiary. The portfolios shift to a more conservative investment allocation over time, eventually transferring to the Short-Term portfolio.

Static investment options: Select among six blended-fund portfolios ranging from aggressive to short-term.

Underlying investments: Mutual funds from Transamerica Corporation, Schwab, American Century, Franklin Templeton, and PIMCO.

Fees and expenses: $27 annual account maintenance fee on accounts less than $25,000 (waived for Kansas residents), 0.39% annualized program management fee charged against the value of the account, and underlying fund expenses recently ranging from approximately 0.58% to 1.12% (portfolio weighted average). There is no enrollment fee and no additional broker expenses.

Maximum contributions: Accepts contributions until all Kansas account balances for the same beneficiary reach $235,000.

Minimum initial contribution: $2,500 or $50 per month ($500 or $25 per month for Kansas residents)

Account changes: The program accepts requests to change beneficiary, transfer account ownership, name a successor owner, and transact rollovers and investment changes that meet the requirements of federal tax law and IRS regulations.

Special considerations:

- Kansas residents receive the same state income tax and creditor protection benefits previously described for the Kansas Learning Quest 529 Education Savings Program.

STATE: KENTUCKY

PROGRAM NAME:	Kentucky Education Savings Plan Trust
529 TYPE:	Savings
STATE AGENCY:	Kentucky Higher Education Assistance Authority
PROGRAM MANAGER:	TIAA-CREF Tuition Financing, Inc.
INITIAL YEAR OF OPERATION:	1990
TELEPHONE:	1–877–598–7878
INTERNET:	www.kysaves.com

Who can purchase a contract? Individuals living in the U.S. who have reached the age of majority, emancipated minors, UTMA/UGMA custodians, and legal entities. Not available through brokers.

Time or age limitations on beneficiary or on use of account assets: None

Age-based investment option: The Managed Allocation Option contains 11 portfolios of underlying mutual funds. Contributions are placed into the portfolio corresponding to the age of the beneficiary. The portfolios shift to a more conservative investment allocation over time.

Static investment options: Select between two portfolios: the 100% Equity Option and the Guaranteed Option. The 100% Equity Option invests approximately 80% in the TIAA-CREF Institutional Growth and Income Fund and 20% in the TIAA-CREF Institutional International Equity Fund. The Guaranteed Option is invested in an instrument that guarantees principal and a minimum 3% annual rate of interest (actual rate is declared quarterly).

Underlying investments: TIAA-CREF institutional mutual funds; the Guaranteed Option consists of a funding agreement issued by TIAA-CREF Life Insurance Company.

Fees and expenses: 0.80% annualized program management fee charged against the value of the account (none for the Guaranteed Option), which includes the expenses of the underlying mutual funds. There are no enrollment or account maintenance fees.

Maximum contributions: Accepts contributions until all Kentucky account balances for the same beneficiary reach $235,000.

Minimum initial contribution: $25, or $15 per month with payroll deduction

Account changes: The program accepts requests to change beneficiary, transfer account ownership, name a successor owner, and transact rollovers and investment changes that meet the requirements of federal tax law and IRS regulations.

Special considerations:

- Under state law, qualified distributions from this program are exempt from Kentucky income tax. Because Kentucky tax law generally conforms to federal tax law, any qualified distributions from other 529 plans that are exempt from federal income tax are also exempt from Kentucky income tax.
- Beneficiaries with at least eight years of participation as a Kentucky resident, and $2,400 in contributions, can lock in their eligibility for in-state tuition rates at Kentucky public institutions, even if they later move out of the state.
- The value of the account will not be counted in determining eligibility and need for student financial aid programs provided by the Commonwealth of Kentucky.
- The program guarantees a 4% minimum return on contributions received before October 1, 1999 (this benefit is targeted to participants who saw their accounts converted when TIAA-CREF was hired as program manager).
- Under Kentucky law, contributions and earnings are exempt from levy of execution, garnishment, distress for rent, or fee bill by a creditor of the account owner or beneficiary.

STATE: **KENTUCKY**

PROGRAM NAME: Kentucky's Affordable Prepaid Tuition (KAPT)
529 TYPE: Prepaid contract
STATE AGENCY: Kentucky Higher Education Assistance Authority
INITIAL YEAR OF OPERATION: 2001
TELEPHONE: 1–888–919–KAPT (1–888–919–5278)
INTERNET: www.getKAPT.com

Who can purchase a contract? Individuals of legal age, UTMA/UGMA custodians, and legal entities. The beneficiary must be a Kentucky resident at the time of program enrollment or intend to attend a participating institution in Kentucky.

Enrollment period: Began August 23, 2004 and ends December 13, 2004

Time or age limitations on beneficiary or on use of benefits: Contract must be purchased at least two years prior to the beneficiary's proposed college enrollment date.

Contract benefits: The Value Plan will pay tuition and fees at any school in the Kentucky Community and Technical College System. The Standard Plan will pay tuition and fees equal to the most expensive Kentucky public university in the year of attendance. The Premium Plan represents the average cost of Kentucky's private institutions and grows in value at the same rate as tuition increases at the University of Kentucky. The value of these contracts can be used at any eligible institution in the country. The value of a contract in excess of actual tuition and fees can be used to pay for other expenses such as books, equipment and room and board.

Contract options: There are three tuition plans: Value (one or two years), Standard (one to five years), and Premium (one to five years).

Costs: There is a $50 program enrollment fee for the first contract ($25 for subsequent contracts). For the enrollment period ending December 13, 2004, lump-sum contract prices range from $3,175 for one year to $6,340 for two years in the Value Plan, from $5,724 for one year to $28,578 for five years in the Standard Plan, and from $16,720 for one year to $83,559 for five years in the Premium Plan. Contract payments may be made in a lump sum or in monthly installments (with or without a down payment) over a variety of terms. Monthly installment payments are computed to include an additional cost for making payments over time along with a $1 per month account maintenance fee.

Cancellation provisions: The contract may be canceled at any time. If the contract is canceled before July 1 of the college enrollment year, the refund will consist of the payments made into the program less administration and cancellation fees. If the contract is canceled after July 1 of the college enrollment year, the refund will consist of the payout value less administration and cancellation fees. The refund may be paid in installments. In the event of the beneficiary's death, disability, or receipt of a scholarship, the refund will consist of the payout value and the cancellation fee will be waived.

Contract changes: The program accepts requests to change beneficiary and name a successor owner. Contract ownership is not transferable except in limited circumstances. There are no special provisions concerning rollovers to another 529 plan (cancellation provisions would apply).

State backing: Contracts are not backed by the full faith and credit of the state of Kentucky, but 75 percent of the abandoned property fund administered by the State Treasurer would be available to meet any unfunded liability of the program trust.

Special considerations:

- Under state law, qualified distributions from this program are exempt from Kentucky income tax. Because Kentucky tax law generally conforms to federal tax law, any qualified distributions from other 529 plans that are exempt from federal income tax are also exempt from Kentucky income tax.
- The value of the contract will not be counted in determining eligibility and need for student financial aid programs provided by the Commonwealth of Kentucky.
- Under Kentucky law, the right to benefits is not subject to attachment, garnishment, or seizure by creditors of the purchaser or beneficiary.

STATE: **LOUISIANA**

PROGRAM NAME:	START Saving Program
529 TYPE:	Savings
STATE AGENCIES/PROGRAM MANAGERS:	Louisiana Tuition Trust Authority (LATTA) and Louisiana State Treasurer
INITIAL YEAR OF OPERATION:	1997
TELEPHONE:	1–800–259–5626
INTERNET:	www.startsaving.la.gov

Who can purchase a contract? Individuals, UTMA/UGMA custodians, and legal entities. The account owner or beneficiary must be a Louisiana resident at the time of program enrollment. Not available through brokers.

Time or age limitations on beneficiary or on use of account assets: A minimum of one year must lapse between opening the account and use of the account for qualified higher education expenses.

Age-based investment options: The Age-Based Option contains four portfolios of underlying mutual funds. Contributions are placed into the portfolio corresponding to the beneficiary's age, and later reassigned to more conservative portfolios as the beneficiary approaches college.

Static investment options: Select among five options: the Louisiana Principal Protection Option is 100% invested in the Fixed Earnings fund managed by the Louisiana State Treasurer; the Total Equity Option is 100% invested in the Vanguard Total Stock Market Index Fund Admiral Shares; and the Balanced Option, Equity-Plus Option, and Principal Preservation-Plus Option each represent a blend of those two underlying investments.

Underlying investments: Vanguard LifeStrategy funds, the Vanguard Total Stock Market Index Fund Admiral Shares, and the Fixed Earnings fund managed by the Louisiana State Treasurer.

Fees and expenses: Underlying fund expenses of approximately 0.28% for the Vanguard LifeStrategy funds and approximately 0.15% for the Vanguard Total Stock Market Index Fund. The Fixed Earnings fund does not incur any investment management fees. There are no enrollment, program management, or account maintenance fees.

Maximum contributions: Accepts contributions until all Louisiana account balances for the same beneficiary reach $205,175.

Minimum initial contribution: $10

Account changes: The program accepts requests to change beneficiary, name a successor owner, and transact rollovers and investments changes that meet the requirements of federal tax law and IRS regulations. Account ownership may not be transferred prior to the owner's death or incapacity.

Special considerations:

- The state of Louisiana also provides an Earnings Enhancement (EE) that matches a portion of contributions into the program. The match percentage ranges from 2% to 14% of contributions based on the account owner's federal adjusted gross income and the classification of the account. Currently, the EE portion of any account must be used for qualified higher education expenses and is not refundable.
- Account owners may deduct up to $2,400 of contributions from their Louisiana taxable income for each beneficiary each year. Any unused portion may be carried forward to subsequent years. Deductions may be subject to recapture if non-qualified withdrawals or rollovers to another state's 529 plan are made in a subsequent year.
- Under state law, qualified distributions from this program are exempt from Louisiana income tax. Because Louisiana tax law generally conforms to federal tax law, any qualified distributions from other 529 plans that are exempt from federal income tax are also exempt from Louisiana income tax.
- The value of the account will not be counted in determining eligibility and need for student financial aid programs provided by the state of Louisiana.
- Under Louisiana law, the right of a beneficiary to the assets of the account is not subject to collation, execution, garnishment, attachment, the operation of bankruptcy or insolvency laws or other process of law.
- The state of Louisiana guarantees the redemption value of accounts that are invested in the Fixed Earnings Fund.

STATE: **MAINE**

PROGRAM NAME:	NextGen College Investing Plan
529 TYPE:	Savings
STATE AGENCIES:	Finance Authority of Maine (FAME) and the State Treasurer
PROGRAM MANAGER:	Merrill Lynch
INITIAL YEAR OF OPERATION:	1999
TELEPHONE:	1–877–463–9843
INTERNET:	www.nextgenplan.com

Who can purchase a contract? Individuals, UTMA/UGMA custodians, and legal entities. The program currently offers two investment series. The Client Direct Series is distributed direct. The Client Select Series is available through Merrill Lynch financial advisors and certain Maine distribution agents.

Time or age limitations on beneficiary or on use of account assets: None

Age-based investment options: The Client Direct Series offers two age-based options, the AIM Age-Based Portfolios and the Merrill Lynch Investment Managers (MLIM) Age-Based Portfolios. The Client Select Series offers four age-based options with portfolios using funds from MLIM, AIM, Franklin Templeton, or MFS. Contributions are placed in the portfolio corresponding to the beneficiary's age and desired investment manager, and later reassigned to more conservative portfolios as the beneficiary approaches college.

Static investment options: Select among seven options in the Client Direct Series: MLIM 100% Equity, MLIM 75% Equity, MLIM Fixed Income, MLIM Equity Index, Franklin Templeton Growth, MFS Fixed Income, and the Principal Plus Portfolio. Select among 27 options in the Client Select Series: 14 blended-fund and 12 individual-fund options separately managed by MLIM, AIM, Franklin Templeton, MFS, and OppenheimerFunds, and the Principal Plus Portfolio.

Underlying investments: The Client Direct Series uses mutual funds managed by MLIM; the Client Select Series uses mutual funds separately managed by MLIM, AIM, Franklin Templeton, MFS, and OppenheimerFunds; the Principal Plus Portfolio invests in a guaranteed investment contract issued by Transamerica Life Insurance Company.

Fees and expenses: $50 annual account maintenance fee on accounts less than $20,000 (waived for Maine residents and for accounts with at least $2,500 in annual contributions, and reduced to $25 for payroll plan participants), annualized program management fee of 0.50% (0.475% for the Principal Plus Portfolio and 0.07% for the MLIM Equity Index Portfolio) in the Client Direct Series, and 0.25% (Class A, except the Principal Plus Portfolio incurs 0.425%) or 1.00% (Class C, except the Principal Plus Portfolios incurs 0.725%) in the Client Select Series charged against the value of the account, and underlying fund expenses recently ranging from approximately 0.61% to 2.00%. There is no enrollment fee, but Class A or Class C shares in the Client Select Series may be subject to an initial sales charge or a contingent deferred sales charge. In the Client Direct Series, Maine residents are eligible to receive up to a 0.15% management fee refund.

Maximum contributions: Accepts contributions until all Maine account balances for the same beneficiary reach $275,000.

Minimum initial contribution: $250, or $50 per month

Account changes: The program accepts requests to change beneficiary, transfer account ownership, name a successor owner, and transact rollovers and investment changes that meet the requirements of federal tax law and IRS regulations.

Special considerations:

- Under state law, qualified distributions from this program are exempt from Maine income tax. Because Maine tax law generally conforms to federal tax law, any qualified distributions from other 529 plans that are exempt from federal income tax are also exempt from Maine income tax. Accounts in this program are also excluded from Maine estate tax.
- Participating Maine residents may be eligible for state programs that offer matching grants and fee rebates or waivers. The matching grant of up to $200 for new accounts and $100 per year for existing accounts requires that the participant or beneficiary be a Maine resident and family adjusted gross income be $50,000 or less in the prior year.
- Under Maine law, accounts are not subject to levy, execution, judgment or other operation of law, garnishment or other judicial enforcement, and accounts are not an asset or property of either the account owner or beneficiary for purposes of Maine insolvency laws.

STATE: **MARYLAND**

PROGRAM NAME:	College Savings Plans of Maryland—College Investment Plan
529 TYPE:	Savings
STATE AGENCY:	College Savings Plans of Maryland Board
PROGRAM MANAGER:	T. Rowe Price Associates, Inc.
INITIAL YEAR OF OPERATION:	2001
TELEPHONE:	1–888–4MD–GRAD (1–888–463–4723)
INTERNET:	www.collegesavingsmd.org

Who can purchase a contract? U.S. citizens and resident aliens, UTMA/UGMA custodians, and legal entities. Not available through brokers.

Time or age limitations on beneficiary or on use of account assets: None

Age-based investment options: The Enrollment-Based Portfolios contain eight portfolios of underlying funds, ranging from 100% equity to 20% equity. Contributions are placed into the portfolio corresponding to the beneficiary's expected year of college enrollment or as selected by the account owner. Seven portfolios shift to a more conservative investment allocation over time, eventually transferring to the Portfolio for College.

Static investment options: Select among four portfolios: the Equity Portfolio, the Bond and Income Portfolio, the Balanced Portfolio (60% equity and 40% fixed income), and the Short-term Bond Portfolio.

Underlying investments: T. Rowe Price mutual funds

Fees and expenses: $90 enrollment fee that covers all accounts opened by the same person for the same beneficiary (reduced to $20 in certain circumstances involving rollovers from the Maryland Prepaid College Trust or for current Maryland Prepaid College Trust account owners), $30 annual account maintenance fee on accounts less than $25,000 (waived for accounts enrolled in an automatic investment or payroll deduction plan), 0.38% annualized program management fee charged against the value of the account, and underlying fund expenses recently ranging from approximately 0.35% to 1.25% (however, the expense ratio cap for the plan as a whole is 1.05%).

Maximum contributions: Accepts contributions until all Maryland account balances for the same beneficiary reach $250,000.

Minimum initial contribution: $250, or $25 per month

Account changes: The program accepts requests to change beneficiary, transfer account ownership, name a successor owner, and transact rollovers and investment changes that meet the requirements of federal tax law and IRS regulations.

Special considerations:

- Up to $2,500 in contributions per beneficiary may be deducted each year from Maryland state taxable income. Excess contributions may be carried forward and deducted for up to ten additional years. Deductions may be subject to recapture if non-qualified withdrawals are made in a subsequent year.
- Under state law, qualified distributions from this program are exempt from Maryland income tax. Because Maryland tax law generally conforms to federal tax law, any qualified distributions from other 529 plans that are exempt from federal income tax are also exempt from Maryland income tax.

STATE:	**MARYLAND**
PROGRAM NAME:	College Savings Plans of Maryland—Prepaid College Trust
529 TYPE:	Prepaid contract
STATE AGENCY:	College Savings Plans of Maryland Board
INITIAL YEAR OF OPERATION:	1998
TELEPHONE:	1–888–4MD–GRAD (1–888–463–4723)
INTERNET:	www.collegesavingsmd.org

Who can purchase a contract? U.S. citizens and resident aliens, UTMA/UGMA custodians, and legal entities. The purchaser or beneficiary must be a resident of Maryland or the District of Columbia at the time of program enrollment.

Enrollment period: Most recent enrollment ended March 19, 2004

Time or age limitations on beneficiary or on use of benefits: The beneficiary must be in the ninth grade or below at the time of program enrollment. After high school graduation, the beneficiary has the number of years purchased in the contract plus ten years and time spent in active military service to use all benefits.

Contract benefits: The contract pays in-state undergraduate tuition and mandatory fees at Maryland public institutions according to the plan and number of years selected. The value derived from the contract will depend in part on the selection of institution, because public institutions in Maryland have different tuition and fee levels. If the beneficiary decides to attend a private or out-of-state school, the contract will pay the weighted average tuition and mandatory fees of the Maryland public colleges in the tuition plan purchased or the actual tuition and mandatory fees, whichever is less. If the beneficiary receives a scholarship or grant, any unused benefits can be used for other qualified expenses including tuition charges in excess of weighted average tuition, graduate school tuition, room and board, and books.

Contract options: One to five years at a Maryland public four-year university, two years at a Maryland community college, or a community/university combination (two years of each).

Costs: There is a one-time $75 enrollment fee. The fee is reduced to $20 in certain circumstances involving purchase of additional years, rollovers, or participation in the Maryland College Investment Plan. In the enrollment period that ended March 19, 2004, lump-sum contract prices for a child in the ninth grade ranged from $7,132 for the two-year community college plan to $40,608 for the five-year university plan. Prices are discounted for younger beneficiaries. Payment options also include annual payments, 60 monthly payments or extended monthly payments, which continue until the beneficiary reaches college age. All installment payments are computed to include an effective annual 7.5% cost of making payments over time.

Cancellation provisions: A contract can be canceled at any time to provide a refund of contract payments less a $75 fee, plus or minus 90% (50% if canceled within three years) of the Trust earnings/losses for the period of program participation.

Contract changes: The program accepts requests to change beneficiary, transfer contract ownership, and name a successor owner. The contract value can be transferred to the Maryland College Investment Plan at an amount equal to contract payments less a $20 fee, plus or minus 100% of the Trust earnings/losses for the period of program participation For rollovers to another state's 529 plan, the fee is $75 and the rollover value is equal to payments plus 100% of Trust earnings/losses (75% if the contract is under three years old).

State backing: The program has a legislative guarantee. If it is unable to pay benefits in any given year, the Governor must include in the annual budget the amount needed to pay full benefits. However, the Maryland General Assembly has final approval of all state appropriations. Any appropriation would need to be repaid by the Trust, without interest, over the following two years.

Special considerations:

- Tuition benefits will be adjusted to ensure that the minimum benefit is equal to contract payments plus a reasonable rate of return pegged to the one-year Treasury bill (less 1.2%). That amount less actual tuition and fees can be used to pay for other qualified higher education expenses.

- Maryland taxpayers may deduct up to $2,500 of their payments, per contract, each year from Maryland taxable income, with carryforward of excess payments until all payments have been deducted. Deductions may be subject to recapture if non-qualified withdrawals are made in a subsequent year.
- Under state law, qualified distributions from this program are exempt from Maryland income tax. Because Maryland tax law generally conforms to federal tax law, any qualified distributions from other 529 plans that are exempt from federal income tax are also exempt from Maryland income tax.
- If favorable investment performance causes projected program assets to exceed projected liabilities by at least 30%, the Board has the option to rebate the excess surplus to program participants.
- Under Maryland law, the right to benefits is not subject to attachment, garnishment, or seizure by creditors of the contract owner or the beneficiary.

STATE: **MASSACHUSETTS**

PROGRAM NAME:	U.Fund College Investing Plan
529 TYPE:	Savings
STATE AGENCY:	Massachusetts Educational Financing Authority (MEFA)
PROGRAM MANAGER:	Fidelity Investments
INITIAL YEAR OF OPERATION:	1999
TELEPHONE:	1–800–544–2776
INTERNET:	www.fidelity.com/ufund

Who can purchase a contract? U.S. citizens and resident aliens 18 years and older, UTMA/UGMA custodians, and trusts. Not available through brokers.

Time or age limitations on beneficiary or on use of account assets: None

Age-based investment option: The Age-Based Strategy contains eight portfolios of underlying mutual funds. Contributions are placed into the portfolio corresponding to the age of the beneficiary or as determined by the account owner. Seven portfolios shift to a more conservative investment allocation over time, eventually transferring to the College portfolio.

Static investment options: Select among three portfolios: 100% Equity, 70% Equity, and Conservative (100% fixed income and money market).

Underlying investments: Fidelity Investments mutual funds

Fees and expenses: $30 annual account maintenance fee on accounts under $25,000 (waived for accounts enrolled in the automatic investment plan), 0.30% annualized program management fee charged against the value of the account, and underlying fund expenses recently ranging from approximately 0.64% to 0.81% (portfolio weighted average). There is no enrollment fee.

Maximum contributions: Accepts contributions until all Massachusetts account balances for the same beneficiary reach $250,000.

Minimum initial contribution: $1,000, or $50 per month

Account changes: The program accepts requests to change beneficiary, name a successor owner, and transact rollovers and investment changes that meet the requirements of federal tax law and IRS regulations. Account ownership may not be transferred prior to the owner's death or incapacity.

Special considerations:

- Under state law, qualified distributions from this program and all other 529 plans are exempt from Massachusetts state income tax.

STATE:	**MASSACHUSETTS**
PROGRAM NAME:	U.Plan
CONTRACT TYPE:	Prepaid contract (but does not qualify as a 529 plan)
STATE AGENCY:	Massachusetts Educational Financing Authority (MEFA)
INITIAL YEAR OF OPERATION:	1995
TELEPHONE:	1–800–449–MEFA (1–800–449–6332)
INTERNET:	www.mefa.org

Who can purchase tuition certificates? Any individual. There are no Massachusetts residency requirements.

Enrollment period: May and June

Contract benefits: U.Plan involves the issuance of special purpose Massachusetts general obligation bonds. Participants purchase tuition certificates that may be redeemed at maturity to pay for tuition and fees at participating Massachusetts colleges. They may not be used to pay for other costs such as books or room and board. There are over 80 Massachusetts institutions participating in the program, including many private colleges. Each tuition certificate is worth a predetermined percentage of each institution's tuition and fees, as agreed to by the institutions. If not redeemed for use at a participating Massachusetts institution (for example, the beneficiary attends an out-of-state school), tuition certificates can be redeemed for the principal plus annually compounded interest equal to the Consumer Price Index.

Contract options: There are sixteen years of maturities available for purchase in each enrollment period, with five years being the shortest.

Costs: There is no enrollment fee. The minimum purchase is $300 per maturity year and the maximum purchase is four years of tuition and fees at the highest cost institution participating in the program. For the 2004/2005 school year, the tuition cost of attending one of the participating institutions for one year ranged from $2,556 to $31,228.

Cancellation provisions: Tuition certificates may not be redeemed before their maturity date. If an emergency sale is needed, the program administrator will attempt to find a buyer, with no assurances given.

Contract changes: The beneficiary may be changed within the owner's family.

State backing: Tuition certificates are backed by the full faith and credit of the Commonwealth of Massachusetts.

Special considerations:

- U.Plan does not rely upon the provisions of Section 529. This means that the special income tax and gift and estate tax provisions contained in Section 529 are not applicable.
- Because a tuition certificate represents a general obligation bond, the interest earned is exempt from Massachusetts state income taxes and presumably exempt from federal income tax, although the IRS has not provided a ruling to this effect. The interest may be taxable as it accrues each year on the state income tax return of an owner who resides outside Massachusetts.

STATE: **MICHIGAN**

PROGRAM NAME:	Michigan Education Trust (MET)
529 TYPE:	Prepaid contract
STATE AGENCIES:	MET Board of Directors and Department of Treasury
INITIAL YEAR OF OPERATION:	1988
TELEPHONE:	1–800–MET–4–KID (1–800–638–4543)
INTERNET:	www.met4kid.com

Who can purchase a contract? U.S. residents 18 years and older, UTMA/UGMA custodians, and legal entities. The beneficiary must be a Michigan resident at the time of program enrollment.

Enrollment period: Began September 1, 2004 and ends June 15, 2005

Time or age limitations on beneficiary or on use of benefits: The beneficiary must be in the twelfth grade or below at the time a contract is purchased. Contract benefits must be used within 9 years after the projected college entrance date.

Contract benefits: The contract pays in-state undergraduate tuition and mandatory fees at a Michigan public institution according to the plan and number of years purchased. The value derived from the contract will depend in part on the selection of institution, because public institutions in Michigan have different tuition and fee levels. Unused credit hours may be used toward graduate school or an advanced program at a Michigan public university or college at the undergraduate tuition rate. If the beneficiary decides to attend a private institution in Michigan, the program will pay the weighted average public tuition. If the beneficiary decides to attend an out-of-state institution, the program will pay the average public tuition.

Contract options: One semester to four years under the Full Benefits Plan, which covers tuition and fees at any Michigan public institution; one semester to four years under the Limited Benefits Plan, which covers tuition and mandatory fees at Michigan public institutions whose tuition does not exceed 105 percent of the weighted average tuition of all Michigan public four-year universities; and one semester to two years under the Community College Plan, which covers in-district tuition and mandatory fees at any Michigan public community college.

Costs: There is a one-time $85 enrollment fee reduced to as low as $25 for early enrollment. In the enrollment period that ends June 15, 2005, lump-sum prices for a student in the twelfth grade range from $4,375 for the one-semester contract to $35,000 for the four-year contract under the Full Benefits Plan, $3,253 for the one-semester contract to $26,024 for the four-year contract under the Limited Benefits Plan, and $1,057 for the one-semester contract to $4,228 for the two-year contract under the Community College Plan. Contract payments may be made in a lump sum, or in monthly installments under specified terms. Monthly installment payments are computed to include an effective annual 8% cost for making payments over time.

Cancellation provisions: If the beneficiary decides not to attend college, the "refund designee" will receive a refund in four annual installments equal to tuition at the lowest cost Michigan public four-year university, or the lowest cost community college if the community college contract was purchased. A $100 termination fee is deducted from the first refund payment. Only a beneficiary who has reached 18 years of age or has received a high school diploma can terminate the contract and request a refund, except in the event of the beneficiary's death or diagnosed learning disability. Once the beneficiary completes more than one-half of the credit hours needed for a four-year degree, the contract may not be terminated. Contracts terminated due to the receipt of a full-tuition scholarship are valued at the average tuition of Michigan's public four-year universities or community colleges.

Contract changes: The beneficiary can transfer contract rights to a spouse, parent, sibling, niece, nephew, or cousin of the first degree after reaching age 18 or receiving a high school diploma. An additional payment may be required if the new beneficiary is older. Beneficiary designation cannot be changed once the original beneficiary earns more than one-half of the four-year degree requirements at a Michigan public institution. The contract purchaser cannot transfer rights in the contract during lifetime. If the contract purchaser dies, the executor of the estate can add an appointee, and change the refund designee (unless the beneficiary is the refund designee). There are no operational provisions concerning rollovers to another state's 529 plan. Any rollover would have to wait until the beneficiary reaches age 18 or receives a high school diploma and would be subject to the contract cancellation provisions.

State backing: Contracts are not backed by the full faith and credit of the state of Michigan. The trustee invests program assets with the goal of creating a reserve to protect against shortfalls in the program fund.

Special considerations:

- Note that in this program contract ownership rights are generally held by the beneficiary, not the purchaser, except that the purchaser may initially name a "refund designee" other than the beneficiary.
- All payments towards the cost of the contract are eligible for a state income tax deduction. Deductions may be subject to recapture if non-qualified withdrawals are made in a subsequent year.
- Michigan does not specifically provide that qualified distributions are exempt from state income tax, but its tax law generally conforms to federal tax law so any qualified distributions that are exempt from federal income tax are also exempt from Michigan income tax.

STATE: **MICHIGAN**

PROGRAM NAME:	Michigan Education Savings Program
529 TYPE:	Savings
STATE AGENCY:	Michigan Department of Treasury
PROGRAM MANAGER:	TIAA-CREF Tuition Financing, Inc.
INITIAL YEAR OF OPERATION:	2000
TELEPHONE:	1–877–861–MESP (1–877–861–6377)
INTERNET:	www.misaves.com

Who can purchase a contract? U.S. citizens and resident aliens with a valid Social Security number or federal taxpayer identification number, UTMA/UGMA custodians, and 501(c)(3) organizations. Not available through brokers.

Time or age limitations on beneficiary or on use of account assets: None

Age-based investment option: The Managed Allocation Option contains 11 portfolios of underlying mutual funds. Contributions are placed into the portfolio corresponding to the age of the beneficiary. The portfolios shift to a more conservative investment allocation over time.

Static investment options: Select between two portfolios: the 100% Equity Option (80% domestic equity and 20% international equity) and the Guaranteed Option which invests in an instrument that guarantees principal and a minimum 3% annual rate of interest (actual rate is declared quarterly).

Underlying investments: TIAA-CREF institutional mutual funds; the Guaranteed Option consists of a funding agreement issued by TIAA-CREF Life Insurance Company.

Fees and expenses: 0.65% annualized program management fee charged against the value of the account (none for the Guaranteed Option), which includes the expenses of the underlying mutual funds. There are no enrollment or account maintenance fees.

Maximum contributions: Accepts contributions until all Michigan account balances for the same beneficiary reach $235,000.

Minimum initial contribution: $25, or $15 with payroll deduction

Account changes: The program accepts requests to change beneficiary, transfer account ownership, name a successor owner, and transact rollovers and investment changes that meet the requirements of federal tax law and IRS regulations.

Special considerations:

- Up to $5,000 ($10,000 for married couples filing joint returns) of total annual contributions to all accounts may be deducted from Michigan taxable income each year. Deductions may not be claimed in the year any withdrawals are made or in any subsequent year (pending legislation would remove this limitation and permit a deduction for contributions in excess of withdrawals). Deductions may be subject to recapture if non-qualified withdrawals are made in a subsequent year.
- Under state law, qualified distributions from this program are exempt from Michigan income tax. Because Michigan tax law generally conforms to federal tax law, any qualified distributions from other 529 plans that are exempt from federal income tax are also exempt from Michigan income tax.
- A contribution may be eligible for a matching grant of up to $200 from the state of Michigan if the beneficiary is a Michigan resident under seven years old, and if the federal adjusted gross income of the beneficiary's custodial parent(s) is $80,000 or less. This is a one-time grant per beneficiary.

STATE: **MINNESOTA**

PROGRAM NAME:	Minnesota College Savings Plan
529 TYPE:	Savings
STATE AGENCIES:	Minnesota State Board of Investment and Minnesota Higher Education Services Office
PROGRAM MANAGER:	TIAA-CREF Tuition Financing, Inc.
INITIAL YEAR OF OPERATION:	2001
TELEPHONE:	1–877–EDU4MIN (1–877–338–4646)
INTERNET:	www.mnsaves.org

Who can purchase a contract? U.S. citizens and resident aliens with a valid Social Security number, UTMA/UGMA custodians, trustees for minors, and legal entities. Not available through brokers.

Time or age limitations on beneficiary or on use of account assets: None

Age-based investment option: The Managed Allocation Option contains six portfolios of underlying mutual funds. Contributions are placed into the portfolio corresponding to the age of the beneficiary, and later reassigned to more conservative portfolios as the beneficiary approaches college.

Static investment options: Select between two portfolios: the 100% Equity Option and the Guaranteed Option which is invested in a funding agreement that guarantees principal and a minimum 3% annual rate of interest (actual rate is declared quarterly).

Underlying investments: TIAA-CREF institutional mutual funds; the Guaranteed Option consists of a funding agreement issued by TIAA-CREF Life Insurance Company.

Fees and expenses: 0.65% annualized program management fee charged against the value of the account (none for the Guaranteed Option), which includes the expenses of the underlying mutual funds. There are no enrollment or account maintenance fees.

Maximum contributions: Accepts contributions until all Minnesota account balances for the same beneficiary reach $235,000.

Minimum initial contribution: $25 per investment option, or $15 per investment option with payroll deduction.

Account changes: The program accepts requests to change beneficiary, transfer account ownership, name a successor owner, and transact rollovers and investment changes that meet the requirements of federal tax law and IRS regulations.

Special considerations:

- The state of Minnesota will make annual matching grants of up to $300 for each beneficiary in the program where certain residency requirements are met, a separate application is filed, and the federal adjusted gross income (AGI) of the beneficiary's family does not exceed $80,000. The matching percentage is 15% for families with AGI of $50,000 or less, and 5% for families with AGI between $50,000 and $80,000. The accumulated grants will be fully or partially forfeited if non-qualified withdrawals are made and under certain other conditions.
- Minnesota does not specifically provide that qualified distributions are exempt from state income tax, but its tax law generally conforms to federal tax law and so any qualified distributions that are exempt from federal income tax are also exempt from Minnesota income tax.

STATE: MISSISSIPPI

PROGRAM NAME:	Mississippi Prepaid Affordable College Tuition Program (MPACT)
529 TYPE:	Prepaid contract
STATE AGENCY:	Mississippi Treasury Department
INITIAL YEAR OF OPERATION:	1997
TELEPHONE:	1–800–987–4450
INTERNET:	www.treasury.state.ms.us or www.collegesavingsmississippi.com

Who can purchase contracts?　Individuals 18 years and older, UTMA/UGMA custodians, and legal entities. The purchaser or beneficiary must be a Mississippi resident at the time of program enrollment.

Enrollment period:　September 1 through November 30 each year

Time or age limitations on beneficiary or on use of benefits:　The beneficiary must be 18 years old or younger at the time of program enrollment. Contract benefits must be used within ten years after the beneficiary's projected college entrance date.

Contract benefits:　The contract pays in-state tuition and mandatory fees at Mississippi's public colleges and universities, up to 160 credit hours (10 semesters). The value derived from the contract will depend in part on the selection of institution, because public institutions in Mississippi have different tuition and fee levels. If the beneficiary receives a scholarship, the unused benefits may be refunded, transferred to another qualified beneficiary, or reserved for future tuition hours. If the beneficiary decides to attend a private college in Mississippi or an out-of-state college, the program will pay the lesser of the weighted average tuition and mandatory fees of the Mississippi public colleges in the tuition plan purchased or the actual tuition and mandatory fees of the institution attended. A one-time $25 administration fee is charged for benefit transfers to a private or out-of-state institution.

Contract options:　A university plan for one to five years, a community college plan for one or two years, or a combination plan.

Costs:　There is a one-time $60 enrollment fee. For the enrollment period that ends November 30, 2004, contract prices for a student in the 12th grade range from $1,595 for a one-year community college contract to $21,000 for a five-year university contract. Contract prices are discounted for younger beneficiaries. Contract payments can be made in a lump sum, annual or monthly installments over a variety of terms, or a combination of the two.

Cancellation provisions: The contract may be terminated at any time for a refund. The refund will equal the actual payments made, plus interest computed at prevailing rates for bank savings accounts, less a cancellation fee of $25.

Contract changes: The program accepts requests to change beneficiary prior to matriculation to a member of the immediate family, transfer contract ownership, and name a successor purchaser, subject to residency requirements. There are no special provisions concerning rollovers to another 529 plan (cancellation provisions would apply).

State backing: Contracts are backed by the full faith and credit of the state of Mississippi.

Special considerations:

- All payments into MPACT are deductible from Mississippi state income tax without limit. Deductions may be subject to recapture if non-qualified withdrawals or rollovers to another state's 529 plan are made in a subsequent year.
- Under state law, qualified distributions are exempt from Mississippi state income tax. Distributions from other state 529 plans may subject a Mississippi resident to Mississippi state tax as Mississippi currently does not conform to federal tax treatment of qualified distributions.
- A beneficiary is considered a resident for purposes of tuition regardless of the beneficiary's residence at the time of college enrollment if the original purchaser was the parent, grandparent, or legal guardian of the beneficiary or the beneficiary was a resident of Mississippi at the time the MPACT contract was purchased.
- Under Mississippi law, any fund surpluses arising from favorable investment performance cannot be allocated to participant accounts.

STATE:	**MISSISSIPPI**
PROGRAM NAME:	Mississippi Affordable College Savings (MACS)
529 TYPE:	Savings
STATE AGENCY:	College Savings Plans of Mississippi
PROGRAM MANAGER:	TIAA-CREF Tuition Financing, Inc.
INITIAL YEAR OF OPERATION:	2001
TELEPHONE:	1–800–486–3670
INTERNET:	www.collegesavingsms.com

Who can purchase a contract? U.S. citizens and resident aliens with a valid Social Security number or federal taxpayer identification number, UTMA/UGMA custodians, and legal entities Not available through brokers.

Time or age limitations on beneficiary or on use of account assets: None

Age-based investment option: The Managed Allocation Option contains 11 portfolios of underlying mutual funds. Contributions are placed into the portfolio corresponding to the age of the beneficiary. The portfolios shift to a more conservative investment allocation over time.

Static investment options: Select between two portfolios: the 100% Equity Option and the Guaranteed Option. The 100% Equity Option invests approximately 80% in the TIAA-CREF Institutional Growth and Income Fund and 20% in the TIAA-CREF Institutional International Equity Fund. The Guaranteed Option is invested in an instrument that guarantees principal and a minimum 3% annual rate of interest (actual rate is declared quarterly).

Underlying investments: TIAA-CREF institutional mutual funds; the Guaranteed Option consists of a funding agreement issued by TIAA-CREF Life Insurance Company.

Fees and expenses: 0.70% annualized program management fee charged against the value of the account (none for the Guaranteed Option), and underlying fund expenses recently ranging from approximately 0.16% to 0.23% (portfolio weighted average). There are no enrollment or account maintenance fees.

Maximum contributions: Accepts contributions until all Mississippi account balances for the same beneficiary reach $235,000.

Minimum initial contribution: $25, or $15 with payroll deduction

Account changes: The program accepts requests to change beneficiary, transfer account ownership, name a successor owner, and transact rollovers and investment changes that meet the requirements of federal tax law and IRS regulations.

Special considerations:

- Contributions of up to $10,000 per year ($20,000 for joint filers) may be deducted from Mississippi taxable income. Deductions may be subject to recapture if non-qualified withdrawals or rollovers to another state's 529 plan are made in a subsequent year.
- Under state law, qualified distributions are exempt from Mississippi state income tax. Distributions from other state 529 plans may subject a Mississippi resident to Mississippi state tax as Mississippi currently does not conform to federal tax treatment of qualified distributions.
- The value of the account will not be counted in determining eligibility and need for student financial aid programs provided by the state of Mississippi.

STATE:	**MISSISSIPPI**
PROGRAM NAME:	Mississippi Affordable College Savings (MACS) Advisor Program
529 TYPE:	Savings
STATE AGENCY:	College Savings Plans of Mississippi
PROGRAM MANAGER:	TIAA-CREF Tuition Financing, Inc.
INITIAL YEAR OF OPERATION:	2002
TELEPHONE:	1–877–ADVS–529 (1–877–238–7529)
INTERNET:	www.529advisorprograms.com

Who can purchase a contract? U.S. citizens and resident aliens with a valid Social Security number or federal taxpayer identification number, UTMA/UGMA custodians, and legal entities. This program is distributed through brokers.

Time or age limitations on beneficiary or on use of account assets: None

Age-based investment options: None

Static investment options: Select among six individual-fund options, a balanced option, and a guaranteed option that invests in an instrument that guarantees principal and a minimum 3% annual rate of interest (actual rate is declared quarterly).

Underlying investments: TIAA-CREF institutional mutual funds; the Guaranteed Option consists of a funding agreement issued by TIAA-CREF Life Insurance Company

Fees and expenses: $25 annual account maintenance fee on accounts under $25,000, 0.70% annualized program management fee charged against the value of the account (none for the Guaranteed Option), and underlying fund expenses that vary by fund. Contributions are subject to a 5% initial sales charge. There is no enrollment fee.

Maximum contributions: Accepts contributions until all Mississippi account balances for the same beneficiary reach $235,000.

Minimum initial contribution: $3,000 per account and $1,000 per investment option

Account changes: The program accepts requests to change beneficiary, transfer account ownership, name a successor owner, and transact rollovers and investment changes that meet the requirements of federal tax law and IRS regulations.

Special considerations:
- Mississippi residents receive the same state income tax and financial aid benefits previously described for the Mississippi Affordable College Savings direct-sold program.

STATE: **MISSOURI**

PROGRAM NAME:	Missouri Saving for Tuition (MO$T) Program
529 TYPE:	Savings
STATE AGENCY:	Missouri Higher Education Savings Program Board
PROGRAM MANAGER:	TIAA-CREF Tuition Financing, Inc.
INITIAL YEAR OF OPERATION:	1999
TELEPHONE:	1–888–414–MOST (1–888–414–6678)
INTERNET:	www.missourimost.org

Who can purchase a contract? U.S. citizens and resident aliens with a valid Social Security number or federal taxpayer identification number, UTMA/UGMA custodians, and legal entities. Not available through brokers.

Time or age limitations on beneficiary or on use of account assets: None

Age-based investment option: The Managed Allocation Option contains 11 portfolios of underlying mutual funds. Contributions are placed into the portfolio corresponding to the age of the beneficiary. The portfolios shift to a more conservative investment allocation over time.

Static investment options: Select between two portfolios: the 100% Equity Option and the Guaranteed Option. The 100% Equity Option is invested in a blend of six institutional mutual funds. The Guaranteed Option is invested in an instrument that guarantees principal and a minimum 3% annual rate of interest (actual rate is declared quarterly).

Underlying investments: TIAA-CREF institutional mutual funds; the Guaranteed Option consists of a funding agreement issued by TIAA-CREF Life Insurance Company.

Fees and expenses: 0.65% annualized program management fee charged against the value of the account (none for the Guaranteed Option), which includes the expenses of the underlying mutual funds. There are no enrollment or account maintenance fees.

Maximum contributions: Accepts contributions until all Missouri account balances for the same beneficiary reach $235,000.

Minimum initial contribution: $25, or $15 with payroll deduction

Account changes: The program accepts requests to change beneficiary, transfer account ownership, name a successor owner, and transact rollovers and investment changes that meet the requirements of federal tax law and IRS regulations.

Special considerations:

- Each account owner may deduct up to $8,000 against Missouri taxable income each year for the contributions made to any accounts established under this program. A married couple can deduct up to $16,000 in a year if they both have Missouri income and separate accounts. Deductions may be subject to recapture if non-qualified withdrawals are made in a subsequent year.
- Under state law, qualified distributions from this program are exempt from Missouri income tax. Because Missouri tax law generally conforms to federal tax law, any qualified distributions from other 529 plans that are exempt from federal income tax are also exempt from Missouri income tax.

STATE: **MISSOURI**

PROGRAM NAME:	MO$T Advisor Program
529 TYPE:	Savings
STATE AGENCY:	Missouri Higher Education Savings Program Board
PROGRAM MANAGER:	TIAA-CREF Tuition Financing, Inc.
INITIAL YEAR OF OPERATION:	2002
TELEPHONE:	1–877–ADVS–529 (1–877–239–7529)
INTERNET:	www.529advisorprograms.com

Who can purchase a contract? U.S. citizens and resident aliens with a valid Social Security number or federal taxpayer identification number, UTMA/UGMA custodians, and legal entities. This program is distributed through brokers.

Time or age limitations on beneficiary or on use of account assets: None

Age-based investment options: None

Static investment options: Select among six individual-fund options, a balanced option, and a guaranteed option that invests in an instrument that guarantees principal and a minimum 3% annual rate of interest (actual rate is declared quarterly).

Underlying investments: TIAA-CREF institutional mutual funds; the Guaranteed Option consists of a funding agreement issued by TIAA-CREF Life Insurance Company.

Fees and expenses: $25 annual account maintenance fee on accounts under $25,000, and 0.65% annualized program management fee charged against the value of the account, which includes the expenses of the underlying mutual funds. There is no enrollment fee. Contributions are subject to a 5% initial sales charge.

Maximum contributions: Accepts contributions until all Missouri account balances for the same beneficiary reach $235,000.

Minimum initial contribution: $3,000 per account and $1,000 per investment option

Account changes: The program accepts requests to change beneficiary, transfer account ownership, name a successor owner, and transact rollovers and investment changes that meet the requirements of federal tax law and IRS regulations.

Special considerations:

- Missouri residents receive the same state income tax benefits previously described for the Missouri Saving for Tuition (MO$T) Program.

STATE:	**MONTANA**
PROGRAM NAME:	Montana Family Education Savings Program
529 TYPE:	Savings
STATE AGENCY:	Montana Board of Regents of Higher Education
PROGRAM MANAGER:	College Savings Bank
INITIAL YEAR OF OPERATION:	1998
TELEPHONE:	1–800–888–2723
INTERNET:	http://montana.collegesavings.com

Who can purchase a contract? U.S. citizens, UTMA/UGMA custodians, trusts, state/local government agencies, and 501(c)(3) organizations. Not available through brokers.

Time or age limitations on beneficiary or on use of account assets: The underlying investments are certificates of deposit (CDs) with maturities ranging from one to twenty-five years, timed to mature in the years the beneficiary attends college and/or graduate school. The CDs are subject to early redemption penalties ranging from 1% to 10% of principal for withdrawals prior to maturity (waived for Montana residents).

Age-based investment options: None

Static investment option: Funds are invested in CollegeSure® Certificates of Deposit, a product of College Savings Bank.

Underlying investments: CollegeSure® CDs issued after August 1, 2003 earn interest at a variable rate pegged to a tuition inflation index, less a 3% margin, not to fall below 2%. The tuition index is the College Board's Independent College 500® Index measuring one full year of average tuition, fees, and room and board at four-year private colleges. The interest rate adjusts each July 31.

Fees and expenses: There are no enrollment or account maintenance fees.

Maximum contributions: Accepts contributions until all Montana account balances for the same beneficiary reach $275,000.

Minimum initial contribution: $250 lump sum, $25 per pay period with payroll deduction, or $100 per month with automatic contributions.

Account changes: The program accepts requests to change beneficiary, transfer account ownership (but only to the beneficiary, or to the owner's spouse as part of a divorce proceeding), and name a successor owner. Fees may be charged on multiple changes.

Special considerations:

- Principal and interest are backed by the full faith and credit of the U.S. Government up to $100,000 per depositor.
- The account is established as a revocable trust with spendthrift provisions, providing additional protection from creditors.
- Montana has obtained from the U.S. Department of Education a letter ruling determining that account balances are generally treated as parental assets rather than a "resource" for purposes of determining eligibility for federal student aid.
- Account owners (or their spouse or child) may deduct contributions of up to $3,000 per year from Montana taxable income ($6,000 for married couples filing jointly). Deductions may be subject to recapture if non-qualified withdrawals or rollovers to another state's 529 plan are made in a subsequent year or if qualified withdrawals are made within three years of establishing the account.
- Under state law, qualified distributions from this program are exempt from Montana income tax. Because Montana tax law generally conforms to federal tax law, any qualified distributions from other 529 plans that are exempt from federal income tax are also exempt from Montana income tax.

STATE: **MONTANA**

PROGRAM NAME:	Pacific Funds 529 College Savings Plan (Montana)
529 TYPE:	Savings
STATE AGENCY:	Montana Board of Regents of Higher Education
PROGRAM MANAGERS:	Pacific Life and College Savings Bank
INITIAL YEAR OF OPERATION:	2002
TELEPHONE:	1–800–722–2333
INTERNET:	www.collegesavings.PacificLife.com (MT residents)
	www.PacificLife.com (nonresidents)

Who can purchase a contract? Individuals (including joint ownership with spouse), UTMA/UGMA custodians, state/local government agencies, and 501(c)(3) organizations. This program is distributed both direct and through brokers. Anyone who does not meet Montana's residency requirements must open their account through a broker.

Time or age limitations on beneficiary or on use of account assets: None

Age-based investment options: None

Static investment options: Select among five fund-of-fund options and fifteen individual-fund options

Underlying investments: Pacific Funds, including subadvised funds with AIM, Goldman Sachs, Invesco, Janus, Lazard, MFS, PIMCO, Pacific Life, Putnam, Salomon Brothers, and Van Kampen.

Fees and expenses: $25 annual account maintenance fee on accounts with $25,000 or less (waived for Montana residents purchasing direct, for accounts in an automatic investment or payroll deduction plan, and all NAV accounts), and the underlying fund expenses which vary by fund and share class. In addition, accounts opened through a broker are subject to one of three alternative broker expense structures that will determine any initial sales charge, contingent deferred sales charge, and/or additional asset-based fees. There is no enrollment fee.

Maximum contributions: Accepts contributions until all Montana account balances for the same beneficiary reach $275,000.

Minimum initial contribution: $500 per fund, or $50 per fund per month

Account changes: The program accepts requests to change beneficiary, transfer account ownership (but only to beneficiary, or to owner's spouse as part of a divorce proceeding), name a successor owner, and transact rollovers and investment changes that meet the requirements of federal tax law and IRS regulations.

Special considerations:

- Account owners (or their spouse or child) may deduct contributions of up to $3,000 per year from Montana taxable income ($6,000 for married couples filing jointly) Deductions may be subject to recapture if non-qualified withdrawals or rollovers to another state's 529 plan are made in any subsequent year or if qualified withdrawals are made within three years of establishing the account.
- Under state law, qualified distributions from this program are exempt from Montana income tax. Because Montana tax law generally conforms to federal tax law, any qualified distributions from other 529 plans that are exempt from federal income tax are also exempt from Montana income tax.

STATE: **NEBRASKA**

PROGRAM NAME:	College Savings Plan of Nebraska
529 TYPE:	Savings
STATE AGENCY:	Nebraska State Treasurer
PROGRAM MANAGER:	Union Bank & Trust Company
INITIAL YEAR OF OPERATION:	2001
TELEPHONE:	1–888–993–3746
INTERNET:	www.PlanForCollegeNow.com

Who can purchase a contract? Individuals, UTMA/UGMA custodians, and legal entities. This program is distributed both direct and through brokers.

Time or age limitations on beneficiary or on use of account assets: None

Age-based investment options: The Age-Based Portfolios offer a choice among four different tracks: Aggressive, Growth, Balanced, and Conservative. Each track contains five portfolios of underlying funds. Contributions are placed into the portfolio corresponding to the selected track and beneficiary's age, and later reassigned to more conservative portfolios as the beneficiary approaches college.

Static investment options: Select among six blended-fund Target portfolios with varying blends of equity, fixed income, and money market funds from different fund families (ranging from a target mix of 100% equities to 100% fixed income and money market) and twenty-one individual-fund portfolios.

Underlying investments: Mutual funds from Vanguard, American Century, Fidelity, State Street, T. Rowe Price and PIMCO.

Fees and expenses: $5 quarterly account maintenance fee, 0.60% annualized program management fee charged against the value of the account, and underlying fund expenses recently ranging from approximately 0.18% to 0.40% for the blended-fund portfolios (portfolio weighted average) and 0.05% to 1.09% for the individual-fund portfolios. There is no enrollment fee. A one-time fee credit of $10 is provided on accounts enrolled in an automatic investment plan of $25 or more per month. In addition, accounts opened through a broker are subject to one of three alternative broker expense structures that will determine any initial sales charge, contingent deferred sales charge, and/or additional asset-based fees.

Maximum contributions: Accepts contributions until all Nebraska account balances for the same beneficiary reach $250,000.

Minimum initial contribution: None

Account changes: The program accepts requests to change beneficiary, transfer account ownership, name a successor owner, and transact rollovers and investment changes that meet the requirements of federal tax law and IRS regulations.

Special considerations:

- Account owners may deduct up to $1,000 of contributions per tax return each year ($500 for married persons filing separate returns) from Nebraska taxable income. Deductions may be subject to recapture if non-qualified withdrawals or rollovers to another state's 529 plan are made in a subsequent year.
- Under state law, qualified distributions from this program are exempt from Nebraska income tax. Because Nebraska tax law generally conforms to federal tax law, any qualified distributions from other 529 plans that are exempt from federal income tax are also exempt from Nebraska income tax.
- The value of the account will not be counted in determining eligibility and need for student financial aid programs provided by the state of Nebraska.
- Under Nebraska law, an account is not susceptible to any levy, execution, judgment, or other operation of law, garnishment, or other judicial enforcement, and the amount is not an asset or property of either the participant or the beneficiary for purposes of any state insolvency laws.

STATE: **NEBRASKA**

PROGRAM NAME:	TD Waterhouse 529 College Savings Plan
529 TYPE:	Savings
STATE AGENCY:	Nebraska State Treasurer
PROGRAM MANAGER:	Union Bank & Trust Company
DISTRIBUTION PARTNER:	TD Waterhouse
INITIAL YEAR OF OPERATION:	2002
TELEPHONE:	1–877–408–4644
INTERNET:	www.tdwaterhouse.com

Who can purchase a contract? Individuals, UTMA/UGMA custodians, and legal entities This program is distributed through TD Waterhouse.

Time or age limitations on beneficiary or on use of account assets: None

Age-based investment options: The Age-Based Portfolios offer a choice among four different tracks: Aggressive, Growth, Balanced, and Conservative. Each track contains five portfolios of underlying funds. Contributions are placed into the portfolio corresponding to the selected track and beneficiary's age, and later reassigned to more conservative portfolios as the beneficiary approaches college.

Static investment options: Select among six blended-fund Target portfolios with varying blends of equity, fixed income, and money market funds from different fund families (ranging from a target mix of 100% equities to 100% fixed income and money market) and twenty-one individual-fund portfolios.

Underlying investments: Mutual funds from Vanguard, American Century, Fidelity, State Street, T. Rowe Price and PIMCO.

Fees and expenses: $7.50 quarterly account maintenance fee, 0.85% annualized program management fee charged against the value of the account, and underlying fund expenses recently ranging from approximately 0.18% to 0.40% for the blended-fund portfolios (portfolio weighted average) and 0.05% to 1.09% for the individual-fund portfolios. There is no enrollment fee and no additional broker expenses.

Maximum contributions: Accepts contributions until all Nebraska account balances for the same beneficiary reach $250,000.

Minimum initial contribution: None

Account changes: The program accepts requests to change beneficiary, transfer account ownership, name a successor owner, and transact rollovers and investment changes that meet the requirements of federal tax law and IRS regulations.

Special considerations:

- Nebraska residents receive the same state income tax, financial aid, and creditor protection benefits described previously for the College Savings Plan of Nebraska.

STATE:	**NEBRASKA**
PROGRAM NAME:	AIM College Savings Plan
529 TYPE:	Savings
STATE AGENCY:	Nebraska State Treasurer
PROGRAM MANAGER:	Union Bank & Trust Company
DISTRIBUTION PARTNER:	AIM Investments
INITIAL YEAR OF OPERATION:	2001
TELEPHONE:	1–877–AIM–PLAN (1–877–246–7526)
INTERNET:	www.aiminvestments.com

Who can purchase a contract? Individuals with a valid Social Security number or federal taxpayer identification number, UTMA/UGMA custodians, trusts, state/local government agencies, and 501(c)(3) organizations. This program is distributed through brokers.

Time or age limitations on beneficiary or on use of account assets: None

Age-based investment options: The Enrollment-Based Portfolios contain seven portfolios of underlying funds, ranging from aggressive (100% equity) to conservative (25% equity, 40% fixed income, and 35% money market). Contributions are placed into the portfolio corresponding to the number of years to expected enrollment, and later reassigned to more conservative investment allocations as the beneficiary approaches college.

Static investment options: Select among three blended-fund portfolios (Aggressive Growth, Growth, and Balanced), and 14 individual-fund portfolios.

Underlying investments: AIM mutual funds

Fees and expenses: $25 annual account maintenance fee on accounts with less than $50,000 (waived for accounts with $25,000 or more if enrolled in an automatic investment plan), and underlying fund expenses recently ranging from approximately 0.90% to 2.02%. In addition, accounts are subject to one of three alternative broker expense structures that will determine any initial sales charge, contingent deferred sales charge, and/or additional asset-based fees. There is no enrollment fee.

Maximum contributions: Accepts contributions until all Nebraska account balances for the same beneficiary reach $250,000.

Minimum initial contribution: $500 per portfolio ($25 with automatic investment).

Account changes: The program accepts requests to change beneficiary, transfer account ownership, name a successor owner, and transact rollovers and investment changes that meet the requirements of federal tax law and IRS regulations.

Special considerations:

- Nebraska residents receive the same state income tax, financial aid, and credito protection benefits described previously for the College Savings Plan of Nebraska.

STATE:	**NEBRASKA**
PROGRAM NAME:	The State Farm College Savings Plan
529 TYPE:	Savings
STATE AGENCY:	Nebraska State Treasurer
PROGRAM MANAGER:	Union Bank & Trust Company
DISTRIBUTION PARTNER:	AIM Investments
INITIAL YEAR OF OPERATION:	2003
TELEPHONE:	1–800–321–7520
INTERNET:	www.statefarm.com/mutual/529.htm

Who can purchase a contract? Individuals, UTMA/UGMA custodians, trusts, state/local government agencies, and 501(c)(3) organizations. This program is distributed through State Farm registered representatives.

Time or age limitations on beneficiary or on use of account assets: None

Age-based investment options: The Enrollment-Based Portfolios contain seven portfolios of underlying funds, ranging from aggressive (100% equity) to conservative (25% equity, 40% fixed income, and 35% money market). Contributions are placed into the portfolio corresponding to the number of years to expected enrollment, and later reassigned to more conservative investment allocations as the beneficiary approaches college.

Static investment options: Select among three blended-fund portfolios: Aggressive Growth, Growth, and Balanced.

Underlying investments: AIM mutual funds

Fees and expenses: $25 annual account maintenance fee on accounts with less than $50,000 (waived for accounts with $25,000 or more if enrolled in an automatic investment plan), and underlying fund expenses recently ranging from approximately 1.06% to 1.43%. In addition, accounts are subject to one of three alternative broker expense structures that will determine any initial sales charge, contingent deferred sales charge, and/or additional asset-based fees. There is no enrollment fee.

Maximum contributions: Accepts contributions until all Nebraska account balances for the same beneficiary reach $250,000.

Minimum initial contribution: $500, or $50 initial plus $25 per month

Account changes: The program accepts requests to change beneficiary, transfer account ownership, name a successor owner, and transact rollovers and investment changes that meet the requirements of federal tax law and IRS regulations.

Special considerations:

- Nebraska residents receive the same state income tax, financial aid, and creditor protection benefits described previously for the College Savings Plan of Nebraska.

STATE: **NEVADA**

PROGRAM NAME:	Nevada Prepaid Tuition Program
529 TYPE:	Prepaid contract
STATE AGENCIES:	Board of Trustees of the College Savings Plans of Nevada and the State Treasurer's Office
INITIAL YEAR OF OPERATION:	1998
TELEPHONE:	1–888–477–2667
INTERNET:	http://NevadaTreasurer.gov/college/prepaid.asp

Who can purchase a contract? Individuals 18 years and older who meet Nevada residency requirements (plus alumni of Nevada colleges and universities and certain military personnel), UTMA/UGMA custodians, and legal entities.

Enrollment period: Began September 7, 2004 and ends January 31, 2005; newborns accepted year-round.

Time or age limitations on beneficiary or on use of benefits: The beneficiary must be in the ninth grade or below and 18 years or younger at the time of program enrollment. Contract benefits must begin no later than ten years beyond initial date of high school graduation or when beneficiary reaches age 30 (extensions granted for military service).

Contract benefits: The contract pays in-state undergraduate tuition limited to 120 credit hours (8 semesters) at any Nevada state college or university. If the beneficiary decides to attend a private college in Nevada or an out-of-state college, the program will pay the weighted-average in-state tuition at a Nevada university or community college or the actual tuition, whichever is less.

Contract options: Four-year university, two-year university, two-year community college, or a combination plan.

Costs: There is a one-time $100 enrollment fee. For the enrollment period that ends January 31, 2005, lump-sum contract prices for a child in the ninth grade range from $3,405 for the two-year community college plan to $14,350 for the four-year university plan. Prices are discounted for younger beneficiaries. Contract payments may be made in a lump sum, under a 5-year monthly payment plan, or under an extended monthly payment plan to the year of college enrollment. Monthly payments include an additional amount to reflect the cost of making payments over time. Payments can be as low as $28 per month (newborn under the two-year community college contract).

Cancellation provisions: A contract may be canceled at any time and the program will provide a refund of contract payments (less a cancellation fee of $100), plus interest at a rate determined by the Board. The cancellation fee is waived in the event of the beneficiary's death, disability, or receipt of scholarship.

Contract changes: The program accepts requests to change beneficiary (an additional payment may be required if the new beneficiary is more than three years older), transfer contract ownership, and name a successor owner, subject to residency requirements. A $20 fee is charged for certain changes. There are no special provisions concerning rollovers to another 529 plan (cancellation provisions would apply).

State backing: Contracts are not backed by the full faith and credit of the state of Nevada. The trustee invests program assets with the goal of creating a reserve to protect against shortfalls in the program fund.

Special considerations:

- If the program trust fund builds an excess surplus due to favorable investment results, the Board may decide to allocate such excess to participant accounts.
- There are no state income tax incentives because Nevada does not have a personal income tax.
- The program is compatible with the Nevada Millennium Scholarship Program.
- Under Nevada law, the right to benefits or refunds is not subject to attachment, garnishment, or seizure by creditors of the contract purchaser or beneficiary.
- The value of the contract will not be counted in determining eligibility and need for student financial aid programs provided by the state of Nevada.

STATE: **NEVADA**

PROGRAM NAME:	American Skandia College Savings Program
529 TYPE:	Savings
STATE AGENCY:	Board of Trustees of the College Savings Plans of Nevada
PROGRAM MANAGER:	Strong Capital Management, Inc.
DISTRIBUTION PARTNER:	American Skandia
INITIAL YEAR OF OPERATION:	2001
TELEPHONE:	1–800–SKANDIA (1–800–752–6342)
INTERNET:	www.americanskandia.prudential.com

Who can purchase a contract? Individuals of legal age with a valid Social Security number or federal taxpayer identification number, UTMA/UGMA custodians, and certain legal entities. This program is distributed through brokers.

Time or age limitations on beneficiary or on use of account assets: None

Age-based investment options: The Enrollment-Based Option offers a choice among three different schedules: Aggressive, Moderate, or Conservative. Each schedule contains five portfolios of underlying funds. Contributions are placed into the portfolio corresponding to the selected schedule and number of years to expected enrollment, and later reassigned to more conservative portfolios as the beneficiary approaches college.

Static investment options: Select among three portfolios: Aggressive (75% equity), Balanced (55% equity), and Conservative (25% equity).

Underlying investments: Advisors and subadvisors include William Blair & Company, Marsico Capital Management, Neuberger Berman, Goldman Sachs Asset Management, Gabelli Asset Management, State Street Research & Management Company, Federated Investors, Dryden, PIMCO, Invesco, and Wells Capital Management.

Fees and expenses: $30 annual account maintenance fee on accounts $25,000 or less (waived for accounts enrolled in an automatic investment or payroll deduction plan), and underlying fund expenses recently ranging from approximately 1.46% to 1.90%. In addition, accounts are subject to one of two alternative broker expense structures that will determine any initial sales charge, contingent deferred sales charge, and/or additional asset-based fees.

Maximum contributions: Accepts contributions until all Nevada account balances for the same beneficiary reach $250,000.

Minimum initial contribution: $250 ($50 with automatic investment)

Account changes: The program accepts requests to change beneficiary, transfer account ownership, name a successor owner, and transact rollovers and investment changes that meet the requirements of federal tax law and IRS regulations.

Special considerations:

- There are no state income tax incentives because Nevada does not have a personal income tax.
- Under Nevada law, an account is exempt from creditor claims, subject to a $500,000 cap and only on those assets in the 529 plan prior to the claim. This protection extends only to those assets eventually used for the beneficiary's college expenses.

STATE:	**NEVADA**
PROGRAM NAME:	The Vanguard 529 College Savings Plan
529 TYPE:	Savings
STATE AGENCY:	Board of Trustees of the College Savings Plans of Nevada
PROGRAM MANAGER:	Upromise Investments, Inc.
INVESTMENT MANAGER:	Vanguard Group
INITIAL YEAR OF OPERATION:	2002
TELEPHONE:	1–866–734–4530
INTERNET:	www.vanguard.com

Who can purchase a contract? U.S. citizens and resident aliens 18 years and older with a valid Social Security number or federal taxpayer identification number, and UTMA/UGMA custodians. Not available through brokers.

Time or age limitations on beneficiary or on use of account assets: None

Age-based investment options: The Age-Based Option offers a choice among three different schedules: Aggressive, Moderate, or Conservative. Each schedule contains five portfolios of underlying funds. Contributions are placed into the portfolio corresponding to the selected schedule and number of years to expected enrollment, and later reassigned to more conservative portfolios as the beneficiary approaches college.

Static investment options: Select among five blended-fund portfolios and twelve individual-fund portfolios.

Underlying investments: Vanguard mutual funds

Fees and expenses: 0.65%–0.86% annualized program management fee charged against the value of the account, which includes the expenses of the underlying mutual funds.

The fee on blended-fund portfolios will be reduced to 0.60% once assets in the program reach $1 billion. There are no enrollment or account maintenance fees.

Maximum contributions: Accepts contributions until all Nevada account balances for the same beneficiary reach $250,000.

Minimum initial contribution: $3,000

Account changes: The program accepts requests to change beneficiary, transfer account ownership, name a successor owner, and transact rollovers and investment changes that meet the requirements of federal tax law and IRS regulations.

Special considerations:

- There are no state income tax incentives because Nevada does not have a personal income tax.
- Under Nevada law, an account is exempt from creditor claims, subject to a $500,000 cap and only on those assets in the 529 plan prior to the claim. This protection extends only to those assets eventually used for the beneficiary's college expenses.

STATE: **NEVADA**

PROGRAM NAME:	Upromise College Fund
529 TYPE:	Savings
STATE AGENCY:	Board of Trustees of the College Savings Plans of Nevada
PROGRAM MANAGER:	Upromise Investments, Inc.
INITIAL YEAR OF OPERATION:	2002
TELEPHONE:	1–800–587–7305
INTERNET:	www.upromisecollegefund.com

Who can purchase a contract? U.S. citizens and resident aliens of legal age with a valid Social Security number or federal taxpayer identification number. Not available through brokers.

Time or age limitations on beneficiary or on use of account assets: None

Age-based investment options: The Age-Based Option offers a choice among three different tracks (Aggressive, Moderate, or Conservative). Each track contains five portfolios of underlying funds. Contributions are placed into the portfolio corresponding to the selected track and beneficiary's age, and later reassigned to more conservative portfolios as the beneficiary approaches college.

Static investment options: Select among five blended-fund portfolios and three individual-fund portfolios.

Underlying investments: Vanguard mutual funds

Fees and expenses: $20 annual account maintenance fee, and 0.65% annualized program management fee charged against the value of the account, which includes the expenses of the underlying mutual funds. There is no enrollment fee.

Maximum contributions: Accepts contributions until all Nevada account balances for the same beneficiary reach $250,000.

Minimum initial contribution: $250 ($50 with automatic investment)

Account changes: The program accepts requests to change beneficiary, name a successor owner, and transact rollovers and investment changes that meet the requirements of federal tax law and IRS regulations.

Special considerations:

- There are no state income tax incentives because Nevada does not have a personal income tax.
- Under Nevada law, an account is exempt from creditor claims, subject to a $500,000 cap and only on those assets in the 529 plan prior to the claim. This protection extends only to those assets eventually used for the beneficiary's college expenses.

STATE:	**NEVADA**
PROGRAM NAME:	USAA College Savings Plan
529 TYPE:	Savings
STATE AGENCY:	Board of Trustees of the College Savings Plans of Nevada
PROGRAM MANAGER:	Upromise Investments, Inc.
DISTRIBUTION PARTNER:	USAA
INITIAL YEAR OF OPERATION:	2002
TELEPHONE:	1–800–292–8825
INTERNET:	www.usaa.com

Who can purchase a contract? U.S. citizens and resident aliens with a valid Social Security number or federal taxpayer identification number, UTMA/UGMA custodians, and trusts. The account owner must be a USAA member. Not available through brokers.

Time or age limitations on beneficiary or on use of account assets: None

Age-based investment option: The Age-Based Option contains six portfolios of underlying funds. Contributions are placed into the portfolio corresponding to the age of the beneficiary, and later reassigned to more conservative portfolios as the beneficiary approaches college.

Static investment options: Select among six portfolios: Aggressive Growth, Growth, Moderate, Balanced, Conservative, and In-College.

Underlying investments: Mutual funds managed by USAA Investment Management Company

Fees and expenses: $15 annual account maintenance fee, $15 minimum balance fee charged annually to accounts with a balance of less than $5,000 (waived for accounts in an automatic investment plan), and 1.10% annualized program management fee charged against the value of the account, which includes the expenses of the underlying mutual funds. There is no enrollment fee.

Maximum contributions: Accepts contributions until all Nevada account balances for the same beneficiary reach $250,000.

Minimum initial contribution: $250

Account changes: The program accepts requests to change beneficiary, transfer account ownership, name a successor owner, and transact rollovers and investment changes that meet the requirements of federal tax law and IRS regulations.

Special considerations:

- There are no state income tax incentives because Nevada does not have a personal income tax.
- Under Nevada law, an account is exempt from creditor claims, subject to a $500,000 cap and only on those assets in the 529 plan prior to the claim. This protection extends only to those assets eventually used for the beneficiary's college expenses.

STATE:	**NEVADA**
PROGRAM NAME:	Columbia 529 Plan
529 TYPE:	Savings
STATE AGENCY:	Board of Trustees of the College Savings Plans of Nevada
PROGRAM MANAGER:	Upromise Investments, Inc.
DISTRIBUTOR:	Columbia Funds Distributor, Inc.
INITIAL YEAR OF OPERATION:	2003
TELEPHONE:	1–877–994–2529
INTERNET:	www.columbia529.com

Who can purchase a contract? U.S. citizens and resident aliens of legal age, and trusts. This program is distributed through brokers.

Time or age limitations on beneficiary or on use of account assets: None

Age-based investment options: The Age-Based Option contains six portfolios of underlying funds. Contributions are placed into the portfolio corresponding to the beneficiary's age, and later reassigned to more conservative portfolios as the beneficiary approaches college.

Static investment options: Select among six blended-fund portfolios and 19 individual-fund portfolios.

Underlying investments: Mutual funds from Liberty Funds, Columbia Management, OppenheimerFunds, and Marsico Capital

Fees and expenses: $25 annual account maintenance fee on accounts under $25,000, 0.30% annualized program management fee charged against the value of the account, and underlying fund expenses recently ranging from approximately 0.67% to 1.61%. In addition, accounts are subject to one of three alternative broker expense structures that will determine any initial sales charge, contingent deferred sales charge, and/or additional asset-based fees. There is no enrollment fee.

Maximum contributions: Accepts contributions until all Nevada account balances for the same beneficiary reach $250,000.

Minimum initial contribution: $1,000 per portfolio

Account changes: The program accepts requests to change beneficiary, name a successor owner, and transact rollovers and investment changes that meet the requirements of federal tax law and IRS regulations.

Special considerations:

- There are no state income tax incentives because Nevada does not have a personal income tax.
- Under Nevada law, an account is exempt from creditor claims, subject to a $500,000 cap and only on those assets in the 529 plan prior to the claim. This protection extends only to those assets eventually used for the beneficiary's college expenses.

STATE: **NEW HAMPSHIRE**

PROGRAM NAME:	UNIQUE College Investing Plan
529 TYPE:	Savings
STATE AGENCY:	State Treasurer
PROGRAM MANAGER:	Fidelity Investments
INITIAL YEAR OF OPERATION:	1998
TELEPHONE:	1–800–544–1722
INTERNET:	www.fidelity.com/unique

Who can purchase a contract? U.S. citizens and resident aliens 18 years and older, UTMA/UGMA custodians, and trusts. Not available through brokers.

Time or age limitations on beneficiary or on use of account assets: None

Age-based investment option: The Age-Based Strategy contains eight portfolios of underlying funds. Contributions are placed into the portfolio corresponding to the age of the beneficiary or as determined by the account owner. Seven portfolios shift to a more conservative investment allocation over time, eventually transferring to the College portfolio.

Static investment options: Select among three portfolios: 100% Equity, 70% Equity, and Conservative (100% fixed income and money market).

Underlying investments: Fidelity Investments mutual funds

Fees and expenses: $30 annual account maintenance fee on accounts less than $25,000 (waived for accounts in the automatic investment plan), 0.30% annualized program management fee charged against the value of the account, and underlying fund expenses recently ranging from approximately 0.65% to 0.81% (portfolio weighted average). There is no enrollment fee.

Maximum contributions: Accepts contributions until all New Hampshire account balances for the same beneficiary reach $270,000.

Minimum initial contribution: $1,000 ($50 with automatic bank transfers or payroll deduction).

Account changes: The program accepts requests to change beneficiary, name a successor owner, and transact rollovers and investment changes that meet the requirements of federal tax law and IRS regulations. Account ownership may not be transferred prior to the owner's death or incapacity.

Special considerations:

- Under state law, qualified distributions from this program and all other 529 plans are exempt from New Hampshire interest and dividends tax. New Hampshire does not have a personal income tax.

STATE: **NEW HAMPSHIRE**

PROGRAM NAME:	Fidelity Advisor 529 Plan
529 TYPE:	Savings
STATE AGENCY:	State Treasurer
PROGRAM MANAGER:	Fidelity Investments
INITIAL YEAR OF OPERATION:	2001
TELEPHONE:	1–800–522–7297
INTERNET:	www.advisor.fidelity.com/529

Who can purchase a contract? U.S. residents and trusts. This program is distributed through brokers.

Time or age limitations on beneficiary or on use of account assets: None

Age-based investment option: The Age-Based Strategy contains eight portfolios of underlying funds. Contributions are placed into the portfolio corresponding to the age of the beneficiary or as determined by the account owner. Seven portfolios shift to a more conservative investment allocation over time, eventually transferring to the College portfolio.

Static investment options: Select among two blended-fund portfolios (100% Equity and 70% Equity) and eleven individual-fund portfolios.

Underlying investments: Fidelity Advisor Funds and Fidelity Cash Reserves

Fees and expenses: $30 annual account maintenance fee on accounts less than $25,000 (waived for accounts in the automatic investment plan), 0.30% annualized program management fee charged against the value of the account, and underlying fund expenses recently ranging from approximately 0.39% to 1.14%. In addition, accounts are subject to one of five alternative broker expense structures that will determine any initial sales charge, contingent deferred sales charge, and/or additional asset-based fees. There is no enrollment fee.

Maximum contributions: Accepts contributions until all New Hampshire account balances for the same beneficiary reach $270,000.

Minimum initial contribution: $1,000 ($50 with automatic investment)

Account changes: The program accepts requests to change beneficiary, transfer account ownership, name a successor owner, and transact rollovers and investment changes that meet the requirements of federal tax law and IRS regulations.

Special considerations:

- Under state law, qualified distributions from this program and all other 529 plans are exempt from New Hampshire interest and dividends tax. New Hampshire does not have a personal income tax.

STATE: **NEW JERSEY**

PROGRAM NAME: New Jersey Better Educational Savings Trust 529 College Savings Plan (NJBEST)
529 TYPE: Savings
STATE AGENCY: New Jersey Higher Education Student Assistance Authority (HESAA)
PROGRAM MANAGER: Franklin Templeton Distributors, Inc.
INITIAL YEAR OF OPERATION: 1998
TELEPHONE: 1–877–4–NJBEST (1–877–465–2378)
INTERNET: www.NJBEST.com

Who can purchase a contract? Individuals who have reached the age of majority, trusts, and legal entities. The account owner or beneficiary must be a New Jersey resident at the time of enrollment. Not available through brokers.

Time or age limitations on beneficiary or on use of account assets: None

Age-based investment option: The Age-Based Investment Portfolios consist of five portfolios of underlying funds, ranging from 100% equity to 100% fixed income. Contributions are placed into the portfolio corresponding to the beneficiary's age, and later reassigned to more conservative portfolios as the beneficiary approaches college. For accounts established prior to March 17, 2003, contributions may be invested in age-based portfolios managed by the New Jersey Division of Investment.

Static investment options: Select among four blended-fund portfolios (Growth, CoreFolio, Growth & Income, and Income), a S&P 500 Index portfolio, and a stable value portfolio.

Underlying investments: Franklin Templeton mutual funds in the blended-fund portfolios, the UBS S&P 500 Index Fund in the S&P 500 Index portfolio, and a Franklin Templeton stable value portfolio.

Fees and expenses: 0.40% annualized program management fee charged against the value of the account, and underlying fund expenses recently ranging from approximately 0.45% to 0.88%. There are no enrollment or account maintenance fees.

Maximum contributions: Accepts contributions until all New Jersey account balances for the same beneficiary reach $305,000.

Minimum initial contribution: $25 per investment option and $300 per year until account balance reaches $1,200

Account changes: The program accepts requests to change beneficiary, transfer account ownership, name a successor owner, and transact rollovers and investment changes that meet the requirements of federal tax law and IRS regulations.

Special considerations:
- A beneficiary may receive a scholarship from the program if he or she enrolls as an undergraduate in a New Jersey college or university or a degree-granting program at a New Jersey proprietary school licensed or approved by the New Jersey Commission on Higher Education, and meets certain participation requirements. Scholarship amounts range from $500 (requires $1,200 in contributions and four years of program participation) to $1,500 (requires $3,600 in contributions and 12 years of program participation).
- Under state law, qualified distributions from this program and all other 529 plans are exempt from New Jersey state income tax.
- Up to $25,000 in account value will not be counted in determining eligibility and need for student financial aid programs provided by the state of New Jersey.
- Under New Jersey state law, accounts are exempt from claims of creditors and are excluded from an estate in bankruptcy, with certain exceptions.

STATE: **NEW JERSEY**

PROGRAM NAME:	Franklin Templeton 529 College Savings Plan
529 TYPE:	Savings
STATE AGENCY:	New Jersey Higher Education Student Assistance Authority (HESAA)
PROGRAM MANAGER:	Franklin Templeton Distributors, Inc.
INITIAL YEAR OF OPERATION:	2003
TELEPHONE:	1–800–223–2141
INTERNET:	www.franklintempleton.com

Who can purchase a contract? Individuals who have reached the age of majority, trusts, and legal entities. This program is distributed through brokers.

Time or age limitations on beneficiary or on use of account assets: None

Age-based investment option: The Age-Based Investment Portfolios consist of five portfolios of underlying funds, ranging from 100% equity to 100% fixed income. Contributions are placed into the portfolio corresponding to the beneficiary's age, and later reassigned to more conservative portfolios as the beneficiary approaches college.

Static investment options: Select among four blended-fund portfolios (Growth, CoreFolio, Growth & Income, and Income), and twelve individual-fund portfolios which include a S&P 500 Index portfolio and a stable value portfolio.

Underlying investments: Franklin Templeton mutual funds in the blended-fund and certain individual-fund portfolios, the UBS S&P 500 Index Fund in the S&P 500 Index portfolio, and a Franklin Templeton stable value portfolio

Fees and expenses: $25 annual account maintenance fee on accounts $25,000 or less (waived for New Jersey residents and accounts in an automatic investment plan), 0.40% annualized program management fee charged against the value of the account, and underlying fund expenses recently ranging from approximately 0.85% to 2.11%. In addition, accounts are subject to one of three alternative broker expense structures that will determine any initial sales charge, contingent deferred sales charge, and/or additional asset-based fees. There is no enrollment fee.

Maximum contributions: Accepts contributions until all New Jersey account balances for the same beneficiary reach $305,000.

Minimum initial contribution: $250 ($50 with automatic investment)

Account changes: The program accepts requests to change beneficiary, transfer account ownership, name a successor owner, and transact rollovers and investment changes that meet the requirements of federal tax law and IRS regulations.

Special considerations:

- A beneficiary will receive a scholarship from the program if he or she enrolls as an undergraduate in a New Jersey college or university or a degree-granting program at a New Jersey proprietary school licensed or approved by the New Jersey Commission on Higher Education, and meets certain participation requirements. Scholarship amounts range from $500 (requires $1,200 in contributions and four years of program participation) to $1,500 (requires $3,600 in contributions and 12 years of program participation).
- Under state law, qualified distributions from this program and all other 529 plans are exempt from New Jersey state income tax.
- Up to $25,000 in account value will not be counted in determining eligibility and need for student financial aid programs provided by the state of New Jersey.
- Under New Jersey state law, accounts are exempt from claims of creditors and are excluded from an estate in bankruptcy, with certain exceptions.

STATE: **NEW MEXICO**

PROGRAM NAME:	The Education Plan's Prepaid Tuition Program
529 TYPE:	Prepaid contract
STATE AGENCY:	Education Trust Board of New Mexico
PROGRAM MANAGER:	Schoolhouse Capital, a division of State Street Corporation
INITIAL YEAR OF OPERATION:	2000
TELEPHONE:	1–877–EdPlan8 (1–877–337–5268)
INTERNET:	www.theeducationplan.com

Who can purchase a contract? U.S. residents 18 years and older, and legal entities. The purchaser or beneficiary must be a New Mexico resident at the time of program enrollment.

Enrollment period: September 1 to December 31 of each year (newborns anytime)

Time or age limitations on beneficiary or on use of benefits: The contract must be purchased at least five years before anticipated use. Contract benefits must be used within ten years of the anticipated college enrollment date as specified at the time of purchase (with extensions for time in the military).

Contract benefits: The contract pays in-state undergraduate tuition and mandatory fees for the normal full-time course load at New Mexico public institutions for the number of years of education purchased. For attendance at a private college in New Mexico, an out-of-state college, or graduate school, the program will pay the lesser of: 1) the average in-state tuition and mandatory fees for the school category purchased or, 2) the amount of net principal contributions to the account plus a reasonable rate of interest as determined by the program. If the beneficiary receives a scholarship, grant, or tuition waiver, excess contract value may be applied toward other qualified expenses or withdrawn without penalty.

Contract options: One to five years of education at New Mexico public branch and community colleges, comprehensive universities, or research universities

Costs: There is no enrollment fee. For the enrollment period that ends December 31, 2004, the per-year cost of a branch/community college contract is $1,043, the per-year cost of a comprehensive university contract is $3,006, and the per-year cost of a research university is $4,367. Contract payments may be made in a lump sum, installment payments, or a combination of lump sum and installment payments. Installment payments are computed to include an additional amount for making payments over time.

Cancellation provisions: A contract can be canceled at any time for a refund equal to contract payments (less a cancellation fee of as much as $150), plus interest at a rate determined by the Board if cancellation occurs after the fifth anniversary of purchase. The cancellation fee is waived if the withdrawal is due to the beneficiary's death, disability, or receipt of scholarship.

Contract changes: The program accepts requests to change beneficiary (the original 10-year time limit for use will not change), transfer contract ownership, name a successor owner, and transact rollovers that meet the requirements of federal tax law and IRS regulations. The amount available for rollover consists of the principal payments made plus a reasonable amount of interest for contracts that are at least five years old. A rollover to The Education Plan's College Savings Program of New Mexico will be credited with interest without regard to the five-year minimum.

State backing: Contracts are not backed by the full faith and credit of the state of New Mexico. The program has an agreement with an affiliate of the program manager that exchanges all investment returns on program assets for an amount equal to the increase in a national tuition index of four-year public undergraduate institutions.

Special considerations:

- All payments made to the program are deductible from New Mexico taxable income. Deductions may be subject to recapture if non-qualified withdrawals are made in a subsequent year.
- Under state law, qualified distributions from this program are exempt from New Mexico income tax. Because New Mexico tax law generally conforms to federal tax law, any qualified distributions from other 529 plans that are exempt from federal income tax are also exempt from New Mexico income tax.
- The value of the contract will not be counted in determining eligibility and need for student financial aid programs provided by the state of New Mexico.

STATE: **NEW MEXICO**

PROGRAM NAME:	The Education Plan's College Savings Program
529 TYPE:	Savings
STATE AGENCY:	Education Trust Board of New Mexico
PROGRAM MANAGER:	Schoolhouse Capital, a division of State Street Corporation
INITIAL YEAR OF OPERATION:	2000
TELEPHONE:	1–877–EdPlan8 (1–877–337–5268)
INTERNET:	www.theeducationplan.com

Who can purchase a contract? U.S. residents 18 years and older, UTMA/UGMA custodians, and legal entities. This program is distributed both direct and through brokers.

Time or age limitations on beneficiary or on use of account assets: For New Mexico resident account owners, there is a one year waiting period from the time the account is established for withdrawals and rollovers.

Age-based investment option: The Age-Based Choice option contains five portfolios of underlying funds, ranging from an 85%/15% blend of stock and fixed income funds to a 20%/80% blend. Contributions are placed into the portfolio corresponding to the beneficiary's age, and later reassigned to more conservative portfolios as the beneficiary approaches college.

Static investment options: Select among eight blended-fund portfolios: the five portfolios under the Age-Based Choice option, a 100% equity portfolio, a 100% fixed income portfolio, and a 100% short-term yield portfolio.

Underlying investments: Mutual funds from State Street Global Advisors, Janus, Fidelity, Baron, and MFS Investment Management.

Fees and expenses: $30 annual account maintenance fee on accounts less than $10,000 (waived for New Mexico residents, and for accounts in an automatic investment or payroll deduction plan), 0.30% annualized program management fee charged against the value of the account, and underlying fund expenses recently ranging from approximately 0.49% to 1.43%. There is no enrollment fee. Accounts opened through a broker are subject to a 3.5% initial sales charge.

Maximum contributions: Accepts contributions until all New Mexico account balances for the same beneficiary reach $294,000.

Minimum initial contribution: $250 ($25 with payroll deduction)

Account changes: The program accepts requests to change beneficiary, transfer account ownership, name a successor owner, and transact rollovers and investment changes that meet the requirements of federal tax law and IRS regulations.

Special considerations:

- All contributions are deductible from New Mexico taxable income. Deductions may be subject to recapture if non-qualified withdrawals are made in a subsequent year.
- Under state law, qualified distributions from this program are exempt from New Mexico income tax. Because New Mexico tax law generally conforms to federal tax law, any qualified distributions from other 529 plans that are exempt from federal income tax are also exempt from New Mexico income tax.
- The value of the account will not be counted in determining eligibility and need for student financial aid programs provided by the state of New Mexico.

STATE:	**NEW MEXICO**
PROGRAM NAME:	CollegeSense 529 Higher Education Savings Plan
529 TYPE:	Savings
STATE AGENCY:	Education Trust Board of New Mexico
PROGRAM MANAGER:	Schoolhouse Capital, a division of State Street Corporation
DISTRIBUTION PARTNER:	New York Life Investment Management
INITIAL YEAR OF OPERATION:	2001
TELEPHONE:	1–866–529–SENSE (1–866–529–7367)
INTERNET:	www.collegesense.com

Who can purchase a contract? U.S. residents 18 years and older, UTMA/UGMA custodians, and legal entities. This program is distributed through brokers.

Time or age limitations on beneficiary or on use of account assets: For New Mexico resident account owners, there is a one year waiting period from the time the account is established for withdrawals and rollovers.

Age-based investment option: The Age-Based Choice option contains five portfolios of underlying funds, ranging from an 85%/15% blend of stock and fixed income funds to a 25%/75% blend. Contributions are placed into the portfolio corresponding to the beneficiary's age, and later reassigned to more conservative portfolios as the beneficiary approaches college.

Static investment options: Select among eight blended-fund portfolios: the five portfolios under the Age-Based Choice option, the Equity Funds Portfolio, the Bond Funds Portfolio, and the Stable Value Portfolio.

Underlying investments: Mutual funds from New York Life Investment Management LLC, State Street Global Advisors, JP Morgan Fleming Asset Management, and Salomon Brothers. The stable value portfolio invests 10% in the Eclipse Money Market Fund and 90% in a funding agreement issued by New York Life Insurance Company.

Fees and expenses: $25 annual account maintenance fee on accounts less than $25,000 (waived for New Mexico residents, and for accounts in an automatic investment plan), 0.35% annualized program management fee charged against the value of the account, and underlying fund expenses recently ranging from approximately 0.49% to 2.27%. In addition, accounts are subject to one of three alternative broker expense structures that will determine any initial sales charge, contingent deferred sales charge, and/or additional asset-based fees. There is no enrollment fee.

Maximum contributions: Accepts contributions until all New Mexico account balances for the same beneficiary reach $294,000.

Minimum initial contribution: $500 ($50 with automatic investment)

Account changes: The program accepts requests to change beneficiary, transfer account ownership, name a successor owner, and transact rollovers and investment changes that meet the requirements of federal tax law and IRS regulations.

Special considerations:

- New Mexico residents receive the same state income tax and financial aid benefits described previously for The Education Plan's College Savings Program of New Mexico.

STATE: **NEW MEXICO**

PROGRAM NAME:	Scholar'sEdge
529 TYPE:	Savings
STATE AGENCY:	Education Trust Board of New Mexico
PROGRAM MANAGER:	Schoolhouse Capital, a division of State Street Corporation
DISTRIBUTOR:	OppenheimerFunds Distributor, Inc.
INITIAL YEAR OF OPERATION:	2001
TELEPHONE:	1–866–529–SAVE (1–866–529–7283)
INTERNET:	www.scholarsedge529.com

Who can purchase a contract? U.S. residents 18 years and older, UTMA/UGMA custodians, and legal entities. This program is distributed through brokers.

Time or age limitations on beneficiary or on use of account assets: For New Mexico resident account owners, there is a one year waiting period from the time the account is established for withdrawals and rollovers.

Age-based investment option: The Age-Based Choice option contains five portfolios of underlying funds, ranging from an 85%/15% blend of stock and fixed income funds to a 25%/75% blend. Contributions are placed into the portfolio corresponding to the beneficiary's age, and later reassigned to more conservative portfolios as the beneficiary approaches college.

Static investment options: Select among sixteen portfolios: the five portfolios under the Age-Based Choice option, a 100% equity portfolio, a 100% fixed-income portfolio, a 100% short-term yield portfolio, and eight individual-fund portfolios.

Underlying investments: Mutual funds from OppenheimerFunds and State Street Global Advisors.

Fees and expenses: $25 annual account maintenance fee on accounts less than $25,000 (waived for New Mexico residents, and for accounts in an automatic investment plan), and underlying fund expenses recently ranging from approximately 0.50% to 1.88%. In addition, accounts are subject to one of three alternative broker expense structures that will determine any initial sales charge, contingent deferred sales charge, and/or additional asset-based fees. There is no enrollment fee.

Maximum contributions: Accepts contributions until all New Mexico account balances for the same beneficiary reach $294,000.

Minimum initial contribution: $250 ($100 with automatic investment) except for the individual-fund portfolios which require $5,000 with a minimum of $1,000 per portfolio

Account changes: The program accepts requests to change beneficiary, transfer account ownership, name a successor owner, and transact rollovers and investment changes that meet the requirements of federal tax law and IRS regulations.

Special considerations:

- New Mexico residents receive the same state income tax and financial aid benefits described previously for The Education Plan's College Savings Program of New Mexico.

STATE:	**NEW MEXICO**
PROGRAM NAME:	Arrive Education Savings Plan
529 TYPE:	Savings
STATE AGENCY:	Education Trust Board of New Mexico
PROGRAM MANAGER:	Schoolhouse Capital, a division of State Street Corporation
DISTRIBUTION PARTNERS:	Evergreen Investments, Prudential Financial, and SunAmerica
INITIAL YEAR OF OPERATION:	2002
TELEPHONE:	1–877–277–4838
INTERNET:	www.arrive529.com

Who can purchase a contract? U.S. residents 18 years and older, UTMA/UGMA custodians, and legal entities. This program is distributed through brokers.

Time or age limitations on beneficiary or on use of account assets: For New Mexico resident account owners, there is a one year waiting period from the time the account is established for withdrawals and rollovers.

Age-based investment option: The Age-Based Portfolio option contains five portfolios of underlying funds, ranging from an 85%/15% blend of stock and fixed income funds to a 25%/75% blend. Contributions are placed into the portfolio corresponding to the beneficiary's age, and later reassigned to more conservative portfolios as the beneficiary approaches college.

Static investment options: Select among twenty-two portfolios: the five portfolios under the Age-Based Choice option, the a 100% Equity Portfolio, a 100% Fixed Income Portfolio, a Stable Value Portfolio, and fourteen individual-fund portfolios.

Underlying investments: Mutual funds from Evergreen Investments, Prudential Financial, State Street Global Advisors, and SunAmerica. The Prudential Insurance Company of America provides the stable value investment.

Fees and expenses: $25 annual account maintenance fee on accounts less than $25,000 (waived for New Mexico residents, and for accounts in an automatic investment plan), 0.40% annualized program management fee charged against the value of the account, and underlying fund expenses recently ranging from approximately 0.44% to 1.47%. In addition, accounts are subject to one of three alternative broker expense structures that will determine any initial sales charge, contingent deferred sales charge, and/or additional asset-based fees. There is no enrollment fee.

Maximum contributions: Accepts contributions until all New Mexico account balances for the same beneficiary reach $294,000.

Minimum initial contribution: $250 ($100 with automatic investment) except for the individual-fund portfolios which require $5,000 with a minimum of $1,000 per portfolio.

Account changes: The program accepts requests to change beneficiary, transfer account ownership, name a successor owner, and transact rollovers and investment changes that meet the requirements of federal tax law and IRS regulations.

Special considerations:

- New Mexico residents receive the same state income tax and financial aid benefits described previously for The Education Plan's College Savings Program of New Mexico.

STATE:	**NEW YORK**
PROGRAM NAME:	New York's 529 College Savings Program Direct Plan
529 TYPE:	Savings
STATE AGENCIES:	Office of the State Comptroller and the New York State Higher Education Services Corporation
PROGRAM MANAGER:	Upromise Investments, Inc.
INVESTMENT MANAGER:	The Vanguard Group
INITIAL YEAR OF OPERATION:	1998
TELEPHONE:	1–877–NYSAVES (1–877–697–2837)
INTERNET:	www.nysaves.org

Who can purchase a contract? U.S. citizens and resident aliens, including minors (with signature of parent or guardian), UTMA/UGMA custodians, and legal entities. Not available through brokers.

Time or age limitations on beneficiary or on use of account assets: None

Age-based investment options: The program offers a choice of three schedules: Aggressive, Moderate, and Conservative. Contributions are placed into a portfolio corresponding to the selected schedule and the age of the beneficiary and later reassigned to more conservative portfolios as the beneficiary approaches college.

Static investment options: Select among twelve portfolios ranging from 100% equity to 100% short-term reserves.

Underlying investments: Vanguard mutual funds

Fees and expenses: 0.58% annualized program management fee charged against the value of the account, which includes the expenses of the underlying mutual funds. There are no enrollment or account maintenance fees.

Maximum contributions: Accepts contributions until all New York account balances for the same beneficiary reach $235,000.

Minimum initial contribution: $25, or $15 with payroll deduction

Account changes: The program accepts requests to change beneficiary, name a successor owner, and transact rollovers and investment changes that meet the requirements of federal tax law and IRS regulations.

Special considerations:
- Up to $5,000 ($10,000 for married couples filing joint returns) of total annual contributions may be deducted from New York taxable income each year. Deductions may be subject to recapture if non-qualified withdrawals or rollovers to another state's 529 plan are made in a subsequent year.
- Under state law, qualified distributions from this program are exempt from New York income tax. Because New York tax law generally conforms to federal tax law, any qualified distributions from other 529 plans that are exempt from federal income tax are also exempt from New York income tax.
- Rollovers to other 529 plans are subject to New York State tax on the earnings and recapture of prior deductions.
- The value of the account will not be counted in determining eligibility and need for student financial aid programs provided by the state of New York.
- Under New York law, up to $10,000 of the aggregate account value is exempt from an application to satisfy a money judgment against the account owner. The entire account is exempt if owned by the minor beneficiary, or if the account is established in connection with a scholarship.

STATE: **NEW YORK**

PROGRAM NAME:	New York's 529 College Savings Program Advisor Plan
529 TYPE:	Savings
STATE AGENCIES:	Office of the State Comptroller and New York State Higher Education Services Corporation
PROGRAM MANAGER:	Upromise Investments, Inc.
INVESTMENT MANAGER:	Columbia Management Group
INITIAL YEAR OF OPERATION:	2003
TELEPHONE:	1–800–774–2108
INTERNET:	www.ny529advisor.com

Who can purchase a contract? U.S. citizens and resident aliens, including minors (with signature of parent or guardian), UTMA/UGMA custodians, and legal entities. This program is distributed through brokers.

Time or age limitations on beneficiary or on use of account assets: None

Age-based investment options: The Age-Based Option contains six portfolios of underlying funds. Contributions are placed into the portfolio corresponding to the age of the beneficiary and later reassigned to more conservative portfolios as the beneficiary approaches college.

Static investment options: Select among eight blended-fund portfolios and twelve individual-fund portfolios.

Underlying investments: Primarily Columbia Funds but with several non-Columbia funds offered as individual-fund portfolios.

Fees and expenses: $25 annual account maintenance fee for accounts $25,000 or less, 0.30% annualized program management fee charged against the value of the account, and underlying fund expenses recently ranging from approximately 0.67% to 2.44%. In addition, accounts are subject to one of three alternative broker expense structures that will determine any initial sales charge, contingent deferred sales charge, and/or additional asset-based fee. There is no enrollment fee.

Maximum contributions: Accepts contributions until all New York account balances for the same beneficiary reach $235,000.

Minimum initial contribution: $1,000 per portfolio

Account changes: The program accepts requests to change beneficiary, name a successor owner, and transact rollovers and investment changes that meet the requirements of federal tax law and IRS regulations.

Special considerations:

- New York residents receive the same state income tax, financial aid, and creditor protection benefits described previously for New York's 529 College Savings Program Direct Plan.

STATE:	**NORTH CAROLINA**
PROGRAM NAME:	North Carolina's National College Savings Program
529 TYPE:	Savings
STATE AGENCY:	North Carolina State Education Assistance Authority
PROGRAM MANAGER:	College Foundation, Inc.
DISTRIBUTION PARTNER (ADVISOR-SOLD ONLY):	Seligman Advisors, Inc.
INITIAL YEAR OF OPERATION:	2001 (predecessor program opened in 1998)
TELEPHONE:	1–800–600–3453
INTERNET:	www.CFNC.org/savings (direct-sold) www.seligman529.com (advisor-sold)

Who can purchase a contract? Individuals who have reached the age of majority and emancipated minors; trusts, estates and business entities such as corporations, partnerships or associations; UTMA/UGMA custodians, state/local government agencies, and 501(c)(3) organizations. This program is distributed both direct and through brokers. Anyone, except for a client of certain fee-only planners, who does not meet North Carolina's residency or employment requirements must open their account through a broker.

Time or age limitations on beneficiary or on use of account assets: None

Age-based investment option: The Seligman CollegeHorizonFunds strategy consists of 22 portfolios of underlying funds based on specified time frames relating to college enrollment, ranging from 18 years before college starts through the senior year of college. Contributions are generally placed into the portfolio corresponding to the number of years to expected enrollment, and later reassigned to more conservative portfolios as the beneficiary approaches college.

Static investment options: Participants enrolling directly have the following options: the Aggressive Stock Fund (100% equity), the Balanced Fund, the Dependable Income Fund (a fixed income portfolio), and the Protected Stock Fund (a funding agreement issued by MetLife that guarantees principal plus the greater of a minimum annualized interest rate or 70% of the price return, excluding dividends, of the S&P 500 Index following a subscription period and five-year index period). Participants enrolling through a broker have the following options: the Seligman Aggressive Allocation, the Seligman Balanced Allocation, the Seligman Income Option, and the MetLife Protected Stock Fund. In addition, any of the portfolios available in the age-based option may be acquired and held as a static investment.

Underlying investments: The CollegeHorizonFunds option and certain static options are invested in mutual funds from J. & W. Seligman & Co. The Aggressive Stock Fund is invested approximately 50% in NCM Capital's Focused Equity Discipline and 50% in the Legg Mason Value Trust. The Balanced Fund is invested in Evergreen mutual funds with approximately 40% in stocks, 30% in Treasury Inflation Securities (TIPS), and 30% in other fixed-income securities. The Dependable Income Fund is invested in the North Carolina state treasurer's short-term investment portfolio. The Protected Stock Fund is provided through an agreement with MetLife.

Fees and expenses: For participants enrolling directly, there is an annualized program management fee of up to 0.25% charged against the value of the account, and underlying fund expenses of 0.05% in the Dependable Income Fund and ranging from approximately 0.63% to 1.39% (portfolio weighted average) in the other options. For participants enrolling through a broker, there is a $25 annual account maintenance fee on accounts less than $25,000 (waived for accounts in the automatic investment plan and for accounts in the MetLife Protected Stock Fund), an annualized program management fee of up to 0.25% charged against the value of the account, and underlying fund expenses for the Seligman options recently ranging from approximately 0.63% to 1.74% (portfolio weighted average). In addition, accounts opened through a broker are subject to one of three alternative broker expense structures that will determine any initial sales charges, contingent deferred sales charges, and/or additional asset-based fees.

Maximum contributions: Accepts contributions until all North Carolina account balances for the same beneficiary reach $297,211.

Minimum initial contribution: $5 with direct enrollment; $100 per portfolio for the Seligman options ($25 with automatic investment or payroll deduction) and $1,000 for the MetLife Protected Stock Fund when enrolling through a broker.

Account changes: The program accepts requests to change beneficiary, transfer account ownership, name a successor owner, and transact rollovers and investment changes that meet the requirements of federal tax law and IRS regulations.

Special considerations:

- North Carolina does not specifically provide that qualified distributions are exempt from state income tax, but its tax law generally conforms to federal tax law and so any qualified distributions that are exempt from federal income are also exempt from North Carolina income tax.

- The program description warns nonresidents of North Carolina that accounts may have sufficient tax situs so as to be subject to North Carolina estate tax.

STATE: **NORTH DAKOTA**

PROGRAM NAME:	College SAVE
529 TYPE:	Savings
STATE AGENCY:	Bank of North Dakota
PROGRAM MANAGER:	Morgan Stanley
INITIAL YEAR OF OPERATION:	2001
TELEPHONE:	1–866–SAVE529 (1–866–728–3529)
INTERNET:	www.collegesave4u.com

Who can purchase a contract? U.S. citizens and resident aliens 18 years and older, UTMA/UGMA custodians, trusts, state/local government agencies, and 501(c)(3) organizations. This program is distributed both direct and through Morgan Stanley brokers.

Time or age limitations on beneficiary or on use of account assets: None

Age-based investment options: The Age-Based Portfolios offer a choice of three different investment schedules (Aggressive, Moderate, and Conservative) and within each schedule an Actively Managed Fund Option or Index Fund Option is offered. Each schedule contains five portfolios of underlying funds. Contributions are placed into the portfolio corresponding to the selected schedule and the beneficiary's age or number of years to anticipated withdrawal. The portfolios shift to a more conservative investment allocation over time.

Static investment options: Select among four portfolios: an aggressive portfolio that includes an actively managed equity fund, an aggressive portfolio that includes an index equity fund, a balanced portfolio that includes an actively managed equity fund, and a balanced portfolio that includes an index equity fund. The aggressive portfolios currently target 90% in stock funds and 10% in bond funds. The balanced portfolios currently target 50% in stock funds, 41% in bond funds, and 9% in cash/money market securities.

Underlying investments: Mutual funds from Morgan Stanley and Van Kampen.

Fees and expenses: $30 annual account maintenance fee (waived for North Dakota residents and for accounts opened by South Dakota residents prior to 2/28/02), 0.50% annualized program management fee charged against the value of the account (also waived for North Dakota residents and for accounts opened by South Dakota residents prior to 2/28/02), and underlying fund expenses recently ranging from approximately 1.17% to 1.71% (portfolio weighted average). There is no enrollment fee and no additional broker expenses.

Maximum contributions: Accepts contributions until all North Dakota account balances for the same beneficiary reach $269,000.

Minimum initial contribution: $30 ($300 minimum account balance required by end of first year)

Account changes: The program accepts requests to change beneficiary, transfer account ownership, name a successor owner, and transact rollovers and investment changes that meet the requirements of federal tax law and IRS regulations.

Special considerations:

- North Dakota does not specifically provide that qualified distributions are exempt from state income tax, but its tax law generally conforms to federal tax law and so any qualified distributions that are exempt from federal income tax are also exempt from North Dakota income tax.
- Under North Dakota law, interests of the account owner and beneficiary in an account are not subject to attachment or alienation by third-party creditors.

STATE: **OHIO**

PROGRAM NAME:	Ohio CollegeAdvantage 529 Savings Plan
529 TYPE:	Savings
STATE AGENCY/PROGRAM MANAGER:	Ohio Tuition Trust Authority (OTTA)
INITIAL YEAR OF OPERATION:	2000
TELEPHONE:	1–800–AFFORD–IT (1–800–233–6734)
INTERNET:	www.collegeadvantage.com

Who can purchase a contract? U.S. citizens and resident aliens, UTMA/UGMA custodians, trusts, and 501(c)(3) organizations. For the Putnam options, either the account owner or the beneficiary must meet Ohio's residency requirements at the time the account is opened. There are no Ohio residency requirements for the Vanguard options.

Time or age limitations on beneficiary or on use of benefits: None

Age-based investment option: One Putnam and three Vanguard Age-Based investment options are offered. The Putnam Age-Based Portfolio contains eight mutual funds. Contributions are allocated between these funds based on the age of the beneficiary. A reallocation of each account is made as the beneficiary ages. The Vanguard Age-Based Options offer a choice among three different schedules: Aggressive, Moderate, and Conservative. Each schedule contains five portfolios of underlying funds. Contributions are placed into the portfolio corresponding to the age of the beneficiary. The portfolios shift to a more conservative investment allocation over time.

Static investment options: Select among several Putnam and Vanguard investment options. The Putnam investment options offer three blended-fund portfolios (Aggressive Growth, Growth, and Balanced), a stable value portfolio, and 12 individual-fund portfolios. The Vanguard investment options offer four blended-fund portfolios and seven individual-fund portfolios.

Underlying investments: Putnam Investments mutual funds and Vanguard funds.

Fees and expenses: Audit and administration expenses of up to 0.04% may be charged against the program fund. A 0.05% OTTA fee is charged for the Putnam investment options and a 0.20% OTTA fee is charged for the Vanguard investment options. The expenses of the underlying funds for the Putnam investment options are 0.94% for the age-based portfolio and a range of approximately 0.52% to 1.35% for the static investment options. The expenses of the underlying funds for the Vanguard investment options range from approximately 0.15% to 0.29% which includes a 0.10% investment fee charged to the program by Vanguard. There are no enrollment or account maintenance fees.

Maximum contributions: Accepts contributions until all Ohio account balances for the same beneficiary reach $256,000.

Minimum initial contribution: $15

Account changes: The program accepts requests to change beneficiary, transfer account ownership, name a successor owner, and transact rollovers and investment changes that meet the requirements of federal tax law and IRS regulations.

Special considerations:
- Up to $2,000 in contributions per beneficiary may be deducted against Ohio taxable income each year, with unlimited carryforward of any excess contributions. Deductions may be subject to recapture if non-qualified withdrawals are made in a subsequent year, unless the withdrawal results from the beneficiary's death, disability, or receipt of scholarship.
- Under state law, qualified distributions from this program, and distributions due to the beneficiary's death, disability, or receipt of a scholarship, are exempt from Ohio income tax. Because Ohio tax law generally conforms to federal tax law, any qualified distributions from other state 529 plans that are exempt from federal income tax are also exempt from Ohio income tax.
- Under Ohio law, an account shall not be subject to execution, garnishment, attachment, the operation of bankruptcy or insolvency laws, or other process of law.

STATE: **OHIO**

PROGRAM NAME:	Putnam CollegeAdvantage
529 TYPE:	Savings
STATE AGENCY:	Ohio Tuition Trust Authority (OTTA)
PROGRAM MANAGER:	Putnam Investments
INITIAL YEAR OF OPERATION:	2000
TELEPHONE:	1–800–225–1581
INTERNET:	www.putnaminvestments.com

Who can purchase a contract? U.S. citizens and resident aliens, UTMA/UGMA custodians, trusts, and 501(c)(3) organizations. This program is distributed through brokers.

Time or age limitations on beneficiary or on use of account assets: None

Age-based investment option: The Age-Based Portfolio contains eight mutual funds. Contributions are allocated between these funds based on the age of the beneficiary. A reallocation of each account is made as the beneficiary ages.

Static investment options: Select among sixteen options: three blended-fund portfolios (Aggressive Growth, Growth, and Balanced), a stable value option, and twelve individual-fund options.

Underlying investments: Putnam Investments mutual funds

Fees and expenses: $15 annual account maintenance fee on accounts with less than $25,000 (waived for Ohio residents and for accounts enrolled in an automatic investment plan with contributions of at least $50), 0.20% annualized program management fee charged against the value of the account, and underlying fund expenses recently ranging from approximately 0.52% to 1.40% (portfolio weighted average). In addition, accounts are subject to one of three alternative broker expense structures that will determine any initial sales charge, contingent deferred sales charge, and/or additional asset-based fees. There is no enrollment fee.

Maximum contributions: Accepts contributions until all Ohio account balances for the same beneficiary reach $256,000.

Minimum initial contribution: $25, or $15 per month

Account changes: The program accepts requests to change beneficiary, transfer account ownership, name a successor owner, and transact rollovers and investment changes that meet the requirements of federal tax law and IRS regulations.

Special considerations:

- Ohio residents receive the same state income tax and creditor protection benefits described previously for the Ohio CollegeAdvantage 529 Savings Plan.

STATE:	**OHIO**
PROGRAM NAME:	Guaranteed Savings Fund
529 TYPE:	Guaranteed savings
STATE AGENCY/PROGRAM MANAGER:	Ohio Tuition Trust Authority (OTTA)
INITIAL YEAR OF OPERATION:	1989
TELEPHONE:	1–800–AFFORD–IT (1–800–233–6734)
INTERNET:	www.collegeadvantage.com

PLEASE NOTE: The Ohio Tuition Trust Authority has suspended contributions into this fund through December 31, 2005. OTTA will decide in 2005 whether to re-open the fund to contributions in 2006.

Who can purchase a contract? Individuals 18 years and older and emancipated minors. Either the account owner or the beneficiary must meet Ohio's residency requirements at the time the account is opened.

Time or age limitations on beneficiary or on use of benefits: Withdrawals may not be taken until the account owner certifies that the beneficiary has reached age 18 or has graduated from high school. Rollovers are permitted prior to age 18.

Benefits: Each unit in the account is worth 1% of the weighted average tuition of Ohio's 13 four-year public universities if held on account until the beneficiary is age 18. As of August 1, 2004, this figure is $74.27 per unit. Tuition units can be redeemed to pay for tuition, fees, room and board, books, and other qualified college expenses at any accredited college or university in the country.

Costs: Pricing of tuition units will be determined prior to the fund accepting new contributions. There are no other annual fees or expenses.

Account changes: The program accepts requests to change beneficiary, transfer account ownership, name a successor owner, and transact rollovers that meet the requirements of federal tax law and IRS regulations. Rollover withdrawals from an account for a beneficiary under age 18 utilize an actuarial formula to determine the account value.

State backing: The Guaranteed Savings Fund is backed by the full faith and credit of the state of Ohio. The state would appropriate funds if the fund had insufficient assets to meet obligations.

Special considerations:

- Ohio residents receive the same state income tax and creditor protection benefits described previously for the Ohio CollegeAdvantage 529 Savings Plan.

STATE: **OKLAHOMA**

PROGRAM NAME:	Oklahoma College Savings Plan
529 TYPE:	Savings
STATE AGENCY:	Oklahoma College Savings Plan Board of Trustees
PROGRAM MANAGER:	TIAA-CREF Tuition Financing, Inc.
INITIAL YEAR OF OPERATION:	2000
TELEPHONE:	1–877–OK4–SAVING (1–877–654–7284)
INTERNET:	www.ok4saving.org

Who can purchase a contract? U.S. citizens and resident aliens 18 years and older with a valid Social Security number or federal taxpayer identification number, UTMA/UGMA custodians, and legal entities. Not available through brokers.

Time or age limitations on beneficiary or on use of account assets: None

Age-based investment option: The Managed Allocation Option contains eight portfolios of underlying funds. Contributions are placed into the portfolio corresponding to the age of the beneficiary. The portfolios shift to a more conservative investment allocation over time.

Static investment options: Select between two portfolios: the 100% Equity Option and the Guaranteed Option. The 100% Equity Option is invested in a blend of five institutional mutual funds. The Guaranteed Option is invested in an instrument that guarantees principal and a minimum 3% annual rate of interest (actual rate is declared quarterly).

Underlying investments: TIAA-CREF institutional mutual funds; the Guaranteed Option consists of a funding agreement with TIAA-CREF Life Insurance Company.

Fees and expenses: 0.55% annualized program management fee charged against the value of the account (none for the Guaranteed Option), and underlying fund expenses recently ranging from approximately 0.11% to 0.13% (portfolio weighted average). There are no enrollment or account maintenance fees.

Maximum contributions: Accepts contributions until all Oklahoma account balances for the same beneficiary reach $235,000.

Minimum initial contribution: $25, or $15 with payroll deduction

Account changes: The program accepts requests to change beneficiary, transfer account ownership, name a successor owner, and transact rollovers and investment changes that meet the requirements of federal tax law and IRS regulations.

Special considerations:

- Up to $2,500 in contributions per account are deductible from Oklahoma taxable income each year.
- Oklahoma does not specifically provide that qualified distributions are exempt from state income tax, but its tax law generally conforms to federal tax law and so any qualified distributions that are exempt from federal income tax are also exempt from Oklahoma income tax.
- Any interest in an account shall be reserved to any person residing in the state, exempt from attachment or execution and every other species of forced sale for the payment of debts.

STATE:	**OREGON**
PROGRAM NAME:	Oregon College Savings Plan
529 TYPE:	Savings
STATE AGENCY:	Oregon College Savings Plan Trust Board, chaired by Oregon State Treasurer
PROGRAM MANAGER:	OppenheimerFunds, Inc.
INITIAL YEAR OF OPERATION:	2001
TELEPHONE:	1–86–OR–SAVINGS (1–866–772–8464)
INTERNET:	www.oregoncollegesavings.com

Who can purchase a contract? U.S. citizens and resident aliens of legal age, UTMA/UGMA custodians, and legal entities. Not available through brokers.

Time or age limitations on beneficiary or on use of account assets: None

Age-based investment option: The Years-to-College option contains five portfolios of underlying funds, ranging from 80% equity to 100% fixed income and money market funds. Contributions are placed into the portfolio corresponding to the number of years to anticipated withdrawal, and later reassigned to more conservative portfolios as the beneficiary approaches college.

Static investment options: Select among six blended-fund portfolios (Aggressive, Moderate, Balanced, Conservative, Ultra Conservative, and 100% Equity), and five individual-fund portfolios.

Underlying investments: Mutual funds from Oppenheimer and The Vanguard Group.

Fees and expenses: $20 annual account maintenance fee per Vanguard Portfolio only (waived for Oregon residents), 0.25% annualized program management fee charged against the value of the account, and underlying fund expenses recently ranging from approximately 0.08% to 0.79%. There is no enrollment fee.

Maximum contributions: Accepts contributions until all account balances in the program for the same beneficiary reach $250,000.

Minimum initial contribution: $250 or $25 per month

Account changes: The program accepts requests to change beneficiary, transfer account ownership, name a successor owner, and transact rollovers and investment changes that meet the requirements of federal tax law and IRS regulations.

Special considerations:
- Up to $2,000 in contributions per taxpayer ($1,000 for married filing separate) are deductible from Oregon taxable income each year, with a four-year carryover of excess contributions. Deductions may be subject to recapture if non-qualified with-drawals are made in a subsequent year.
- Under state law, qualified distributions from this program are exempt from Oregon income tax. Because Oregon tax law generally conforms to federal tax law, any qualified distributions from other 529 plans that are exempt from federal income tax are also exempt from Oregon income tax.
- The value of the account will not be counted in determining eligibility and need for student financial aid programs provided by the state of Oregon.
- Investors are precluded from investing simultaneously in more than one 529 plan sponsored by the state of Oregon for the same beneficiary.

STATE:	**OREGON**
PROGRAM NAME:	OppenheimerFunds 529 Plan
529 TYPE:	Savings
STATE AGENCY:	Oregon College Savings Plan Trust Board, chaired by Oregon State Treasurer
PROGRAM MANAGER:	OppenheimerFunds, Inc.
INITIAL YEAR OF OPERATION:	2004
TELEPHONE:	1–86–OR–SAVINGS (1–866–772–8464)
INTERNET:	www.oregoncollegesavings.com or www.opp529.com

Who can purchase a contract? U.S. citizens and resident aliens of legal age, UTMA/UGMA custodians, and legal entities. This program is distributed through brokers.

Time or age limitations on beneficiary or on use of account assets: None

Age-based investment option: The Years-to-College option contains five portfolios of underlying funds, ranging from 80% equity to 100% fixed income and money market funds. Contributions are placed into the portfolio corresponding to the number of years to anticipated withdrawal, and later reassigned to more conservative portfolios as the beneficiary approaches college.

Static investment options: Select among seven portfolios (100% Equity, Aggressive, Moderate, Balanced, Conservative, Ultra Conservative, and Money Market).

Underlying investments: Mutual funds from Oppenheimer

Fees and expenses: 0.25% annualized program management fee charged against the value of the account, and underlying fund expenses recently ranging from approximately 0.52% to 0.79%. In addition, accounts are subject to one of three alternative broker expense structures that will determine any initial sales charge, contingent deferred sales charge, and/or additional asset-based fees. There are no enrollment or account maintenance fees.

Maximum contributions: Accepts contributions until all account balances in the program for the same beneficiary reach $250,000.

Minimum initial contribution: $250 or $25 per month

Account changes: The program accepts requests to change beneficiary, transfer account ownership, name a successor owner, and transact rollovers and investment changes that meet the requirements of federal tax law and IRS regulations.

Special considerations:
- Oregon residents receive the same state income tax and financial aid benefits described previously for the Oregon College Savings Plan.
- Investors are precluded from investing simultaneously in more than one 529 plan sponsored by the state of Oregon for the same beneficiary.

STATE: **OREGON**

PROGRAM NAME: MFS 529 Savings Plan
529 TYPE: Savings
STATE AGENCY: Oregon College Savings Plan Trust Board, chaired by Oregon State Treasurer
PROGRAM MANAGER: MFS Investment Management
INITIAL YEAR OF OPERATION: 2002
TELEPHONE: 1–866–637–7526
INTERNET: www.mfs.com

Who can purchase a contract? U.S. citizens and resident aliens of legal age, UTMA/UGMA custodians, and legal entities. This program is distributed through brokers.

Time or age limitations on beneficiary or on use of account assets: None

Age-based investment option: The Age-Based Investment Option contains five portfolios of underlying funds. Contributions are placed into the portfolio corresponding to the beneficiary's age, and later reassigned to more conservative portfolios as the beneficiary approaches college.

Static investment options: Select among four blended-fund options (Aggressive Growth, Growth, Moderate, and Conservative) and 20 individual-fund options.

Underlying investments: MFS mutual funds

Fees and expenses: $25 annual account maintenance fee on accounts with less than $25,000 (waived for Oregon residents), 0.25% annualized program management fee charged against the value of the account, and underlying fund expenses which vary by fund. In addition, accounts are subject to one of three alternative broker expense structures that will determine any initial sales charge, contingent deferred sales charge, and/or additional asset-based fees. There is no enrollment fee.

Maximum contributions: Accepts contributions until all account balances in the program for the same beneficiary reach $250,000.

Minimum initial contribution: $250 or $50 per month

Account changes: The program accepts requests to change beneficiary, transfer account ownership, name a successor owner, and transact rollovers and investment changes that meet the requirements of federal tax law and IRS regulations.

Special considerations:

- Oregon residents receive the same state income tax and financial aid benefits described previously for the Oregon College Savings Plan.
- Investors are precluded from investing simultaneously in more than one 529 plan sponsored by the state of Oregon for the same beneficiary.

STATE:	**OREGON**
PROGRAM NAME:	USA CollegeConnect
529 TYPE:	Savings
STATE AGENCY:	Oregon College Savings Plan Trust Board, chaired by Oregon State Treasurer
PROGRAM MANAGER:	Schoolhouse Capital
INITIAL YEAR OF OPERATION:	2003
TELEPHONE:	1–800–457–9001
INTERNET:	www.usacollegeconnect.com

Who can purchase a contract? U.S. residents 18 years and older, UTMA/UGMA custodians, and legal entities. This program is distributed through brokers.

Time or age limitations on beneficiary or on use of account assets: None

Age-based investment option: The Age-Based Option contains five portfolios of underlying funds, ranging from 85% equity to 80% fixed income and money market funds. Contributions are placed into the portfolio corresponding to the number of years to anticipated withdrawal, and later reassigned to more conservative portfolios as the beneficiary approaches college.

Static investment options: Select among eleven individual-fund options

Underlying investments: Federated Investors mutual funds

Fees and expenses: $30 annual account maintenance fee on accounts less than $25,000 (waived for Oregon residents and for accounts enrolled in the automatic investment plan), 0.45% annualized program management fee charged against the value of the account, and underlying fund expenses which vary by fund. In addition, accounts are subject to one of three alternative broker expense structures that will determine any initial sales charge, contingent deferred sales charge, and/or additional asset-based fees. There is no enrollment fee.

Maximum contributions: Accepts contributions until all account balances in the program for the same beneficiary reach $250,000.

Minimum initial contribution: $500 or $50 per month in the Age-Based Option; $5,000 in the Individual-Fund Options (with at least $1,000 per portfolio option).

Account changes: The program accepts requests to change beneficiary, transfer account ownership, name a successor owner, and transact rollovers and investment changes that meet the requirements of federal tax law and IRS regulations.

Special considerations:

- Oregon residents receive the same state income tax and financial aid benefits described previously for the Oregon College Savings Plan.
- Investors are precluded from investing simultaneously in more than one 529 plan sponsored by the state of Oregon for the same beneficiary.

STATE: **PENNSYLVANIA**

PROGRAM NAME:	TAP 529 Guaranteed Savings Plan
529 TYPE:	Guaranteed savings
STATE AGENCY:	Pennsylvania State Treasury
PROGRAM MANAGER:	Delaware Investments
INITIAL YEAR OF OPERATION:	1993
TELEPHONE:	1–800–440–4000
INTERNET:	www.TAP529.com

Who can open an account? A person who has reached the age of majority in their state of residence, UTMA/UGMA custodians, and legal entities. The purchaser or beneficiary must be a Pennsylvania resident at the time of enrollment.

Enrollment period: Open year-round

Time or age limitations on beneficiary or on use of benefits: There is an approximate one-year wait after a contribution is made before it can be withdrawn for college.

Guaranteed Savings: Each contribution to an account is pegged to one of five average tuition levels, or specific tuition levels for 34 publicly-funded schools. Accounts can be used at any eligible educational institution and for all qualified higher education expenses as defined by Section 529. The five average tuition levels correspond to the approximate average tuition charges for that year at 1) Pennsylvania community colleges, 2) the Pennsylvania State System of Higher Education Universities, 3) state-related universities (Penn State, Pitt, Temple, and Lincoln), 4) Ivy League schools, and 5) private four-year colleges. The tuition level used for this purpose is selected by the participant when enrolling, but can be changed at any time and the change is made retroactively. If the account is used for attendance at one of the Pennsylvania publicly-funded schools, the tuition level will be automatically changed to the tuition level at that specific school, recalculating the account based on that school's specific tuition increases. For attendance at any other school, a change in the tuition level can be made by the participant retroactive to the first contribution made.

Costs: There is a one-time $50 enrollment fee (reduced to $25 if account is opened within three weeks of materials being sent) and a $25 annual account maintenance fee (waived for accounts in an automatic investment plan). Within each tuition level a rate for one TAP Credit is established each academic year and is based on the actual tuition or average actual tuition for the school(s) comprising that level. The TAP Credit rate may also contain a premium amount for the purpose of maintaining the actuarial soundness of the program.

Maximum contributions: Accepts contributions until all Pennsylvania accounts for the same beneficiary reach $300,000.

Minimum initial contribution: $25

Cancellation provisions: Cancellation of the account results in a refund of the lesser of (1) the amount that would be obtained by multiplying the number of TAP Credits applied to such distribution by the actual per-credit tuition or average actual per-credit tuition in effect in the academic year of the distribution at the institution(s) comprising the tuition level designated at the time of such distribution, or (2) the market value of the account as determined daily by the program. Additionally, the refund amount will not be less than the amount contributed into the account (less any cancellation fees). If the tuition level was changed within the last twelve months prior to the cancellation, the tuition level that results in the lower refund amount will be used.

Account changes: The program accepts requests to change beneficiary, transfer account ownership, and name a successor owner, subject to residency requirements. A transfer between the TAP 529 Guaranteed Savings Plan and the TAP 529 Investment Plan may be made once in a calendar year. There are no special provisions concerning rollovers to another 529 plan (Pennsylvania taxpayers may be subject to Pennsylvania income tax on the earnings portion of a distribution rolled over to another 529 plan).

State backing: Accounts are not backed by the full faith and credit of the Commonwealth of Pennsylvania. The trustee invests program assets with the goal of creating a reserve to protect against shortfalls in the program fund.

Special considerations:

- Each year the Guaranteed Savings Program fund will be evaluated to determine if the investment performance of the fund has created an excess surplus (above the amount needed to cover future withdrawals as determined by actuarial calculations). The Treasury Department can decide to allocate a portion of the surplus to accounts in the program.

- Qualified distributions are exempt from Pennsylvania income tax. The earnings portion of distributions from other state 529 plans may subject a Pennsylvania resident to Pennsylvania income tax as Pennsylvania currently does not conform to federal tax treatment of qualified distributions.
- Accounts are not subject to Pennsylvania inheritance tax. Accounts owned by a Pennsylvania resident in another state's 529 plan could be subject to Pennsylvania inheritance tax.
- The value of the account will not be counted in determining eligibility and need for student financial aid programs provided by the Commonwealth of Pennsylvania.
- Under Pennsylvania law, a TAP 529 account or any legal interest therein shall not be subject to attachment, levy, or execution by any creditor of an account owner or beneficiary.
- Savings in TAP 529 Guaranteed Savings Plan are eligible for earning "Tuition Rewards" which are guaranteed tuition discounts at over 160 colleges participating in the privately-run SAGE Scholars program.
- Pennsylvania low-income families (200% of the poverty level) may be eligible to have their contributions matched with government funds by participating in the Family Savings Account Program offered through the Pennsylvania Department of Community and Economic Development.

STATE: **PENNSYLVANIA**

PROGRAM NAME:	TAP 529 Investment Plan
529 TYPE:	Savings
STATE AGENCY:	Pennsylvania State Treasury
PROGRAM MANAGER:	Delaware Investments
INITIAL YEAR OF OPERATION:	2002
TELEPHONE:	1–800–440–4000
INTERNET:	www.TAP529.com

Who can purchase a contract? A person who has reached the age of majority in their state of residence, UTMA/UGMA custodians, and legal entities. This program is distributed both direct and through brokers. Anyone who does not meet Pennsylvania's residency requirements must open their account through a broker.

Time or age limitations on beneficiary or on use of account assets: None

Age-based investment options: The Age-Based Portfolios offer a choice between two schedules: Aggressive and Conservative. Each schedule contains seven portfolios of underlying funds. Contributions are placed into the portfolio corresponding to the beneficiary's age, and later reassigned to more conservative portfolios as the beneficiary approaches college.

Static investment options: Select among seven portfolios: Most Aggressive, Aggressive, Balanced, Conservative, Most Conservative, Socially Responsible Equity, and Socially Responsible Bond.

Underlying investments: Mutual funds from Delaware Investments and Calvert Asset Management.

Fees and expenses: $25 annual account maintenance fee on accounts $20,000 or less (waived for accounts in an automatic investment plan), 0.35% annualized program management fee charged against the value of the account, and underlying fund expenses recently ranging from approximately 0.45% to 1.29% (portfolio weighted average). There is no enrollment fee. In addition, accounts opened through a broker are subject to one of three alternative broker expense structures that will determine any initial sales charge, contingent deferred sales charge, and/or additional asset-based fees.

Maximum contributions: Accepts contributions until all Pennsylvania account balances for the same beneficiary reach $300,000.

Minimum initial contribution: $1,000 ($50 with automatic investment)

Account changes: The program accepts requests to change beneficiary, transfer account ownership, name a successor owner, and transact investment changes that meet the requirements of federal tax law and IRS regulations. A transfer between the TAP 529 Investment Plan and the TAP 529 Guaranteed Savings Plan may be made once in a calendar year. There are no special provisions concerning rollovers to another 529 plan (Pennsylvania taxpayers may be subject to Pennsylvania income tax on the earnings portion of a distribution rolled over to another 529 plan).

Special considerations:
- Qualified distributions are exempt from Pennsylvania income tax. The earnings portion of distributions from other state 529 plans may subject a Pennsylvania resident to Pennsylvania income tax as Pennsylvania currently does not conform to federal tax treatment of qualified distributions.
- Accounts are not subject to Pennsylvania inheritance tax. Accounts owned by a Pennsylvania resident in another state's 529 plan could be subject to Pennsylvania inheritance tax.

- The value of the account will not be counted in determining eligibility and need for student financial aid programs provided by the Commonwealth of Pennsylvania.
- Under Pennsylvania law, a TAP 529 account or any legal interest therein shall not be subject to attachment, levy, or execution by any creditor of an account owner or beneficiary.
- Savings in TAP 529 Investment Plan are eligible for earning "Tuition Rewards" which are guaranteed tuition discounts at over 160 colleges participating in the privately-run SAGE Scholars program.
- Pennsylvania low-income families (200% of the poverty level) may be eligible to have their contributions matched with government funds by participating in the Family Savings Account Program offered through the Pennsylvania Department of Community and Economic Development.

STATE: RHODE ISLAND

PROGRAM NAME:	CollegeBoundfund
529 TYPE:	Savings
STATE AGENCY:	Rhode Island Higher Education Assistance Authority
PROGRAM MANAGER:	Alliance Capital
INITIAL YEAR OF OPERATION:	1998
TELEPHONE:	1–888–324–5057
INTERNET:	www.collegeboundfund.com/ri (Rhode Island residents)
	www.collegeboundfund.com (nonresidents)

Who can purchase a contract? U.S. citizens and resident aliens, UTMA/UGMA custodians, and legal entities. This program is distributed both direct and through brokers. Anyone who does not meet Rhode Island's residency requirements must open their account through a broker.

Time or age limitations on beneficiary or on use of account assets: None

Age-based investment options: The Age-Based Portfolios offer a choice between two schedules: Aggressive Growth Emphasis and Growth Emphasis. Each schedule contains seven portfolios of underlying funds, ranging from 100% equity to 25% equity. Contributions are placed into the portfolio corresponding to the selected schedule and the age of the beneficiary. The portfolios shift to a more conservative investment allocation over time.

Static investment options: Select among three blended-fund portfolios (Aggressive Growth, Growth, and Balanced), a stable value portfolio, and nine individual-fund portfolios. A dollar-cost averaging option provides for automatic monthly reallocations to any from any investment option.

Underlying investments: Mutual funds from AllianceBernstein

Fees and expenses: $25 annual account maintenance fee on accounts less than $25,00 (waived for Rhode Island residents, and for accounts in an automatic investment plan and underlying fund expenses recently ranging from approximately 0.76% to 0.95% (port folio weighted average) for the blended-fund portfolios and that vary by fund for the ind vidual-fund portfolios. There is no enrollment fee. In addition, accounts opened throug a broker are subject to one of three alternative broker expense structures that will dete mine any initial sales charge, contingent deferred sales charge, and/or additional asset based fees.

Maximum contributions: Accepts contributions until all Rhode Island account balances fc the same beneficiary reach $315,270.

Minimum initial contribution: $250 for Rhode Island accounts (no minimum with autc matic investment or payroll deduction plan) and $1,000 for broker-sold accounts ($50 wit automatic investment or payroll deduction plan)

Account changes: The program accepts requests to change beneficiary, transfer accour ownership, name a successor owner, and transact rollovers and investment changes tha meet the requirements of federal tax law and IRS regulations.

Special considerations:

- Up to $500 ($1,000 for married couples filing joint returns) in total contribution may be deducted by the account owner from Rhode Island taxable income eac year (excluding rollover contributions from other 529 plans), with unlimited carry over of excess contributions. Deductions may be subject to recapture if non-quali fied withdrawals or rollovers to another state's 529 plan are made within two year of the deductions.
- Under state law, qualified distributions from this program are exempt from Rhod Island income tax. Because Rhode Island tax law generally conforms to federal ta law, any qualified distributions from other 529 plans that are exempt from federa income tax are also exempt from Rhode Island income tax.
- The program will match up to $500 in contributions made by eligible Rhode Islan residents on a 2-for–1 or 1-for–1 basis. To be eligible for a match, the beneficiar must be the contributor's dependent child and family income must fall below pre scribed levels. The account must be opened before the child reaches age 11, an the match can extend for a maximum of five consecutive years.
- The value of the account will not be counted in determining eligibility and need fc student financial aid programs provided by the state of Rhode Island.

- Under Rhode Island law, an account balance, right or interest of a person in the program is exempt from attachment, with limited exceptions.

STATE: SOUTH CAROLINA

PROGRAM NAME:	South Carolina Tuition Prepayment Program
529 TYPE:	Prepaid contract
STATE AGENCY:	Office of the State Treasurer
INITIAL YEAR OF OPERATION:	1998
TELEPHONE:	1–888–7SC–GRAD (1–888–772–4723)
INTERNET:	www.scgrad.org

Who can purchase a contract? U.S. citizens and resident aliens, UTMA/UGMA custodians, and legal entities. The beneficiary must be a South Carolina resident for at least 12 months prior to enrollment.

Enrollment period: The most recent enrollment period began on October 1, 2003 and ended on January 15, 2004. Newborns are accepted year-round.

Time or age limitations on beneficiary or on use of benefits: The beneficiary must be in the 10th grade or below at the time of enrollment. Contract benefits must be used by the time the beneficiary is 30 years old with an extension for up to four years for military service.

Contract benefits: The contract pays in-state undergraduate tuition and mandatory fees at a South Carolina public institution according to the plan and number of years selected. The value derived from the contract will depend in part on the selection of institution, because public institutions in South Carolina have different tuition and fee levels. If the beneficiary decides to attend a private college in South Carolina or an out-of-state college, the program will pay the lesser of the in-state contract value or the actual tuition cost. There is a $25 out-of-state school transfer fee charged each semester.

Contract options: Two-year and four-year contracts are available.

Costs: There is a one-time $85 enrollment fee. In the enrollment period that ended January 15, 2004, lump-sum contract prices for a child in the tenth grade ranged from $12,996 for the two-year plan to $25,566 for the four-year plan. Prices are discounted for younger beneficiaries. Contract payments may be made in a lump sum, in 48 monthly installments, or in monthly installments (with or without a down payment) through the year of projected enrollment. Monthly installment payments are computed to include an effective annual 7% cost for making payments over time along with a small account maintenance fee.

Cancellation provisions: The contract may be canceled at any time after one year for a refund of all contract payments, plus a share of the earnings in the program trust, less a penalty of 10% of the earnings and a $150 cancellation fee. Cancellation within one year will forfeit any share of earnings. Cancellation due to the beneficiary's death, disability, or receipt of scholarship results in a refund of the lesser of contract payments plus the compounded rate of return earned by the fund or the current tuition charged at colleges and universities in South Carolina, and the $150 cancellation fee is waived.

Contract changes: The program accepts requests to change beneficiary prior to matriculation to a younger family member, transfer contract ownership, and name a successor owner. There are no special provisions concerning rollovers to another 529 plan (cancellation provisions would apply).

State backing: Contracts are not backed by the full faith and credit of the state of South Carolina. If the program is discontinued, contract owners are entitled to a refund of all payments plus 4% annual interest. If the program fund does not have sufficient assets to make this payment, the state must consider appropriating the shortfall from the South Carolina general fund.

Special considerations:
- All payments are deductible form South Carolina taxable income each year. Deductions may be subject to recapture if non-qualified distributions are made in a subsequent year.
- Under state law, qualified distributions from this program are exempt from South Carolina income tax. Because South Carolina tax law generally conforms to federal tax law, any qualified distributions from other 529 plans that are exempt from federal income tax are also exempt from South Carolina income tax.
- Under South Carolina law, interests in the program are exempt from attachment under bankruptcy proceedings.

STATE: SOUTH CAROLINA

PROGRAM NAME:	Future Scholar 529 College Savings Plan
529 TYPE:	Savings
STATE AGENCY:	Office of the State Treasurer
PROGRAM MANAGER:	BACAP Distributors, LLC (a subsidiary of Bank of America)
INITIAL YEAR OF OPERATION:	2002
TELEPHONE:	1–888–244–5674 (in-state)
	1–800–765–2668 (out-of-state)
INTERNET:	www.futurescholar.com

Who can purchase a contract? U.S. citizens and resident aliens, and UTMA/UGMA custodians. The Treasurer and Program Manager may permit other persons and legal entities to open accounts. This program is distributed both direct and through brokers. Anyone who does not meet South Carolina's residency requirements must open their account through a broker.

Time or age limitations on beneficiary or on use of account assets: Accounts must be used within 30 years of either the beneficiary's expected date of college matriculation or the beneficiary's 18th birthday.

Age-based investment option: The Automatic Allocation Choice contains six portfolios of underlying funds. Contributions are placed into the portfolio corresponding to the beneficiary's age or number of years to expected enrollment, and later reassigned to more conservative portfolios as the beneficiary approaches college.

Static investment options: Select among six blended-fund portfolios (Aggressive Growth, Growth, Balanced Growth, Balanced, Income and Growth, and Income) and a stable value portfolio. In addition, the direct-sold program offers two index individual-fund portfolios while the broker-sold program offers 14 individual-fund portfolios.

Underlying investments: Nations Funds; the stable value portfolio consists of a funding agreement issued by Transamerica Life.

Fees and expenses: $25 annual account maintenance fee on accounts less than $10,000 (waived for South Carolina residents and employees, and for accounts in an automatic investment plan), 0.20% (0.30% for broker-sold accounts) annualized program management fee charged against the value of the account, and underlying fund expenses recently ranging from approximately 0.10%–0.41% (0.10% to 1.30% in the broker-sold options). There is no enrollment fee. In addition, accounts opened through a broker are subject to one of three alternative broker expense structures that will determine any initial sales charge, contingent deferred sales charge, and/or additional asset-based fees.

Maximum contributions: Accepts contributions until all South Carolina account balance for the same beneficiary reach $277,000.

Minimum initial contribution: $250, or $50 per month with payroll deduction

Account changes: The program accepts requests to change beneficiary, transfer account ownership, name a successor owner, and transact rollovers and investment changes that meet the requirements of federal tax law and IRS regulations.

Special considerations:

- All contributions are deductible against South Carolina taxable income each year. Deductions may be subject to recapture if non-qualified withdrawals are made in a subsequent year.
- Under state law, qualified distributions from this program are exempt from South Carolina income tax. Because South Carolina tax law generally conforms to federal tax law, any qualified distributions from other 529 plans that are exempt from federal income tax are also exempt from South Carolina income tax.
- Under South Carolina law, interests in the program are exempt from attachment under bankruptcy proceedings.

STATE: **SOUTH DAKOTA**

PROGRAM NAME:	CollegeAccess 529
529 TYPE:	Savings
STATE AGENCY:	South Dakota Investment Council
PROGRAM MANAGER:	PA Distributors, LLC (a PIMCO affiliate)
INITIAL YEAR OF OPERATION:	2002
TELEPHONE:	1–866–529–7462
INTERNET:	www.CollegeAccess529.com

Who can purchase a contract? U.S. citizens and resident aliens 18 years and older (individually or as joint owners), UTMA/UGMA custodians, 501(c)(3) organizations, and other legal entities. This program is distributed both direct and through brokers. Anyone who does not meet South Dakota's residency requirements must open their account through a broker.

Time or age limitations on beneficiary or on use of account assets: None

Age-based investment option: The Age-Based Option consists of five portfolios of underlying funds. Contributions are placed into the portfolio corresponding to the age of the beneficiary or the anticipated years to matriculation. The portfolios shift to a more conservative investment allocation over time.

Static investment options: In the direct-sold plan, select among two portfolios (the Real Return Plus Portfolio which invests primarily in inflation-indexed bonds and short and moderate-term fixed-income instruments, and the All Asset individual-fund portfolio which is an actively-managed tactical fund that invests in 14 underlying PIMCO funds). For broker-sold accounts, select among five blended-fund portfolios (Capital Appreciation, Core Equity, Total Return Plus, Real Return Plus, and Money Market Plus) and fourteen individual-fund portfolios.

Underlying investments: Mutual funds from American, Franklin, Heritage, MFS, NFJ, Nicholas-Applegate, Northern, OppenheimerFunds, PEA, PIMCO, RCM, and Templeton.

Fees and expenses: $4 quarterly account maintenance fee on investment options below $2,500 (waived for South Dakota residents and for accounts in an automatic investment plan), 0.35% annualized program management fee charged against the value of the account (waived for South Dakota residents), and underlying fund expenses recently ranging from approximately 0.21% to 1.42%. Expenses for South Dakota residents enrolling directly are capped at 0.65% all-inclusive. There is no enrollment fee. In addition, accounts opened through a broker are subject to one of three alternative broker expense structures that will determine any initial sales charge, contingent deferred sales charge, and/or additional asset-based fees.

Maximum contributions: Accepts contributions until all South Dakota account balances for the same beneficiary reach $305,000.

Minimum initial contribution: $250 ($50 with automatic investment) for direct-sold accounts; $1,000 ($250 with automatic investment) for accounts opened through a broker.

Account changes: The program accepts requests to change beneficiary, transfer account ownership, name a successor owner, and transact rollovers and investment changes that meet the requirements of federal tax law and IRS regulations.

Special considerations:

- There are no state income tax incentives because South Dakota does not have a personal income tax.
- Under South Dakota law, except for funds contributed within one year of a Chapter 11 bankruptcy filing by the account owner or contributor, amounts in an account are not an asset or property of the account owner, contributor, or beneficiary for purposes of paying any debt or liability, and the account is exempt from any levy, execution or judgment, or other operation of law, garnishment, or other judicial enforcement.

STATE: **SOUTH DAKOTA**

PROGRAM NAME:	Legg Mason Core4College 529 Plan
529 TYPE:	Savings
STATE AGENCY:	South Dakota Investment Council
PROGRAM MANAGER:	PA Distributors, LLC (a PIMCO affiliate)
DISTRIBUTION PARTNER:	Legg Mason Wood Walker
INITIAL YEAR OF OPERATION:	2003
TELEPHONE:	1–800–800–3609
INTERNET:	www.leggmasonfunds.com

Who can purchase a contract? U.S. citizens and resident aliens 18 years and older (individually or as joint owners), UTMA/UGMA custodians, and legal entities. This program is distributed through Legg Mason financial advisors and dedicated account representatives. Others may enroll directly, but are limited to investing in the Age-Based Portfolio.

Time or age limitations on beneficiary or on use of account assets: None

Age-based investment option: The Age-Based Portfolios consist of four portfolios of underlying funds, ranging from 75% equity to 15% equity. Contributions are placed into the portfolio corresponding to the beneficiary's age, and later reassigned to more conservative portfolios as the beneficiary approaches college.

Static investment options: Select among the four blended-fund portfolios used in the age-based option and eleven individual-fund portfolios.

Underlying investments: Legg Mason & Royce mutual funds managed by various firms owned by Legg Mason, Inc.

Fees and expenses: $25 annual account maintenance fee on accounts less than $25,000 (waived for accounts in an automatic investment plan), 0.30% annualized program management fee charged against the value of the account, and underlying fund expenses combined with annual distribution fees recently ranging from approximately 0.69% to 2.25%. There is no enrollment fee.

Maximum contributions: Accepts contributions until all South Dakota account balances for the same beneficiary reach $305,000.

Minimum initial contribution: $1,000 per Age-Based Portfolio and $2,500 per Core Fund Investment Portfolio (may be reduced under an automatic contribution plan)

count changes: The program accepts requests to change beneficiary, transfer account vnership, name a successor owner, and transact rollovers and investment changes that eet the requirements of federal tax law and IRS regulations.

ecial considerations:

- There are no state income tax incentives because South Dakota does not have a personal income tax.
- Under South Dakota law, except for funds contributed within one year of a Chapter 11 bankruptcy filing by the account owner or contributor, amounts in an account are not an asset or property of the account owner, contributor, or beneficiary for purposes of paying any debt or liability, and the account is exempt from any levy, execution or judgment, or other operation of law, garnishment, or other judicial enforcement.

STATE: **TENNESSEE**

PROGRAM NAME:	Tennessee's BEST Prepaid College Tuition Plan
529 TYPE:	Prepaid unit / Guaranteed savings
STATE AGENCIES:	Treasury Department and nine-member Board chaired by State Treasurer
INITIAL YEAR OF OPERATION:	1997
TELEPHONE:	1–888–486–BEST (1–888–486–2378)
INTERNET:	www.treasury.state.tn.us/best

ho can purchase a contract? Individuals with a valid Social Security number (including inors) and legal entities. The purchaser or beneficiary must be a Tennessee resident at e time of enrollment.

rollment period: Open year-round

me or age limitations on beneficiary or on use of benefits: The first payout date must e at least two calendar years after the beneficiary is enrolled in the plan and after the eneficiary has reached age 17.

ntract benefits: Each unit in the account is worth 1% of the weighted average tuition t Tennessee's public four-year universities. Units may be redeemed at any eligible educa- onal institution in the country for any qualified higher education expense that is billed by e institution. The redemption value of a unit based on tuition and fees for the 2004/2005 ear is $43.15. If the beneficiary attends an out-of-state or private school, the tuition units ill be paid out to the institution at the same rate paid for Tennessee public schools.

Costs: The purchase price of a tuition unit is based on the current tuition as adjusted f actuarial considerations and expenses. As of August 1, 2004, the purchase price is $48.9 per unit (will increase to $50.80 on January 1, 2005). There is no enrollment fee.

Maximum contributions: Accepts contributions until all Tennessee account balances f the same beneficiary reach $235,000.

Minimum initial contribution: $48.96 (one unit), or $25 with automatic contributions, $15 with payroll deduction

Cancellation provisions: The designated refund recipient (purchaser or beneficiary) m request a refund after the beneficiary reaches the age of 18 by sending a written not rized notice signed by the refund recipient that tuition units will not be used for colleg The refund is equal to the total purchase price of tuition units purchased and not us and 100% of the difference between the purchase price and 1% of the weighted avera tuition minus any termination fee.

Contract changes: The program accepts requests to change beneficiary, name a succe sor purchaser, and transact rollovers that meet the requirements of federal tax law ar IRS regulations.

State backing: Units are not backed by the full faith and credit of the state of Tennesse The trustee invests program assets with the goal of creating a reserve to protect again shortfalls in the program fund.

Special considerations:
- Contributions to BEST or any other 529 plan, along with any earnings, are exem from Tennessee state, county, and municipal taxes.
- Under state law, BEST units are exempt from execution, attachment, garnishmer and bankruptcy proceedings.

STATE: TENNESSEE

PROGRAM NAME:	Tennessee's BEST Savings Plan
529 TYPE:	Savings
STATE AGENCY:	Tennessee Baccalaureate Education System Trust
PROGRAM MANAGER:	TIAA-CREF Tuition Financing, Inc.
INITIAL YEAR OF OPERATION:	2000
TELEPHONE:	1–888–486–BEST (1–888–486–2378)
INTERNET:	www.tnbest.com

Who can purchase a contract? U.S. citizens and resident aliens, including minors. Not available through brokers.

Time or age limitations on beneficiary or on use of account assets: None

Age-based investment option: The Managed Allocation option consists of 11 portfolios of underlying funds. Contributions are placed into the portfolio corresponding to the age of the beneficiary. The portfolios shift to a more conservative investment allocation over time.

Static investment option: 100% Equity option

Underlying investments: TIAA-CREF institutional mutual funds

Fees and expenses: 0.95% annualized program management fee charged against the value of the account, which includes the expenses of the underlying mutual funds. There are no enrollment or account maintenance fees.

Maximum contributions: Accepts contributions until all Tennessee account balances for the same beneficiary reach $235,000.

Minimum initial contribution: $25, or $15 with payroll deduction

Account changes: The program accepts requests to change beneficiary, name a successor purchaser, and transact rollovers and investment changes that meet the requirements of federal tax law and IRS regulations.

Special considerations:

- Contributions to BEST or any other 529 plan, along with any earnings, are exempt from Tennessee state, county, and municipal taxes.
- Under state law, BEST assets are exempt from execution, attachment, garnishment, and bankruptcy proceedings.

STATE:	**TEXAS**
PROGRAM NAME:	Texas Guaranteed Tuition Plan
529 TYPE:	Prepaid contract
STATE AGENCIES:	State Comptroller's Office and the Texas Prepaid Higher Education Tuition Board
INITIAL YEAR OF OPERATION:	1996
TELEPHONE:	1–800–445–GRAD (1–800–445–4723)
INTERNET:	www.texastomorrowfunds.org

Who can purchase a contract? Individuals 18 years and older, UTMA/UGMA custodians, and legal entities. The beneficiary must be either a Texas resident for at least 12 months prior to enrollment or a non-resident child of a purchaser who is a Texas resident.

Enrollment period: The program has suspended new enrollments. The most recent enrollment ended May 23, 2003.

Time or age limitations on beneficiary or on use of benefits: The beneficiary must not have graduated from high school at the time of enrollment. Contract benefits must be used within a 10-year period beginning on the date the beneficiary is projected to graduate from high school (extended for active-duty time spent in the military).

Contract benefits: The contract pays the actual in-state cost (for public school contracts) or the estimated average cost (for private school contracts) of undergraduate tuition and required fees for up to 160 credit hours (10 semesters) at any accredited college or university in Texas. The value derived from the contract may depend in part on the selection of institution, because public institutions in Texas have different tuition and fee levels. The value of the contract benefits, based on the average in-state tuition and fees for public schools, or estimated average tuition and fees for private schools, can also be transferred to any accredited out-of-state college or university or accredited Texas proprietary school. There is a $25 fee for each academic term that benefits are paid to an out-of-state college.

Contract options: One or two year contracts for junior public college plans, one to five year contracts for senior public and private college plans, and a four year contract for the junior/senior public college plan.

Costs: There is a one-time $50 enrollment fee. For the enrollment period that ended May 23, 2003, lump-sum contract prices for a child in the twelfth grade ranged from $1,820 for the one-year community college plan to $65,391 for the five-year private college and university plan. Prices may be slightly discounted for younger beneficiaries. Contract payments may be made in a lump sum or in monthly installments over five years, ten years, or an extended term to the beneficiary's projected high school graduation date.

installment payments are computed to include an effective annual 8% cost of making payments over time.

Cancellation provisions: The contract can be canceled at any time for a refund of at least the amount of payments, less a cancellation fee of $25 and an account maintenance fee of $3 per month for monthly or annual pay contracts or $20 for lump sum contracts. Cancellations due to the death or disability of the beneficiary or purchaser are based on the greater of the current average tuition rate or the total contract payments made and do not incur the cancellation fee. If the beneficiary is 18 years old or has graduated from high school, the refund is based on the greater of the current average tuition rate or total contract payments made. Special refund provisions apply in the event the beneficiary receives a scholarship.

Contract changes: The program accepts requests to change beneficiary prior to use of any contract benefits by the current beneficiary, transfer contract ownership, and name a successor owner, subject to residency requirements. There are no special provisions concerning rollovers to another 529 plan (cancellation provisions would apply).

State backing: Contracts are backed by the full faith and credit of the state of Texas.

Special considerations:

- A beneficiary who moves to another state after enrolling in the program remains eligible for Texas in-state tuition rates while using program benefits.
- There are no state income tax incentives because Texas does not have a personal income tax.
- Under Texas law, contract benefits are exempt from claims of creditors of a purchaser or beneficiary.

STATE:	**TEXAS**
PROGRAM NAME:	Tomorrow's College Investment Plan
529 TYPE:	Savings
STATE AGENCY:	Texas Prepaid Higher Education Tuition Board
PROGRAM MANAGER:	Enterprise Capital Management, Inc.
INITIAL YEAR OF OPERATION:	2002
TELEPHONE:	1–800–445–GRAD (1–800–445–4723)
INTERNET:	www.enterprise529.com

Who can purchase a contract? Individuals, UTMA/UGMA custodians, and legal entities. This program is distributed both direct and through brokers. Anyone who does not meet Texas residency requirements must open their account through a broker.

Time or age limitations on beneficiary or on use of account assets: None

Age-based investment option: The Age-Based Portfolios consist of five portfolios o underlying funds. Contributions are placed into the portfolio that corresponds to the ag of the beneficiary or number of years to expected enrollment. The portfolios automaticall shift to a more conservative investment allocation over time.

Static investment options: Select among two blended-fund portfolios (100% Stock Alloca tion and Balanced Allocation), 12 individual-fund portfolios, and a stable value portfolio.

Underlying investments: Mutual funds managed by Enterprise Capital Management Gabelli Asset Management, Marsico Capital Management, Montag & Caldwell, PIMCO Rockefeller & Co., SSgA Funds Management, TCW Investment Management, UBS Globa Asset Management, Wellington Management Company, and William D. Witter, Inc.; plu a guaranteed investment contract (GIC) issued by Transamerica Life Insurance Company.

Fees and expenses: $30 annual account maintenance fee on accounts less than $25,00C (waived for Texas residents, and for accounts in an automatic investment or payrol deduction plan). Direct-sold units (Class T) incur an annualized program managemen fee of 1.00% for the age-based and blended-fund options (including all underlying fund expenses), 0.45% for the stable value option, and 0.45% plus the cost of the underlying funds (recently ranging from 0.15% to 1.75%) for the individual-fund options. Broker-sold units incur a 0.45% (Class A) and 0.95% (Classes B and C) annualized program manage ment fee, and underlying fund expenses that vary by investment option. In addition, the broker-sold units are subject to an initial sales charge (Class A) or contingent deferree sales charge (Classes B and C). Beginning May 1, 2005, expenses incurred by the state for administering the plan are reimbursable to the state from the program assets. There i no enrollment fee.

Maximum contributions: Accepts contributions until all Texas account balances for the same beneficiary reach $257,460.

Minimum initial contribution: $25 per portfolio, or $15 with automatic investment or pay roll deduction plans.

Account changes: The program accepts requests to change beneficiary, transfer accoun ownership, name a successor owner, and transact rollovers and investment changes tha meet the requirements of federal tax law and IRS regulations.

Special considerations:
- There are no state income tax incentives because Texas does not have a persona income tax.

- Under Texas state law, money in any 529 plan is exempt from attachment, execution, and seizure for the satisfaction of debt or liability of an account owner or beneficiary.

STATE: UTAH

PROGRAM NAME:	Utah Educational Savings Plan (UESP) Trust
529 TYPE:	Savings
STATE AGENCY/PROGRAM MANAGER:	Utah Higher Education Assistance Authority
INITIAL YEAR OF OPERATION:	1996
TELEPHONE:	1–800–418–2551
INTERNET:	www.uesp.org

Who can purchase a contract? Individuals with a valid Social Security number or federal taxpayer identification number, UTMA/UGMA custodians, and legal entities. Not available through brokers.

Time or age limitations on beneficiary or on use of account assets: Withdrawals must begin by the time the beneficiary reaches the age of 27 or the account has been open 10 years, whichever is later. The program has the authority to grant further extensions.

Age-based investment options: Under Investment Options 2, 3, 7, 8, and 9, contributions are invested in a blend of underlying investments corresponding to the number of years to expected enrollment, and later reassigned to more conservative blends as the beneficiary approaches college. Option 2 has a 95% equity investment for the youngest age group and 100% money market investment for the oldest age group. Option 3 is more aggressive, with the equity concentration never going below 65%. For the youngest age group, the diversified equity investment is 100% for Option 7, 80% for Option 8, and 50% for Option 9. For the oldest age group in Options 7–9, investment is 100% money market funds.

Static investment options: Select among the State Treasurer's Investment Fund (invested in money market securities), two individual-fund portfolios (a Vanguard equity index fund and a Vanguard bond index fund), and a blended-fund portfolio consisting of Vanguard equity index funds.

Underlying investments: Vanguard institutional index funds and the Utah State Treasurer's Investment Fund.

Fees and expenses: $5 per $1,000 of account balance (up to a maximum of $25) annual account maintenance fee (waived for Utah residents and investment Option 1 which is the State Treasurer's Investment Fund), 0.25% annualized program management fee charged against the value of the account (none for Option 1), and underlying fund expenses of approximately 0.025% for the S&P 500 stock index fund, 0.05% for the bond index fund, 0.10% for the small and mid cap index funds, and 0.51% to 0.62% for international stocks. There is no enrollment fee.

Maximum contributions: Accepts contributions until all Utah account balances for the same beneficiary reach $300,000.

Minimum initial contribution: $25

Account changes: The program accepts requests to change beneficiary, transfer account ownership, name a successor owner, and transact rollovers and investment changes that meet the requirements of federal tax law and IRS regulations.

Special considerations:

- Up to $1,470 ($2,940 for a married couple filing jointly) of contributions per beneficiary may be deducted by an account owner from Utah taxable income in 2004, with the limit to adjust each year based on inflation, but only for accounts that were established while the beneficiary was 18 or younger. Deductions may be subject to recapture if non-qualified withdrawals are made in a subsequent year.
- Under state law, qualified distributions from this program are exempt from Utah income tax. Because Utah tax law generally conforms to federal tax law, any qualified distributions from other 529 plans that are exempt from federal income tax are also exempt from Utah income tax.
- Utah beneficiaries who move out of the state after at least eight years in the program remain eligible for resident tuition rates at any Utah public institution.
- The value of the account will not be counted in determining eligibility and need for student financial aid programs provided by the state of Utah.
- Accounts in the State Treasurer's Investment Fund are supplemented with earnings from a separate endowment fund if the beneficiary uses withdrawals for qualified expenses.
- Under a pilot program, up to $300 of contributions are matched each year for up to four years for low-income Utah participants.

STATE:	**VERMONT**

PROGRAM NAME:	Vermont Higher Education Investment Plan
529 TYPE:	Savings
STATE AGENCY:	Vermont Student Assistance Corp. (VSAC)
PROGRAM MANAGER:	TIAA-CREF Tuition Financing, Inc.
INITIAL YEAR OF OPERATION:	1999
TELEPHONE:	1–800–637–5860
INTERNET:	www.vsac.org

Who can purchase a contract? U.S. citizens and resident aliens with a valid Social Security number or federal taxpayer identification number, UTMA/UGMA custodians, corporations, and certain other legal entities. Not available through brokers.

Time or age limitations on beneficiary or on use of account assets: None

Age-based investment option: The Managed Allocation Option contains 10 portfolios of underlying mutual funds. Contributions are placed into the portfolio corresponding to the age of the beneficiary. The portfolios shift to a more conservative investment allocation over time.

Static investment options: Select between two portfolios: the 100% Equity Option and the Interest Income Option. The 100% Equity Option is currently invested 80% in a growth and income fund and 20% in an international fund. The Interest Income Option provides a return pegged to the 91-day T-bill rate.

Underlying investments: TIAA-CREF institutional mutual funds for the Managed Allocation Option and 100% Equity Option, and an interest-bearing note (backed by guaranteed student loans) for the Interest Income Option.

Fees and expenses: 0.80% annualized program management fee charged against the value of the account (none for the Interest Income Option), which includes the expenses of the underlying mutual funds. There are no enrollment or account maintenance fees.

Maximum contributions: Accepts contributions until all Vermont account balances for the same beneficiary reach $240,100.

Minimum initial contribution: $25, or $15 with payroll deduction plans

Account changes: The program accepts requests to change beneficiary, transfer account ownership, name a successor owner, and transact rollovers and investment changes that meet the requirements of federal tax law and IRS regulations.

Special considerations:

- A Vermont state income tax credit may be claimed each year for 5% of up to $2,000 in annual contributions per beneficiary. The credit is nonrefundable and may be subject to recapture if non-qualified withdrawals are made in a subsequent year.
- Under state law, qualified distributions from this program are exempt from Vermont income tax. Because Vermont tax law generally conforms to federal tax law, any qualified distributions from other 529 plans that are exempt from federal income tax are also exempt from Vermont income tax.

STATE: **VIRGINIA**

PROGRAM NAME:	Virginia Prepaid Education Program (VPEP)
529 TYPE:	Prepaid contract
STATE AGENCY:	Virginia College Savings Plan Board
INITIAL YEAR OF OPERATION:	1996
TELEPHONE:	1–888–567–0540
INTERNET:	www.virginia529.com

Who can purchase a contract? U.S. citizens and resident aliens 18 years and older, UTMA/UGMA custodians, and legal entities. The purchaser, beneficiary, or parent of a non-resident beneficiary must be a Virginia resident.

Enrollment period: Began October 1, 2004 and ends January 31, 2005

Time or age limitations on beneficiary or on use of benefits: The beneficiary must be in the ninth grade or below at the time the contract is purchased (tenth-grade students are being accepted in the current enrollment period only). Contract benefits must be used within ten years after the projected date of high school graduation; extensions may be requested.

Contract benefits: The contract pays in-state undergraduate tuition and mandatory fees at a Virginia public institution according to the plan and number of years selected. The value derived from the contract will depend in part on the selection of institution, because public institutions in Virginia have different tuition and fee levels. At any time, contracts may be rolled over from VPEP to VEST or CollegeAmerica (Virginia's 529 savings program options) at an amount that includes payments plus a reasonable rate of return (the institutional money-market fund index). If the beneficiary decides to attend an in-state private school, the contract will pay an amount equal to the payments made plus the actual rate of return earned on program fund investments, capped at the highest tuition and mandatory fees at a Virginia public institution. For attendance at an out-of-state school, the contract will pay an amount equal to payments made plus a reasonable rate of interest based on institutional money market rates, capped at the average tuition and mandatory fees at Virginia public institutions.

Contract options: One to five years at a Virginia public four-year university, one to three years at a Virginia community college, or any combination of university and community college (maximum of eight years).

Costs: There is a one-time $85 application fee ($25 for each additional Virginia account opened and owned by the same person). In the enrollment period that ends January 31, 2005, lump-sum contract prices for a child in the tenth grade range from $2,498 for the one-year community college plan to $38,230 for the five-year university plan. The contract price may also be paid in 60 monthly installments or over an extended period until the beneficiary reaches college age (with or without a down payment). All installment payments are computed to include an effective annual 8% cost of making payments over time.

Cancellation provisions: If the contract is canceled within three years, the program will provide a refund of contract payments less a $25 cancellation fee. If the contract is canceled after three years, the program will provide a refund of contract payments plus a reasonable rate of return (the institutional money-market index) less a $25 cancellation fee. Cancellation fees are waived in the event of the beneficiary's death, disability, or receipt of a scholarship.

Contract changes: The program accepts requests to change beneficiary (an additional payment may be required if the new beneficiary is older than the current beneficiary), transfer contract ownership, and name a successor owner. Contract payments, including reasonable interest, may be rolled over to Virginia's VEST or CollegeAmerica programs at any time. The program also permits rollover of contract payments to another state's 529 plan, except that interest is included only on contracts that are at least three years old, and a $25 fee is charged.

State backing: If the investment return on program funds is not sufficient to cover the plan's contractual obligations, Virginia law requires that the Governor include in the budget an appropriation providing for such contingency.

Special considerations:

- Up to $2,000 of contract payments per account are deductible from Virginia taxable income each year, with unlimited carryforward of excess payments. The $2,000 limit is removed for individuals who are at least 70 years old. Deductions may be subject to recapture if non-qualified distributions or rollovers to another state's 529 plan are made in a subsequent year, unless the distribution results from the beneficiary's death, disability, or receipt of scholarship.

- Under Virginia law, qualified distributions from this program, and distributions due to the death, disability, or receipt of a scholarship, are exempt from Virginia income tax. Because Virginia tax law generally conforms to federal tax law, any qualified distributions from other 529 plans that are exempt from federal income tax are also exempt from Virginia income tax.
- The value of the contract will not be counted in determining eligibility and need for student financial aid programs provided by the Commonwealth of Virginia.
- Under Virginia law, contracts are protected from the claims of creditors of the purchaser or the beneficiary.

STATE: **VIRGINIA**

PROGRAM NAME:	Virginia Education Savings Trust (VEST)
529 TYPE:	Savings
STATE AGENCY/PROGRAM MANAGER:	Virginia College Savings Plan Board and its Executive Director
INITIAL YEAR OF OPERATION:	1999
TELEPHONE:	1–888–567–0540
INTERNET:	www.virginia529.com

Who can purchase a contract? U.S. citizens and resident aliens 18 years and older, UTMA/UGMA custodians, and legal entities. Not available through brokers.

Time or age limitations on beneficiary or on use of account assets: Accounts must be used within 10 years after the projected date of high school graduation, or within 10 years after the account is opened if the beneficiary has already graduated from high school; extensions may be requested.

Age-based investment option: The Age-Based Portfolios contain seven portfolios of underlying investments. Contributions may be invested in any portfolio. The portfolios automatically shift to a more conservative investment allocation over time.

Static investment options: Select among four portfolios: Aggressive, Moderate, Conservative and Money Market.

Underlying investments: Mutual funds or separate accounts managed by Vanguard, Rothschild Asset Management, Capital Guardian, Franklin Templeton, Western Asset Management, and Invesco.

Fees and expenses: $85 enrollment fee ($25 for each additional Virginia account opened by the same account owner), and operating and investment expenses at an annual rate recently ranging from approximately 0.85% to 1.00%. There is no account maintenance fee.

Maximum contributions: Accepts contributions until all Virginia account balances for the same beneficiary reach $250,000.

Minimum initial contribution: $25; $250 minimum in first 12 months

Account changes: The program accepts requests to change beneficiary, transfer account ownership, name a successor owner, and transact rollovers and investment changes that meet the requirements of federal tax law and IRS regulations.

Special considerations:

- Up to $2,000 of contributions per account are deductible from Virginia taxable income each year, with unlimited carryforward of excess contributions. The $2,000 limit is removed for individuals who are at least 70 years old. Deductions may be subject to recapture if non-qualified withdrawals or rollovers to another state's 529 plan are made in a subsequent year, unless the withdrawal results from the beneficiary's death, disability, or receipt of scholarship.
- Under Virginia law, qualified distributions from this program, and distributions due to the death, disability, or receipt of a scholarship, are exempt from Virginia income tax. Because Virginia tax law generally conforms to federal tax law, any qualified distributions from other 529 plans that are exempt from federal income tax are also exempt from Virginia income tax.
- Under Virginia law, accounts are protected from the claims of creditors of the account owner or the beneficiary.

STATE:	**VIRGINIA**
PROGRAM NAME:	CollegeAmerica
529 TYPE:	Savings
STATE AGENCY/PROGRAM MANAGER:	Virginia College Savings Plan Board and its Executive Director
INVESTMENT MANAGER:	American Funds
INITIAL YEAR OF OPERATION:	2002
TELEPHONE:	1–800–421–4120
INTERNET:	www.americanfunds.com

Who can purchase a contract? U.S. citizens and resident aliens, UTMA/UGMA custodians, and legal entities. This program is distributed through brokers.

Time or age limitations on beneficiary or on use of account assets: Must use the assets in the account or designate a new beneficiary within 30 years after the beneficiary graduates from high school or within 30 years after opening the account, whichever comes later.

Age-based investment options: None

Static investment options: Select among 21 individual American Funds. Contributions may be directed to one fund or allocated among them.

Underlying investments: American Funds

Fees and expenses: $10 enrollment fee, $10 annual account maintenance fee, and underlying fund expenses that vary by fund. In addition, accounts are subject to one of three alternative broker expense structures that will determine any initial sales charge, contingent deferred sales charge, and/or additional asset-based fees.

Maximum contributions: Accepts contributions until all Virginia account balances for the same beneficiary reach $250,000.

Minimum initial contribution: $250 per fund ($1,000 for the Cash Management Trust of America)

Account changes: The program accepts requests to change beneficiary, transfer account ownership, name a successor owner, and transact rollovers and investment changes that meet the requirements of federal tax law and IRS regulations.

Special considerations:
- Virginia residents receive the same state income tax and creditor protection benefits as described previously for the Virginia Education Savings Trust (VEST).

STATE: # WASHINGTON

PROGRAM NAME:	Guaranteed Education Tuition (GET)
529 TYPE:	Prepaid unit / Guaranteed savings
STATE AGENCY:	Washington State Higher Education Coordinating Board
INITIAL YEAR OF OPERATION:	1998
TELEPHONE:	1–877–438–8848
INTERNET:	www.get.wa.gov

Who can purchase a contract? Individuals with a valid Social Security number (including minors), UTMA/UGMA custodians, and legal entities. The beneficiary must be a Washington resident.

Enrollment period: September 15 to March 31 each year

Time or age limitations on beneficiary or on use of benefits: There are no age restrictions. Tuition units purchased can be redeemed or refunded after two years from account opening. Units must be used within 10 years after the beneficiary's projected college entrance year or the first use of units, whichever is later.

Contract benefits: Each unit in the account is worth 1% of the resident undergraduate tuition for one year at the highest-priced Washington state public university. Up to 125 units may be redeemed each year to pay for tuition and fees at any eligible institution, and excess units can be used to pay for other qualified higher education expenses. The redemption value of a unit based on tuition and fees at the highest-priced Washington state public university for the 2004/2005 school year is $51.54. If the beneficiary attends an out-of-state or private school, the tuition units will be paid out to the institution at the same rate paid to Washington's highest-priced public college or university.

Costs: There is a one-time $50 enrollment fee with a maximum fee of $100 per family. The purchase price of a tuition unit is based on the current tuition as adjusted for actuarial considerations and expenses. The purchase price for any units acquired by April 30, 2005 is $61 per unit. Rather than making separate purchases of additional units in the future, a quantity of 50 to 500 units may be purchased at one time under a customized monthly payment arrangement over a maximum 18-year period at an additional cost equivalent to annual interest of 7.5%.

Maximum contributions: $30,500 for 500 units; installment payments available

Minimum initial contribution: One unit

Cancellation provisions: The program will consider a request for refund after the account has been open at least two years (exceptions to the two-year period exist in cases of death, disability, and financial hardship). Units are valued at 1% of the current annual tuition at the highest-priced Washington state public university when the refund is due to the beneficiary's death, disability, receipt of a scholarship, or graduation or program completion. Units are valued based on weighted average public tuition if a refund is requested because the beneficiary decides not to attend college. A refund penalty will be assessed equal to 10% of the increase in unit value (minimum $100 penalty). A withdrawal made on account of the beneficiary's death or disability, or to the extent the beneficiary receives a scholarship, is not subject to the penalty.

Contract changes: Subject to residency requirements, the program accepts requests to change beneficiary, transfer contract ownership, and name a successor owner. There are no special provisions concerning rollovers to another 529 plan (cancellation provisions would apply).

State backing: Tuition units are backed by the full faith and credit of the state of Washington.

Special considerations:
- There are no state income tax incentives because Washington does not have a personal income tax.
- The value of the account will not be counted in determining eligibility and need for student financial aid programs provided by the state of Washington (the state of Washington does not include any assets in its consideration for financial aid).
- Proposed legislative changes would make adjustments to certain payout provisions, permit Washington residents to open accounts for non-resident children or grandchildren, and protect units held for more than two years from the claims of creditors.

STATE:	**WEST VIRGINIA**
PROGRAM NAME:	SMART529 Prepaid Tuition Plan
529 TYPE:	Prepaid contract
STATE AGENCY:	West Virginia College Prepaid Tuition and Savings Program Board of Trustees
PROGRAM MANAGER:	Hartford Life Insurance Company
INITIAL YEAR OF OPERATION:	1998
TELEPHONE:	1–866–574–3542
INTERNET:	www.SMART529.com

Who can purchase a contract? Individuals 18 years and older, and approved legal entities. The purchaser, beneficiary, or parent of a non-resident beneficiary must be a West Virginia resident at the time the contract is purchased.

Enrollment period: Currently closed to new enrollments. The most recent enrollment period ended December 31, 2002.

Time or age limitations on beneficiary or on use of benefits: The beneficiary must be in the ninth grade or below at the time the contract is purchased. Contract benefits must be used within 10 years after the projected college entrance date.

Contract benefits: The contract pays in-state undergraduate tuition and mandatory fees at a West Virginia public institution according to the number of units purchased. If the beneficiary receives a scholarship, any remaining contract value can be refunded or applied to room and board, books, or supplies. The value derived from the contract will depend in part on the selection of institution, because public institutions in West Virginia have different tuition and fee levels. If the beneficiary decides to attend a private college in West Virginia or an out-of-state college, the program will pay the plan benefit value based on the weighted average tuition and mandatory fees at West Virginia public institutions.

Contract options: One to ten semester units (up to five years).

Costs: In the enrollment period that ended December 31, 2002, the lump-sum contract price for a child in the ninth grade was $1,832 per unit. Prices are discounted for younger beneficiaries. Payments may be made in a single lump sum or in monthly installments (with or without a down payment) over a variety of terms. Installment payments are computed to include an effective annual 7.25% to 8.50% cost of making payments over time. There is no enrollment fee.

Cancellation provisions: A contract may be canceled at any time and the cancellation value will be distributed to the contract owner. The cancellation value is the lesser of (1) payments made and accumulated at the actual rate of return, with realized and unrealized gains and losses, less administrative expenses, or (2) payments made and accumulated at a 1.5% annual rate of return, less administrative expenses.

Contract changes: The program accepts requests to change beneficiary (an additional payment may be required if the new beneficiary's projected college enrollment date is different), transfer contract ownership, name a successor owner, and transact rollovers that meet the requirements of federal tax law and IRS regulations.

State backing: Contracts are not backed by the full faith and credit of the state of West Virginia. A prepaid tuition escrow account was created to ensure payment of prepaid tuition contracts. Up to $500,000 annually is placed in the escrow account if an unfunded liability exists in the trust fund.

Special considerations:

- All contract payments are deductible from West Virginia taxable income each year. Deductions may be subject to recapture if non-qualified withdrawals are made in a subsequent year.
- West Virginia does not specifically provide that qualified distributions are exempt from state income tax, but its tax law generally conforms to federal tax law and so any qualified distributions that are exempt from federal income tax are also exempt from West Virginia income tax.
- The value of the account will not be counted in determining eligibility and need for student financial aid programs provided by the state of West Virginia.
- Moneys in the trust fund are exempt from creditor process in West Virginia, and payments made on behalf of a designated beneficiary to the trust fund are exempt from the property of an estate in bankruptcy proceedings in West Virginia.

STATE:	**WEST VIRGINIA**
PROGRAM NAME:	SMART529 College Savings Option
529 TYPE:	Savings
STATE AGENCY:	West Virginia College Prepaid Tuition and Savings Program Board of Trustees
PROGRAM MANAGER:	Hartford Life Insurance Company
INITIAL YEAR OF OPERATION:	2002
TELEPHONE:	1–866–574–3542
INTERNET:	www.SMART529.com

Who can purchase a contract? U.S. citizens and resident aliens, UTMA/UGMA custodians, and legal entities. This program is distributed both direct and through brokers. Anyone who does not meet West Virginia's residency requirements must open their account through a broker.

Time or age limitations on beneficiary or on use of account assets: None

Age-based investment option: The Age-Based Option contains four portfolios of underlying mutual funds. Contributions are placed into the portfolio corresponding to the beneficiary's age, and later reassigned to more conservative portfolios as the beneficiary approaches college, unless otherwise instructed by the account owner.

Static investment options: In the direct-sold program, select among five blended-fund portfolios (Aggressive Growth, Growth, Balanced, Conservative Balanced, and Conservative Bond), and a stable value fund portfolio. In the broker-sold program, select among three blended-fund portfolios (Aggressive Growth, Growth, and Balanced), a stable value fund, and eight individual-fund portfolios.

Underlying investments: Mutual funds from Hartford Funds and Invesco

Fees and expenses: $25 annual account maintenance fee for accounts less than $25,000 (waived for West Virginia residents and for accounts in an automatic investment plan), and a 1.16% annualized program management fee charged against the value of the account, which includes the expenses of the underlying mutual funds. There is no enrollment fee. In addition, accounts opened through a broker are subject to one of three alternative broker expense structures that will determine any initial sales charge, contingent deferred sales charge, and/or additional asset-based fees.

Maximum contributions: Accepts contributions until all West Virginia account balances for the same beneficiary reach $265,620.

Minimum initial contribution: $100, or $15 per month with automatic investments ($500, or $50 per month with automatic investments, for accounts opened by nonresidents through a broker)

Account changes: The program accepts requests to change beneficiary, transfer account ownership, name a successor owner, and transact rollovers and investment changes that meet the requirements of federal tax law and IRS regulations.

Special considerations:

- All contributions are deductible from West Virginia taxable income each year. Deductions may be subject to recapture if non-qualified withdrawals are made in a subsequent year.
- West Virginia does not specifically provide that qualified distributions are exempt from state income tax, but its tax law generally conforms to federal tax law and so any qualified distributions that are exempt from federal income tax are also exempt from West Virginia income tax.
- The value of the account will not be counted in determining eligibility and need for student financial aid programs provided by the state of West Virginia.
- Moneys in the trust fund are exempt from creditor process in West Virginia, and payments made on behalf of a designated beneficiary to the trust fund are exempt from the property of an estate in bankruptcy proceedings in West Virginia.

STATE:	**WEST VIRGINIA**
PROGRAM NAME:	SMART529 Select
529 TYPE:	Savings
STATE AGENCY:	West Virginia College Prepaid Tuition and Savings Program Board of Trustees
PROGRAM MANAGER:	Hartford Life Insurance Company
INITIAL YEAR OF OPERATION:	2004
TELEPHONE:	1–877–767–8529
INTERNET:	www.smart529select.com

Who can purchase a contract? U.S. citizens and resident aliens, UTMA/UGMA custodians, and legal entities. This program is not available through brokers.

Time or age limitations on beneficiary or on use of account assets: None

Age-based investment option: The Age-Based Option contains seven portfolios of underlying mutual funds. Contributions are placed into the portfolio corresponding to the beneficiary's age, and later reassigned to more conservative portfolios as the beneficiary approaches college, unless otherwise instructed by the account owner.

Static investment options: Select among ten blended-fund portfolios ranging from 100% equity to 100% fixed income.

Underlying investments: Mutual funds from Dimensional Fund Advisors

Fees and expenses: $25 annual account maintenance fee for accounts less than $25,000 (waived for West Virginia residents and for accounts in an automatic monthly investment plan of $50 or more), 0.68% annualized program management fee charged against the value of the account, and underlying fund expenses recently ranging from approximately 0.20% to 0.51%. There is no enrollment fee.

Maximum contributions: Accepts contributions until all West Virginia account balances for the same beneficiary reach $265,620.

Minimum initial contribution: $500, or $50 per month

Account changes: The program accepts requests to change beneficiary, transfer account ownership, name a successor owner, and transact rollovers and investment changes that meet the requirements of federal tax law and IRS regulations.

Special considerations:

- West Virginia residents receive the same state income tax, financial aid, and creditor protection benefits previously described for West Virginia's SMART529 College Savings Option.

STATE:	**WEST VIRGINIA**
PROGRAM NAME:	Leaders SMART529
529 TYPE:	Savings
STATE AGENCY:	West Virginia College Prepaid Tuition and Savings Program Board of Trustees
PROGRAM MANAGER:	Hartford Life Insurance Company
INITIAL YEAR OF OPERATION:	2003
TELEPHONE:	1–866–574–3542
INTERNET:	www.SMART529.com

Who can purchase a contract? U.S. citizens and resident aliens 18 years and older, UTMA/UGMA custodians, and legal entities. This program is distributed through brokers.

Time or age limitations on beneficiary or on use of account assets: None

Age-based investment option: The Age-Based Portfolios consist of four portfolios of underlying funds, ranging from 100% equity to 20% equity. Contributions are placed into the portfolio corresponding to the beneficiary's age, and later reassigned to more conservative portfolios as the beneficiary approaches college.

Static investment options: Select among four blended-fund portfolios (Aggressive Growth, Growth, Balanced, and Conservative), a stable value fund, and fifteen individual-fund portfolios.

Underlying investments: Mutual funds from AIM, American Funds, Franklin Templeton, MFS, and Invesco

Fees and expenses: $25 annual account maintenance fee for accounts less than $25,000 (waived for West Virginia residents and for accounts in an automatic investment plan), 0.44% annualized program management fee charged against the value of the account, and underlying fund expenses recently ranging from approximately 0.83% to 1.01% for the age-based and blended-fund portfolios, and from approximately 0.70% to 1.38% for the individual-fund portfolios. In addition, accounts are subject to one of three alternative broker expense structures that will determine any initial sales charge, contingent deferred sales charge, and/or additional asset-based fees. There is no enrollment fee.

Maximum contributions: Accepts contributions until all West Virginia account balances for the same beneficiary reach $265,620.

Minimum initial contribution: $500, or $50 per month with automatic investments ($100 or $15 per month with automatic investments for West Virginia residents)

Account changes: The program accepts requests to change beneficiary, transfer account ownership, name a successor owner, and transact rollovers and investment changes that meet the requirements of federal tax law and IRS regulations.

Special considerations:

- West Virginia residents receive the same state income tax, financial aid, and creditor protection benefits previously described for West Virginia's SMART529 College Savings Option.

STATE: **WEST VIRGINIA**

PROGRAM NAME:	Cornerstone SMART529
529 TYPE:	Savings
STATE AGENCY:	West Virginia College Prepaid Tuition and Savings Program Board of Trustees
PROGRAM MANAGER:	Hartford Life Insurance Company
INITIAL YEAR OF OPERATION:	2003
TELEPHONE:	1–866–574–3542
INTERNET:	www.SMART529.com

Who can purchase a contract? U.S. citizens and resident aliens 18 years and older, UTMA/UGMA custodians, and legal entities. This program is distributed through Edward Jones financial advisors.

Time or age limitations on beneficiary or on use of account assets: None

Age-based investment option: The Age-Based Portfolios consist of four portfolios of underlying funds, ranging from 100% equity to 20% equity. Contributions are placed into the portfolio corresponding to the beneficiary's age, and later reassigned to more conservative portfolios as the beneficiary approaches college.

Static investment options: Select among four blended-fund portfolios (Aggressive Growth, Growth, Balanced, and Conservative), a stable value fund, and twenty-one individual-fund portfolios.

Underlying investments: Mutual funds from Hartford Funds, Invesco, American Funds, Federated Investors, Goldman Sachs Asset Management, Lord Abbett, Putnam Investments, and Van Kampen Investments.

Fees and expenses: $25 annual account maintenance fee for accounts less than $25,000 (waived for West Virginia residents and for accounts in an automatic investment plan), 0.44% annualized program management fee charged against the value of the account, and underlying fund expenses recently ranging from approximately 0.76% to 0.96% for the age-based and blended-fund portfolios, and from approximately 0.72% to 1.31% for the individual-fund portfolios. In addition, accounts are subject to one of three alternative broker expense structures that will determine any initial sales charge, contingent deferred sales charge, and/or additional asset-based fees. There is no enrollment fee.

Maximum contributions: Accepts contributions until all West Virginia account balances for the same beneficiary reach $265,620.

Minimum initial contribution: $500, or $50 per month with automatic investments ($100 or $15 per month with automatic investments for West Virginia residents)

Account changes: The program accepts requests to change beneficiary, transfer account ownership, name a successor owner, and transact rollovers and investment changes that meet the requirements of federal tax law and IRS regulations.

Special considerations:

- West Virginia residents receive the same state income tax, financial aid, and creditor protection benefits previously described for West Virginia's SMART529 College Savings Option.

STATE: **WISCONSIN**

PROGRAM NAME:	EdVest
529 TYPE:	Savings
STATE AGENCY:	Wisconsin Office of the State Treasurer
PROGRAM MANAGER:	Strong Capital Management, Inc.
INITIAL YEAR OF OPERATION:	1997
TELEPHONE:	1–888–EdVest–WI (1–888–338–3789)
INTERNET:	www.edvest.com

Who can purchase a contract? U.S. citizens and resident aliens of legal age, UTMA/UGMA custodians, and legal entities. This program is distributed both direct and through brokers.

Time or age limitations on beneficiary or on use of account assets: None

Age-based investment option: The Age-Based Option contains four portfolios of underlying funds, ranging from a 90%/10% blend of stock and fixed income funds to a 100% fixed income portfolio. Contributions are placed into the portfolio corresponding to the number of years to expected enrollment, and later reassigned to more conservative portfolios as the beneficiary approaches college.

Static investment options: Select among four blended-fund portfolios (Aggressive, Moderate, Balanced, and Bond), a stable value portfolio, and four individual-fund portfolios.

Underlying investments: Mutual funds from Strong, RW Baird, Legg Mason, and Vanguard.

Fees and expenses: $10 annual account maintenance fee on accounts $25,000 and less (waived for accounts in an automatic investment plan), annualized program management fee charged against the value of the account of 0.30% for the blended-fund portfolios, 0.40% for the individual-fund portfolios, or 0.25% for the stable value portfolio, and underlying fund expenses recently ranging from approximately 0.40% to 1.02% (portfolio weighted average) for the blended-fund portfolios, 0.05% to 0.78% for the individual-fund portfolios, and 0.50% for the stable value portfolio. There is no enrollment fee. In addition, accounts opened through a broker are subject to one of three alternative broker expense structures that will determine any initial sales charge, contingent deferred sales charge, and/or additional asset-based fees.

Maximum contributions: Accepts contributions until all Wisconsin account balances for the same beneficiary reach $246,000.

Minimum initial contribution: $250, or $25 per month

Account changes: The program accepts requests to change beneficiary, transfer account ownership, name a successor owner, and transact rollovers and investment changes that meet the requirements of federal tax law and IRS regulations.

Special considerations:
- Up to $3,000 in contributions per beneficiary (provided that the beneficiary is either the claimant, or claimant's dependent child, grandchild, great-grandchild, nephew, or niece) may be deducted from Wisconsin state taxable income each year.
- Under state law, qualified distributions from this program are exempt from Wisconsin income tax. Because Wisconsin tax law generally conforms to federal tax law, any qualified distributions from other 529 plans that are exempt from federal income tax are also exempt from Wisconsin income tax.

- The value of the account will not be counted in determining eligibility and need for student financial aid programs provided by the state of Wisconsin.
- Under state law, a beneficiary's right to qualified withdrawals is not subject to garnishment, attachment, execution, or other process of law.

STATE: WISCONSIN

PROGRAM NAME:	tomorrow's scholar
529 TYPE:	Savings
STATE AGENCY:	Wisconsin Office of the State Treasurer
PROGRAM MANAGER:	Strong Capital Management, Inc.
DISTRIBUTION PARTNER:	American Express Financial Advisors
INITIAL YEAR OF OPERATION:	2001
TELEPHONE:	1–866–677–6933
INTERNET:	www.tomorrowsscholar.com

Who can purchase a contract? Individuals of legal age with either a valid Social Security number or federal taxpayer identification number, UTMA/UGMA custodians, and certain legal entities. This program is distributed through American Express Financial Advisors and other approved brokers.

Time or age limitations on beneficiary or on use of account assets: None

Age-based investment options: The Age-Based Option offers a choice among three different schedules: Aggressive Growth, Moderate Growth, or Conservative Growth. Each schedule contains five portfolios of underlying funds, ranging from 90% equity to 20% equity. Contributions are placed into the portfolio corresponding to the selected schedule and the number of years to expected enrollment, and later reassigned to more conservative portfolios as the beneficiary approaches college.

Static investment options: Select among three blended-fund portfolios: Aggressive (75% equity), Balanced (50% equity), and Conservative (20% equity).

Underlying investments: Mutual funds from American Express and Strong

Fees and expenses: $15 annual account maintenance fee for accounts with balances $25,000 or less (waived for accounts in an automatic investment plan), 0.25% annualized program management fee charged against the value of the account, and underlying fund expenses recently ranging from approximately 0.76% to 1.10% (portfolio weighted average). In addition, accounts are subject to one of three alternative broker expense structures that will determine any initial sales charge, contingent deferred sales charge, and/or additional asset-based fees. There is no enrollment fee.

Maximum contributions: Accepts contributions until all Wisconsin account balances for the same beneficiary reach $246,000.

Minimum initial contribution: $250, or $25 per month with automatic investments

Account changes: The program accepts requests to change beneficiary, transfer account ownership, name a successor owner, and transact rollovers and investment changes that meet the requirements of federal tax law and IRS regulations.

Special considerations:
* Wisconsin residents receive the same state income tax, financial aid, and creditor protection benefits previously described for the Wisconsin's EdVest program.

STATE:	**WYOMING**
PROGRAM NAME:	College Achievement Plan
529 TYPE:	Savings
STATE AGENCY:	Wyoming Family College Savings Program Trust
PROGRAM MANAGER:	Mercury Advisors
DISTRIBUTION PARTNER:	MFS Investment Management
INITIAL YEAR OF OPERATION:	2000
TELEPHONE:	1–877–529–2655
INTERNET:	www.collegeachievementplan.com

Who can purchase a contract? Individuals with a valid Social Security number, UTMA/ UGMA custodians, and legal entities. This program is distributed both direct and through brokers.

Time or age limitations on beneficiary or on use of account assets: None

Age-based investment option: The Age-Adjusted Option contains nine portfolios of underlying mutual funds. Contributions are placed into the portfolio corresponding to the number of years to expected enrollment. Eight portfolios shift to a more conservative investment allocation over time, eventually transferring to the Short-Term Portfolio.

Static investment options: Select among four blended-fund portfolios: 100% Equity, 75% Equity, Balanced (50% equity), and Fixed-Income.

Underlying investments: Mutual funds from Merrill Lynch and MFS Investments

Fees and expenses: $25 annual account maintenance fee on accounts less than $25,000 (waived for Wyoming residents), 0.95% annualized program management fee charged against the value of the account, and underlying fund expenses recently ranging from approximately 0.85% to 1.45% (portfolio weighted average). There is no enrollment fee. Accounts opened through a broker are not subject to an additional expense structure.

Maximum contributions: Accepts contributions until all Wyoming account balances for the same beneficiary reach $245,000.

Minimum initial contribution: $1,000 ($250 for Wyoming residents).

Account changes: The program accepts requests to change beneficiary, transfer account ownership, name a successor owner, and transact rollovers and investment changes that meet the requirements of federal tax law and IRS regulations.

Special considerations:

- There are no state income tax incentives because Wyoming does not have a personal income tax.

- The program description warns that Wyoming residents should be careful to discuss the treatment of an account in this program (or any other 529 plan) with their attorney or other advisor for purposes of the state inheritance tax. The value of the account may be includable as an asset of the account owner for this purpose.

Notes

Index

Additional Copies

THE BEST WAY TO SAVE FOR COLLEGE
A Complete Guide to 529 Plans

TELEPHONE ORDERS: 1–800–400–9113
Please have your Visa, MasterCard, or American Express ready.

FAX ORDERS: 585–419–7820
MAIL ORDERS: Savingforcollege.com LLC
1151 Pittsford-Victor Road
Suite 103
Pittsford, NY 14534, USA

SOLD TO

Name _____

Company _____

Address _____

City / ST / Zip _____

Phone _____

Email _____

DESCRIPTION	QUANTITY	COST	TOTAL
The Best Way to Save for College	_____	$22.95	_____
2005 Edition			
ISBN 0–9742977-5-5			
New York State residents, add 8% state sales tax			_____
Shipping and handling*	_____	$4.85	
*Call for shipping cost on multiple book orders			
TOTAL			_____

PAYMENT METHOD

❑ Check Enclosed   ❑ VISA ❑ MasterCard ❑ American Express

Credit Card # _____

Expiration Date _____

Name on Card _____

Authorized Signature _____

We offer discounts for purchases of 10 or more books.
Please contact us.

Also Available from Savingforcollege.com

Guide to College Savings—booklet explaining 529 plans and other college savings options in simple and easy-to-understand language. In English or Spanish.

529PRO Solutions—subscriber-only access to specialized 529 content and planning tools for financial advisers, attorneys, accountants, and those involved in higher education.

For more information,
visit www.savingforcollege.com
or call 1–800–400–9113.